Disloyal Mothers and Scurrilous Citizens

WOMEN AND SUBVERSION
DURING WORLD WAR I

Kathleen Kennedy

INDIANA UNIVERSITY PRESS

Bloomington and Indianapolis

This book is a publication of

Indiana University Press
601 North Morton Street
Bloomington, IN 47404-3797 USA

http://www.indiana.edu/~iupress

Telephone orders 800-842-6796
Fax orders 812-855-7931
Orders by e-mail iuporder@indiana.edu

The paper used in this publication meets the minimum
requirements of American National Standard for Information
Sciences—Permanence of Paper for Printed Library
Materials, ANSI Z39.48-1984.

Manufactured in the United States of America

Library of Congress Cataloging-in-Publication Data

Kennedy, Kathleen, date
Disloyal mothers and scurrilous citizens : women and
subversion during World War I / Kathleen Kennedy.
p.   cm.
Includes bibliographical references and index.
ISBN 0-253-33565-5 (cl. : alk. paper)
1. World War, 1914–1918—Women—United States. 2. Subversive activities—
United States. 3. World War, 1914–1918—Protest movements—United States.
4. Political persecution—United States—History—20th century.   I. Title.
D639.W7T69   1999
940.3'082—dc21   98-55989

1   2   3   4   5   04   03   02   01   00   99

For Lori and Denise
with love

CONTENTS

ACKNOWLEDGMENTS

Throughout my life, I have been blessed with wonderful teachers. At Ausable Valley Central High, I learned the art of historical research from Miss Mary Haney and from my father, John Kennedy. At the State University of New York, Plattsburgh, I developed a passion for history and women's studies in classes taught by Anita Rapone, Carol Leonard, and Harriette Walker. At the University of California, Irvine, I learned how to think more creatively and critically. I am grateful to my dissertation advisor, Jon Wiener, and to Amy Dru Stanley, Leslie Rabine, James Given, and Spencer Olin for their criticisms and encouragement. At Irvine I also found the support of friends and colleagues who made my graduate career a true pleasure. In particular I would like to thank Ellen Broidy, Joan Ariel, Robert Sieber, Bill Billingsly, Anne Marie Scholtz, Linda Peterson, Scott Howlett, Kyle Cuordileone, Jennifer Reed, Anne Walthall, Sharon Ullman, and Robert Moeller.

As they always do with such studies, research librarians played a central role in this project. In particular, I would like to thank the research staffs at the University of California, Irvine, the Swarthmore College Peace Collection, the Tamiment Institute of Labor History, the National Archives, the State Historical Society of Wisconsin, the University of Texas at Dallas and Western Washington University. The University of Texas at Dallas and Western Washington University provided financial assistance during this project.

Frances Early has been a constant source of support throughout my career and has on many occasions shared her research. She is a model of a feminist scholar and was especially generous to a new colleague. I also want to thank Ruth Alexander and Sally Miller for reading parts of this manuscript. This work has also benefited from many anonymous readers who have offered their criticism through the years. I would also like to thank Michael Wilson, Julie Reuben, and Linda Williamson for their support.

The editorial staff at Indiana University Press, in particular, Joan Catapano, Jane Lyle, and Michael Lundell, guided this manuscript through the various publication processes with care and diligence. Kathy Babbitt saved me from many embarrassing sins against the English language and offered insightful comments about the manuscript's content and argument. I appreciate the care and interest that my manuscript received while in their hands.

I am fortunate to come from a family that values education and that encouraged me from a young age to seek knowledge. My father, John Kennedy, and my aunt, Mary Patricia Kennedy, both extraordinary teachers, have been models of professionalism throughout my career. My mother, Mary Kennedy, has kindly tolerated her daughter's decision to study and live thousands of miles from home. I know how difficult it has been for her to let me go, and I am grateful for the fact that she still provides me with a home. My sisters, Colleen Kennedy and Maureen Kennedy Badger, have been constant boosters and have even agreed to buy this book.

Finally, I want to thank my family and friends here in Bellingham. My colleagues and students at Western Washington have provided me with a place at which I love to teach. I am especially grateful to Nancy van Deusen, Cecilla Danysk, Alan Galley, Midori Takagi, and Chris Friday for their advice on this project. My immediate family has, of course, meant everything to me—Eliot for demanding that I take him to the beach every morning rain or shine and Rigel for leaving his special mark on this project.

This work is dedicated to two women who have changed my life and who, for different reasons, I love very much. Lori Hiris has been a friend and colleague for almost two decades. In that time we have argued about feminist theory, taken motorcycle tours of NYC, and have just hung in there. Denise Seibert simply continues to take my breath away and provides the most important reason for getting up every morning.

INTRODUCTION

On the eve of American participation in World War I, Anna Strunsky and William English Walling exchanged a series of angry letters. Walling, a socialist who supported Wilson's war plans, denounced Strunsky's anti-war position as Quakerism, warning her that her stance constituted treason:

> Of course I think your proposal to attack in the back those who are giving up their lives for democracy, peace, and anti-militarism is criminal to the last degree. But the world is moving in spite of all you do to help the militarists and reactionaries. You are their accomplice and neither I nor mankind, nor the genuine idealists and revolutionists of the world will ever forget or forgive what your kind has said and done in this great hour. If I fight it will be against the traitors to internationalism—I trust you will not be among them.[1]

Strunsky's tone was mild in comparison. She admonished Walling for trivializing her position. "A statement does not offer a condition," she noted, "you cannot turn me into a [Quaker] by saying so." Her anti-war stance, she argued, no more constituted Quakerism than his pro-war position made him "cruel and bloodthirsty." Rather, she based her opposition to the war on the same principles that in 1905 had led her into the streets of Petrograd to support Russian workers who were protesting the tsar. The present crisis, she reminded Walling, had led many rational individuals to hyperbole and to politically dubious positions. She hoped that he would not be among them. Once the present crisis was over Strunsky anticipated a reconciliation, telling Walling that he would "understand me as well as I understand you and then we will laugh together."[2]

In themselves Walling's recriminations against Strunsky were unremarkable. Many pro-war socialists bitterly denounced their former colleagues, who often responded in kind.[3] But Walling and Strunsky were married. Their letters provide a personal glimpse into the effects of wartime political culture and at the same time reveal the social and political factors that fueled their argument. Strunsky and Walling were from two different worlds that were separated by gender, ethnicity, and class. Their marriage, like that of their friends Rose Pastor Stokes and Graham Stokes, symbolized the partnership between upper-class altruistic reform and working-class politics that characterized the socialism of American intellectuals. Yet, when the war came, both marriages fractured along class, ethnic, and gender lines.[4]

Gender and ethnicity separated Strunsky and Walling; so too did each one's conception of citizenship. Walling argued that Strunsky had forfeited her citizenship by opposing the war. Defining her as a traitor both to her adopted nation and to socialism, Walling warned Strunsky that she would never be forgiven by the "true revolutionists of the world." Like other pro-war socialists, Walling believed that Wilson's war programs would promote industrial democracy and further the programs of constructive and loyal socialists like himself.[5] Yet, the ferocity and character of Walling's attack suggests that he also accepted an important tenet of wartime political culture—that opposition to the war was not only un-American but also "criminal to the last degree."

In contrast to Walling's characterization of her position, Strunsky forged her position from her understanding of a revolutionary's responsibilities as a member of an international community rather than from absolute pacifism. Although Strunsky eventually "capitulated" to Walling's demands that she cease her anti-war activity, she viewed the war as a "an intellectual and spiritual battle" that threatened to bring "pitiless vengeance" in the name of patriotism to all those defined as un-American. "A revolutionist," Strunsky asserted, "believes in the people and opposes the established order."[6] Rejecting the racial thinking that characterized social Darwinist interpretations of some nationalist thinkers, Strunsky argued that true revolutionists "do not wipe people off the face of the earth. [They] do not believe in artificial selection—the killing off of all the bad that the good may remain. [They] do not punish, [they] educate." When socialists resort to war, Strunsky warned, "we lose our humanity."[7] Strunsky anguished over her reluctant decision to join her husband and vote for war believing that she had condemned other women's children to war.[8] For her war did not represent opportunity but a tragedy that fundamentally threatened rather than preserved internationalism.

President Woodrow Wilson ended such debates on April 2, 1914, when he asked Congress for a declaration of war. Initially, his plan faced stiff opposition from Strunsky's "kind"—peace advocates, socialists, and some immigrant groups. By defining American participation in the war as a crusade to preserve an endangered liberal democratic tradition, Wilson sought to preempt this opposition. And historians suggest that Wilson was successful. His ability to define American participation in the war as a democratic crusade quelled much of this opposition, especially among liberals and progressives.[9]

For those Americans still unpersuaded by the merits of his mission, Wilson promised a "firm hand of repression."[10] His administration fashioned internationalism to the liberal democratic state, which outlawed Strunsky's competing vision of internationalism that stressed allegiances between workers. Five days after his war message, Wilson asked Congress to take steps against potential disloyalty. The centerpiece of this effort—the Espionage Act—became law on June 15, 1917. Although ostensibly aimed at foreign agents, its ambiguity encouraged prosecutions of individuals who were critical of the war.[11] Its key passage read as follows:

> Any person who shall willfully make or convey false reports or false statements with intent to interfere with the operation or success of the military or naval forces . . . [or] shall willfully cause or attempt to cause insubordination, disloyalty, mutiny, or refusal of duty in the military or naval forces of the United States, or shall willfully obstruct the recruiting or enlistment service of the United States . . . shall be punished by a fine of not more than $10,000 or imprisonment for not more than twenty years or both.[12]

In addition to restricting speech, the Espionage Act gave the postmaster general broad powers to deny second-class mailing privileges to any newspaper or magazine that he believed violated the law. Federal officials used the Espionage Act to prosecute a wide range of utterances against the war by arguing that they were intended to prevent men from enlisting or complying with the draft.[13]

On its face the Espionage Act limited wartime prosecutions to utterances that directly criticized the war and that were intended to interfere with enlistment and conscription. Responding to charges that these restrictions limited the government's response to subversion, Congress amended the Espionage Act in 1918 to include the Sedition Act. The Sedition Act included utterances that merely criticized the American government. Specifically, it forbade

> uttering, printing, writing, or publishing any disloyal, profane, scurrilous, or abusive language intended to cause contempt, scorn, contumely or disrepute as regards the form of government of the United States, or the Constitution, or the flag, or the uniform of the Army and Navy, or any language intended to incite resistance to the United States or to promote the cause of its enemies; urging any curtailment of production of anything necessary to the prosecution of the war with intent to hinder its prosecution; advocating, teaching, defending, or suggesting the doing of any of these acts; and words or acts supporting or favoring the cause of any country at war with the United States, or opposing the cause of the United States therein.[14]

The Sedition Act defined any criticism of American policy as sedition, regardless of its relationship to the war. Augmented by the Immigration Act of 1917 that increased the government's ability to deport aliens who were convicted of a crime and by state anti-syndicalist laws, the Espionage Act virtually outlawed free speech.[15]

The wartime emergency laws obtained their clout from the courts. Preserving a pre-war hostility to free speech, the courts either ignored first amendment concerns or applied the "bad tendency doctrine" to free speech cases. Assuming that radical speech had a "bad tendency to cause unrest in an impressionable public," the courts set a pre-war precedent against socialist and anarchist speech.[16] As long as there was no prior restraint on speech, the government could legitimately control utterances that might cause social disorder.[17] Developed primarily as a response to labor unrest, the "bad tendency doctrine" allowed federal and state authorities to arrest leaders of radical or workers' organizations whenever violence accompanied their protests regardless of who was responsible for inciting or carrying out that violence.[18]

The "bad tendency doctrine" assumed that certain types of speech were inherently suspect; it encouraged the broad definition of intent that characterized wartime convictions. Opponents of the war generally avoided utterances that directly criticized conscription or the war programs of the government. Yet jurists, relying on the bad tendency doctrine, ruled that even indirect criticism of the war violated the Espionage Act because such utterances potentially disrupted the recruitment of soldiers.[19]

Wartime repression is a popular subject among historians. Scholars writing just prior to World War II examined wartime repression as an aberration caused by the hysteria of war. They used their work to warn against repeating the excesses of World War I.[20] John Higham's study of nativism changed the direction of these studies. He examined wartime repression as an extension of a long-standing tradition of nativism that had characterized American politics since the middle of the nineteenth century. Nativism, he wrote, was an

> intense opposition to an internal minority on the ground of its foreign (i.e. "un-American") connections. Specific nativist antagonisms may, and do, vary widely in response to the changing character of minority irritants and the shifting conditions of the day; but through each separate hostility runs the connecting, energizing force of modern nationalism. While drawing on much broader cultural and ethnocentric judgements, nativism translates them into a zeal to destroy the enemies of a distinctly American way of life.[21]

American participation in the war, he argued, enabled the federal government to develop agencies and pass laws that controlled dissent in general and subversion within the country's alien population in particular. Higham understood repression to be part of this nativist tradition rather than a product of wartime hysteria, and as such an integral part of the processes by which American politics incorporated or failed to incorporate ethnic differences. The wartime emergency laws and other wartime measures that controlled domestic dissent, Higham suggested, were tools in an increasingly focused attack against class and ethnic differences that was often conducted under the guise of protecting "a distinctly American way of life."[22]

Following Higham's lead, historians now see the roots of wartime repression in progressivism in particular and in American political culture in general.[23] Wartime repression was unique for its intensity and its creation of a bureaucracy designed to control domestic subversion.[24] Responding to fears that immigrants and radicals were fomenting disloyalty, state authorities developed internal agencies and a legal structure that criminalized particular political ideas. The war permanently changed the tempo and character of the anti-radical crusade. Unlike the pre-war years, wartime repression used federal troops and judicial trials and committed the state to a permanent program whose goal was the destruction of domestic subversion. By the end of the war, both federal and state governments had in place an apparatus designed solely to control domestic dissent.[25] These changes resulted in the modern surveillance state.

Although historians have demonstrated the class and ethnic dimensions of wartime repression, they have yet to explore its gendered components. Nor have they examined its impact on women and women's politics. In fact, with the notable exception of Richard Polenberg's study of the Abrams case, women's wartime cases have served only as footnotes to the political history of World War I.[26] Historians have viewed women's cases as significant only when they confirmed the excesses of wartime anti-radicalism.[27]

This project examines how wartime expectations of loyalty in general and the anti-radical crusades in particular shaped women's citizenship. It takes as its centerpiece the arrests, trials, and defenses of women charged under the wartime emergency laws passed during World War I. Women were the primary defendants in about twenty of the approximately eight hundred federal cases that resulted in convictions.[28] Despite these small numbers, the demographics of the defendants are significant. Most of the women charged under the wartime laws were doctors, teachers, and/or political leaders.[29] Half were single; only two had children. Such women were uniquely conspicuous; they violated both wartime prescriptions of loyalty and middle-class definitions of gender-appropriate behavior.[30]

I argue that issues of gender appropriate behavior appeared regularly in women's confrontations with legal authorities. For example, in June of 1917 the Justice Department indicted Kate Richards O'Hare under the Espionage Act for alleging that war corrupted motherhood.[31] O'Hare's case was not an isolated incident. In Oregon, federal authorities arrested Dr. Marie Equi for an anti-conscription speech. The prosecuting attorney asked the jury to consider Equi's condition as an "unnatural woman" in their deliberations.[32] Similarly in New York City, after her arrest for distributing leaflets that protested American involvement in the Russian Civil War, the presiding judge questioned Mollie Steimer about her views on "free love" and marriage during her testimony.[33] As disorderly women, O'Hare, Equi, and Steimer posed a unique threat to the political order. They were, in historian Natalie Davis's words, "women on top"—women who subverted the political order through gender transgressions that were often understood as appropriations of a male gender role and/or as a misuse of women's sexual/reproductive roles.[34] To their detractors, disorderly women embodied the social and political chaos that could accompany the entrance of women into the public sphere.

As written, the federal wartime laws were not gendered. It was in their application that the wartime laws gave statutory power to the particular definitions of manhood and womanhood demanded by wartime political culture. The broad definition of intent that characterized espionage convictions assumed that all men of a particular age were potential soldiers and that all women acted as mothers in their relationships with such men. If utterances critical of the war even had the potential to reach men of that age group, juries would convict under the Espionage and Sedition Acts, even if there was no evidence that those utterances specifically targeted draft-aged men.[35]

Wilson's concern that a draft would undercut support for the war shaped how his administration approached the draft and its enforcement. After much debate, Wilson decided to institute the draft as the most efficient method of "assigning . . . men to the necessary labor of the country." Wilson argued that a draft would allow the government to control the distribution of manpower and would assure a plentiful supply of both soldiers and laborers.[36] Wilson recognized, however, that a draft was controversial. Remembering the anti-draft riots of the Civil War, he took steps to preempt protests by ensuring fairness in the selection of soldiers. The Selective Service Act of 1917 provided for local administration of the draft and established geographical quotas.[37]

Federal authorities combined rigorous prosecution of those who opposed conscription with a massive propaganda campaign to gain maximum compliance with the draft law. By all accounts, their efforts were successful. Draft day saw little organized resistance and a high rate of registration. Still, a fear that the draft could become a focal point for anti-war activity continued to shape how state authorities prosecuted wartime cases and how they defined subversion. Federal authorities prosecuted utterances that did not directly attack the draft and actions that did not block registration because they potentially caused dissension among draft-aged men.

The draft and these concerns over the nation's ability to produce an efficient and effective fighting force dictated that the most important wartime roles of women would be the production of soldiers. The Selective Service Act gave the state an increased stake in carefully defining and enforcing patriotic motherhood.[38] If mothers did "not let their sons grow up to be soldiers," they could disrupt the draft.[39]

Although European studies about the ways in which the nationalism and patriotism of the Great War affected definitions of woman's citizenship abound, few American historians have examined this problem. Current studies generally argue that the war marked a "regress . . . in postwar gender relations, the attitude of the state towards women, and most pronouncedly, postwar feminism."[40] The experience of war re-masculinized society as men's roles as soldiers were privileged over women's roles at home. According to these arguments, the gendering of the front (as well as its memory) as masculine and of the home front as feminine preserved and even strengthened sexual asymmetry even as women undertook traditionally masculine tasks. Wartime patriotism and nationalism reinforced women's roles as mothers and defined women's rights arguments as selfish. The net result was a divided feminist movement that was focused on pronatalist state-building in the face of a post-war anti-feminist backlash.[41]

My study is indebted to much of this work as it explores how state authorities used patriotic motherhood to shape the type of political activity in which women could engage. But the effects of wartime repression on women and their political roles and identities is more complicated than a status decline model alone suggests. "To study women in wartime," the editors of *Behind the Lines: Gender and the Two World Wars* argue, "a new historical perspective is called for, one in which women are studied in relation to men and as part of identifiable gender systems." War, they stress, "must be understood as a *gendering* activity, one that ritually marks the gender of all members of a society . . . [by drawing on] preexisting definitions of gender at the same time that it restructures gender relations."[42] In the ten years since *Behind the Lines* appeared, historians and literary critics have augmented questions of status with those that "take stock of the mutations in the borderlines of femininities and masculinities."[43]

Influenced by this literature, my study reexamines wartime anti-radicalism as an "event of gender politics" that was instrumental in forging the definitions of women's citizenship that emerged from early twentieth-century state-building.[44] Within this framework, issues of status fall to the background as questions of how wartime discourses such as anti-radicalism, nativism, patriotism, and Americanism shaped women's relationship to the state take center stage. My study examines "the structural components between gender identity and wartime nationalism" that, according to one historian, still remain "peripheral to the study of gender and war."[45]

My study is at the intersection of recent efforts to gender political history and more traditional projects that write women back into history. It both tells the story of women's encounters with the wartime legal system and dissects the meanings that those encounters acquired.[46] It is within those meanings, I argue, that state authorities and defendants negotiated women's roles and responsibilities in the twentieth-century state. In particular, I assert that those encounters revealed and helped clarify the shifting relationships between the citizenship of women and their responsibility for social reproduction and state formation.[47]

State appropriations of social reproduction and public morality are essential to our understanding of wartime repression. How women understood their role in social reproduction and the preservation of public morality was key to how they constructed their place in early twentieth-century political culture. In her pathbreaking essay "The Domestication of Politics," Paula Baker shifted the terms by which political historians understood the role of white, middle-class women in early twentieth-century state-building and perhaps even more significantly, how they used gender analysis. Baker argues that progressivism represented an important change not only in women's participation in formal politics but also in how politics itself encoded gender identities and roles. Women's increasing participation in formal politics, including suffrage, was made possible by a breakdown in separate spheres that divided the men and women of the nineteenth century. As women entered the political, they lost, in Baker's words, "their place above politics and their position as a force in the moral order." It was the government that "now carried moral authority and the obligations it implied."[48] To rephrase Baker's argument, a central component of early twentieth-century state formation was the transfer of moral authority from white middle-class women to the state.

Recent historical studies of the welfare state have complicated and added important specificity to Baker's observations, but they have confirmed her key observations—the importance of the deconstruction and reconstruction of social reproduction in general and motherhood in particular to the process of state formation.[49] Yet their emphasis on social reform and the welfare state tell only part of the story. My study suggests another dimension to early twentieth-century state-building: how the wartime legal system and its attendant definitions of loyalty, patriotism, and subversion gendered citizenship.

Like social welfare, anti-radicalism raised questions about the state's role in defining motherhood, public morality, and social reproduction and their relationships to the public roles of women. With the notable exception of O'Hare, most women charged under the wartime laws did not define their political behavior within the terms set by maternalism. Instead, defendants used liberal arguments of equality, justice, and citizenship or, like Strunsky, their membership in an international workers' community, to argue their cases. Such claims brought them into conflict not only with state authorities but also with their defense teams, who generally preferred strategies that emphasized women's futility as citizens. When they are examined from the perspective of both the accusers and the accused, arguments that women either subsumed their politics to the needs of the nation-state or that they accepted the tenets of nationalist discourses prove to be too simplistic.

I begin this study by examining patriotic motherhood, the construction used by historians to define the ways in which pro-war literature and propaganda defined women's obligations to the state. I argue that patriotic motherhood emerged from a variety of sources, including nationalists who were concerned about the increasing role of women in the public sphere and women who supported preparedness activities as a way to expand the role of women in politics. Women in preparedness organizations argued that patriotic mothers sacrificed their sons to war not only in defense of their country but also in defense of the characters of their sons. Those women who rejected patriotic motherhood, supporters of preparedness activities and war argued, endangered the nation through their production of sons who were incapable of fulfilling their duties as citizens. I argue that the values of patriotic motherhood formed a framework that helped to construct definitions of women's subversion once the United States entered the war.

Chapters two and three examine the trials of Kate Richards O'Hare and Emma Goldman. Both were respected leaders in the American left and both spoke extensively against the war. Their arrests took place within a few weeks of each other, and, as two of the first women tried under the wartime laws, their cases drew national attention. Yet, O'Hare and Goldman were fundamentally different types of political actors. Goldman was an anarchist who defined her right to protest the war as a matter of individual conscience. She challenged not only the state's right to exist but also conventional morality and middle-class constructions of motherhood. Although she was a long-standing member of the Socialist Party, O'Hare was not as easily characterized as a disorderly woman. She advocated evolutionary socialism and legitimized her own political activity through middle-class constructions of motherhood. Despite these differences, federal authorities tried both Goldman and O'Hare for being disorderly women; that is, for how they integrated their political and gender identities rather than for their specific utterances against the war. As significantly, O'Hare's and Goldman's cases reveal a pattern in which female defendants are charged with corrupting women's roles as social mothers; that is, women's responsibility to teach and instill patriotic and nationalist values. This failure, when framed within nativist languages, suggested that defendants had corrupted women's reproductive powers, in particular women's ability to and responsibility for producing loyal citizens.

My fourth chapter examines the case of Rose Pastor Stokes, who was convicted of violating the newly amended Espionage Act in May of 1918. Like O'Hare and Goldman, Stokes was a nationally known figure whose trial and conviction received nationwide coverage. What distinguishes Stokes's case from Goldman's and O'Hare's was the explicit link that prosecutors drew between Stokes's support for the Bolshevik Revolution and the nature of her political subversion. Stokes's case then provides a rich case study for an exploration of the ways in which state authorities grafted anti-Bolshevism onto patriotic motherhood. Like the trials of O'Hare and Goldman, Stokes's trial did not focus on the specifics of her opposition to war (it was not even apparent that Stokes opposed the war itself) but rather on how Stokes's support of Bolshevism represented a corruption of women's reproductive roles. Stokes's trial also underscores how court officials explicitly framed this corruption of reproduction within classic nativist languages, further illustrating the often-overlooked links among gender disorder, class conflict, and ethnic heterogeneity in the countersubversive discourses that emerged during World War I.

Chapters five and six further refine this argument by examining the federal cases of lesser-known women who were charged, seemingly at random, for violating wartime laws. In chapter five, I examine the cases of four women who were charged under the wartime laws for their political work. In chapter six, I further complicate my analysis by focusing on how women's professional identities influenced the charges against them. Unlike the cases of O'Hare, Goldman, and Stokes, these cases did not generate national publicity nor did defendants have the luxury of the same networks of support available to leaders of socialist and workers' movements. In part for these reasons, there is less evidence available; consequently, it is often impossible to draw complete profiles of their cases. These cases illustrate the pervasiveness of gendered discourses at the wartime trials of women. They also illustrate how these gendered discourses were applied to a wider variety of women's political and professional identities.

This study does not claim to examine the whole of women's political culture during World War I nor does it suggest that the wartime emergency laws alone imposed patriotic motherhood on women. But the trials of women accused under the wartime emergency laws do lend insight into the relationships drawn in that culture between gender and subversion, relationships that continue to form core values of Americanism and patriotism.

1

⚜

Loyal Mothers and Virtuous Citizens

WOMEN'S CITIZENSHIP ON THE EVE OF THE ARMAGEDDON

Two years before the United States entered World War I, women in the preparedness movement defined the role of women in national defense. Disturbed by the sinking of the *Lusitania* and the formation of the Woman's Peace Party (WPP), they reassured the public that American women stood willing to protect the nation from its domestic and foreign enemies. To demonstrate this resolve, one preparedness organization asked its members to sign the following pledge in support of "patriotic motherhood":

> I pledge to think, talk, and work for patriotism, Americanism and sufficient national defense to keep the horrors of war from America's home and shores forever.
>
> In these days of world strife and peril, I will strive to do my share to awaken our nation and our lawmakers to the dangers of our present undefended condition so that we may continue to dwell in peace and prosperity and may not have to mourn states desolated by war within our own borders.
>
> Insofar as I am able, I will make my home a center of American ideals and patriotism, and endeavor to teach the children in my care to cherish and revere our country and its history and to uphold its honor and fair repute in their generation.[1]

Those who signed the pledge promised to uphold the ideals of patriotic motherhood, ideals that defined women's most significant political role as producing citizens who would stand firm against America's foes. For those who signed the pledge, preparedness offered a unique opportunity for national service, which they increasingly defined as a central component of motherhood and women's citizenship.

Yet the fact that preparedness organizations made a public spectacle of women's signatures suggests that patriotic motherhood was not universally valued.[2] The war sharpened debates over women's citizenship and its implied relationship between women's obligations to the state and to their families. Those women who signed the pledge took a strong stand in these debates by publicly affirming the relationship between women's duties in the home and their role in shaping national-ism, Americanism, and military preparedness. As women joined pre-paredness organizations, published magazines, and lobbied congress, the tenets of patriotic motherhood pulled women from their homes. The war required women to play a more public role in shaping motherhood and its relationship to citizenship.

Like those women who signed the pledge, government authorities were concerned that some women's rejection of patriotic motherhood threatened the character of the nation. The cases of women who were charged under the wartime emergency laws exposed this anxiety. Most often state authorities and the press operated within nationalist dis-courses that emphasized a close relationship between women's roles as mothers and their responsibilities in reproducing Americanism and patriotism. It was patriotic motherhood that state authorities claimed that the women who were accused under the Espionage and Sedition Acts had violated. And, not surprisingly, it was patriotic motherhood that the accused women rejected in their constructions of themselves as citizens. This chapter sets the context for women's prosecutions under the wartime emergency laws by examining how the war influenced arguments over women's citizenship and the consequences of women's increasing role in American political culture.

Patriotic motherhood emerged from the maternalist discourses that shaped the political activities and identities of white middle-class wom-en throughout the nineteenth and early twentieth centuries.[3] Loosely defined, maternalism was a series of "ideologies and discourses that exalted women's capacity to mother and applied to society as a whole the values they attached to that role: care, nurturance, and morality."[4] Maternalism did not have a uniform or even stable meaning. Instead, "[m]aternalism necessarily operated in relation to other discourses—about citizenship, class relations, gender difference, and national iden-tity, to name only a few—and in relation to a wide array of concrete social and political practices."[5]

Discussions about American participation in the war took place while white, middle-class women were carving out a place within the emerg-ing state bureaucracy by claiming primary responsibility for programs that affected mothers and children.[6] The state, these reformers argued, should reward mothers for their service and protect mothers and their children from the worst effects of industrial society. Such efforts re-shaped women's relationship to American politics and, in turn, "domes-ticated" politics as the state took over some of the functions of the home.[7]

Although pro-natalist state-building remained a key facet of wom-en's politics, class, race, and ideological differences led women to as-sert varied and often oppositional constructions of women's citizenship.[8] Women's rights advocates often disagreed about the meaning of women's citizenship. Social feminists, who argued for women's political rights on the basis of their sexual difference, were challenged by equity feminists, who argued that as citizens women had the same inherent rights and responsibilities as men.[9] Equity feminists stressed that as individuals, rather than as mothers, women were entitled to the same basic civil and human rights promised to their male counterparts by the American Revolution. It was from these ideas of equal citizenship and from socialist and progressive ideas of internationalism that women who were accused under the wartime laws defined their political identities.

Historians argue that World War I accentuated gender differences and facilitated pro-natalist state-building at the cost of feminist discourses that stressed sexual equality.[10] For both men and women, the war provided an opportunity to rethink the relationships between manhood, womanhood, and citizenship. The result was a highly dynamic and complex political culture in which women's actual political participation may have increased, but one in which the meanings attached to that increased participation confined women's access to key components of citizenship, such as patriotism and Americanism, to narrow constructions of maternalism.[11] The pro-war and countersubversive discourses that accompanied American participation in the war facilitated this process because they focused attention on women's mothering and its relationship to a healthy and well-ordered state.

As war approached, nationalists linked maternalism to Americanism and patriotism while opponents of war emphasized its relationship to internationalism and peace politics. American participation in the war limited, at least for the duration, any substantive public debate between maternalist peace advocates and supporters of patriotic motherhood. Most liberal peace advocates bowed to the Wilson administration's pressure for absolute loyalty and shifted their focus toward affecting the peace rather than opposing the war. That participation established patriotic motherhood, at least for the war's duration, as the only acceptable definition of the relationships among motherhood, internationalism, and women's citizenship.

The fact that the war could provide anti-feminists with a language and opportunity to reconstruct a masculine and Anglo political community was not lost on women's rights advocates. As I will discuss below, many women's rights activists ultimately supported the war for both pragmatic and patriotic reasons. But before January of 1917, women's rights advocates linked women's citizenship to pacifism as they asserted women's influence over liberal and socialist internationalism. Their efforts resulted in a new peace movement that was clearly associated with women's politics. The WPP was, not surprisingly, the feminist organization that pro-war nationalists most vilified.

The WPP was the most influential arm of the new peace movement that emerged during the European war. Before 1914 business interests had dominated the peace movement. Business leaders who were concerned about the impact of war on international economic stability had argued for a system of international arbitration. Specifically, they turned toward international law and a world court to regulate international disputes. The European war, however, changed the face and character of the peace movement.[12]

Unlike the pre-war peace movement, the WPP defined peace politics within the context of reform. Before American entrance into World War I, the WPP played a central role in shaping progressive internationalism and Wilson's own peace initiatives. In fact, members of this new peace movement were essential to the left-liberal coalition that narrowly re-elected Wilson in 1916.[13]

Members of the women's peace movement were concerned with more than shaping progressive internationalism and Wilson's peace initiatives. They also sought to define a privileged space for women within the new world order they hoped would accompany Wilson's programs. Arguing that women's opposition to war was instinctive, members of the WPP viewed peace politics as a rational extension of maternalism.[14] They believed that their role as nurturers gave women a unique commitment to peace that men did not share, a perspective that led women to view social relations differently than their male counterparts.[15] WPP members asserted that as mothers, women approached relationships less competitively and more cooperatively than men, which led them to seek mutually agreeable solutions to international disputes. Peace politics, they insisted, required a reorientation of political and international citizenship that women were more qualified than men to undertake. Partly because of this ability to connect domestic and international politics, the WPP enjoyed support from a broad spectrum of women who were committed to social reform and civil liberties politics, not all of whom may have shared the maternalism espoused by the WPP's leadership and national statements.[16]

As Wilson came to the pragmatic decision that he could only have a seat at the peace table if the United States entered the war, his administration worried that "women, especially those in the prewar women's peace movement, might constitute a subversive element in the nation, detrimental to wartime unity and the smooth functioning of selective service."[17] To its detractors, the WPP symbolized the dangers of unchecked maternal influence.[18] Although the WPP was not the first or only organization to foster women's interests and influence in international affairs, its ability to fundamentally question and redefine the relationships among citizenship, democracy, and militarism sharpened attacks on the values that white middle-class women brought to politics. To many of its critics, the WPP represented a particularly unwelcome and dangerous intrusion into the last frontier for masculine politics—foreign affairs.[19]

Pre-war critics of the WPP contended that its maternal politics exposed a fundamental flaw in women's participation in international politics. Responding to the formation of the WPP, the editors of the *New Republic*, a leading vehicle for pro-war Progressives, berated the WPP for venturing into international relations:

> The American women who have formed the Woman's Peace Party are sane in their insistence upon human values, but their sanity is the sanity of isolation, and their horror of war is that of the spectator. They will never know the reality of their own sentiment until they have tested it in the face of a personal crisis, until, like the women of Europe, they have lived in the tensions that may ultimately lead to war.... What better work could the Woman's Peace Party undertake than to cut its wisdom teeth on a thoroughly domestic issue? Surely, women cannot hope to intervene in Europe until they have shown what they can do in a country where women are powerful.[20]

In the words of historian David Kennedy, progressives shared "the hopeful premise that men and women in the mass were rational beings, uniformly responsive to reasoned argument and incapable of serious disagreement in the face of scientifically demonstrated facts."[21] Progressives dismissed dissenting positions as irrational. Using this framework, the *New Republic* transformed a disagreement about policy into a judgment against women's political capacities. Its editors simply asserted that members of the WPP lacked the political experience to make rational decisions, especially in international politics. Once they had the same political experience as men, then perhaps members of the WPP would recognize their own fallacies and join the political community as rational decision makers. Until then, they should leave international politics to men such as themselves who were guided by a higher ideal of citizenship.

Pro-war progressives believed that the experience of war would make American society more efficient and would promote nationalism. A "moral adventure of war," they argued, not only strengthened formal political structures but also promoted the idea of a less selfish citizenry that would be ready to sacrifice for a national culture rather than a local community.[22] These ideas were compatible with those of female reformers who likewise argued for a stronger state and a national political community that would be dedicated to the promotion of universal moral values.[23] At the same time, progressives emphasized that this search for a national identity must be free from sentiment and emotional attachments. The editors of the *New Republic* implied, through their critique of the WPP, that women's lack of political experience made them more susceptible to such sentimentality than were men.

But members of the WPP were no less experienced in the business of war than the editors of the *New Republic*, and many, such as Jane Addams and Lillian Wald, had significant experience in domestic politics. The *New Republic's* relegation of women to domestic politics was not based on significant differences between the actual experiences of the editors of the *New Republic* and members of the WPP, but instead on their possible experiences. As men, the editors of the *New Republic* could make war. Pro-war progressives, such as the editors of the *New Republic*, claimed that men's potential experience as soldiers gave them insight that American women lacked because women remained behind the lines of battle. By privileging the rational decision making that they argued derived from this uniquely male experience, the editors of the *New Republic* reserved the highest ideals of citizenship for men.

Like the editors of the *New Republic*, Theodore Roosevelt criticized the WPP for undermining the rational pursuit of the nation's interest. In a now-famous letter written to the Chicago *Herald* and reprinted in the pages of *Literary Digest*, Roosevelt characterized the WPP as "silly and base." He argued that its protests against American intervention in the European war were futile, timid, and immoral; they betrayed the entire peace movement with sentimentality and hypocrisy. "There is nothing easier, there is nothing on the whole less worthwhile," Roosevelt wrote, "than vague and hysterical demands for the right in the abstract, coupled with the unworthy and timid refusal even to allude to frightful wrongs that are at the very moment being committed in the concrete."[24] Roosevelt argued that moral action derived from the careful application of scientific principles that had been discovered and tested through action. In contrast, he defined those values that the WPP claimed distinguished women's politics as "sentimentalism" and consequently antithetical to national interests.

The WPP focused specific anxieties about the status of masculine citizenship on women's politics. Yet, the origins of that fear went deeper than women's claims to political authority. "To a significant degree," writes Kennedy, "the concern for preparedness and the concern for forced assimilation flowed from the same anxiety about the flabbiness of American society in a hostile world."[25] Historians have long noted the "virility impulse" that shaped the languages of nationalism in the three decades that preceded American intervention in the war; a more active nationalism, which included American participation in the war, promised to change the character of citizenship.[26]

Until recently historians have not examined this virility impulse in relation to the changes brought about by women's participation in public life beyond observing that feminism had produced in middle-class men anxiety about the status of their sons.[27] Women's political participation facilitated important structural changes that, at least according to one historian, changed the character of politics such that "politics was no longer a public space where ideas of manhood and womanhood could be acted out." Unlike nineteenth-century politics, which were intimately defined by gender difference, progressive politics posited a new vision of expertise that advanced a strong state run by professional bureaucrats. On its face, this new vision of expertise was gender neutral, because education and training rather than participation in a manly political culture defined one's role in politics.[28] Yet political discourses of war continued as a forum in which "ideas of manhood and womanhood could be acted out." In particular, pro-war nationalists believed that a war would reinscribe citizenship with the manly ideals that feminism and industrialization had threatened.[29]

Nationalists ranged in their expectations of how the experience of war would lead to a higher ideal of citizenship. Some, like Roosevelt, argued that preparation for war produced virtuous citizens. To that end he advocated compulsory military training. Although many pro-war progressives found Roosevelt's ideas extreme, they shared his belief that participation in the war would champion the civic virtue, commonality of purpose, and heroic action that American citizenship lacked.[30]

The war provided nationalists with a language for reconstructing a homosocial political community that reconfirmed sexual and racial differences under the guise of national unity. Nationalists felt that this community provided an alternative set of moral values than those espoused by women, values that were grounded in nationalism and Americanism. As the American ambassador to the Court of St. James explained to his son,

> 1. It [World War I] will break up and tear away our isolation; 2. It will unhorse our cranks and soft-brains; 3. It will make us less promiscuously hospitable to every kind of immigrant; 4. It will reestablish in our mind and conscience and policy our true historic genesis, background, kindred and destiny—kill the Irish and German influence; 5. It will revive our real manhood—put mollycoddles in disgrace, as idiots and dandies are; 6. It will make our policies frank and manly by restoring true nationality; 7. It will make us again [into] a great sea-faring people; 8. Break our education —make a boy [a] vigorous animal and make our education rest on [a] wholesome physical basis; 9. Bring men [of] a higher type [into] our political life.[31]

Like many nationalists of the period, Ambassador Page subscribed to the Teutonic view of history that endowed the Anglo-Saxon race with those characteristics necessary for democratic government.[32] But Page also linked racial heterogeneity with anxieties about feminization and its effects on masculine citizenship. Although many nationalist thinkers such as Page did not argue that women should not participate in politics, they were concerned that politics itself retain the manly qualities that they felt were essential to the preservation of the Anglo-Saxon race.[33]

As Gail Bederman has argued in *Manliness and Civilization: A Cultural History of Gender and Race in the United States, 1880–1917*, these links between civilization, racial identity, and gender were pervasive in the years before the war. For middle-class men, Bederman contends, "whiteness was both a palpable fact and a manly ideal." She demonstrates how middle-class white men forged ideas of manliness and masculinity in response to both their own economic dislocation and the increasing participation of women in public life. Most significantly for our purposes, Bederman illustrates how manliness itself was constructed as a racial and nationalist identity.[34] Within this framework, those qualities that peace activists brought to politics were dismissed as irrational, weak, and, consequently, un-American.

Not surprisingly, Roosevelt was among the loudest advocates for this vision of a racialized and gendered nationalist identity. Roosevelt believed that political heterogeneity resulted in a "hyphenated Americanism" or "dual loyalties" that "emasculated" the nation by breaking down the homogenous community in which "national manliness" flourished. In Roosevelt's words:

> A flabby cosmopolitanism, especially if it expresses itself through flabby pacifism, is not only silly but degrading. It represents a national emasculation. The professors of every form of hyphenated Americanism are as truly the foes of this country as if they dwelt outside its borders and made active war against it.[35]

Although Roosevelt believed that the American character was generally sound, he worried that it could slip into decay. Influenced by Lamarckian racial theories, Roosevelt feared that Americans could inherit inferior racial characteristics if those characteristics flourished within its borders. To avoid this fate, Roosevelt believed that Americans must protect a manly political culture capable of resisting the infections of racial and gender heterogeneity.[36]

As Bederman points out, Roosevelt had a long history of racial thinking that linked a distinctly American character with the conquest of "savage" races. His book *The Winning of the West* described how this character emerged "in the act of winning a new and virgin continent."[37] This conquest, followed by what he considered to be the "civilization" of a new frontier, preserved racial purity and national manliness. Roosevelt characterized American participation in the war as a test of and a necessary prerequisite for racial fitness.

The fact that proponents of war described both their expectations and their fears about America's response to war in gendered as well as racialized terms is significant. It illustrates the intricate relationship between the family and American political culture.[38] On the most basic level, proponents of war argued that maintaining middle-class gender roles was essential to the preservation of political order and racial fitness. To enforce this family ideal, they encouraged interventions in the way women socialized male children.[39]

For some proponents of war, the military served as a check on the maternal influence of women.[40] Although they agreed that women's primary contribution to the war effort was as mothers, some proponents of war were profoundly ambivalent about women's socialization of their sons. This concern motivated calls for compulsory military service. "The average boy is neither obedient, helpful nor well-mannered," argued Rear Admiral Goodrich. "We have learned that these things cannot be taught in the homes. Something is needed and that is universal service."[41] For Goodrich and other advocates of compulsory service, American homes were ill-suited for citizenship training.[42] Fearful that American citizenship had lost its virility, they looked to a distinctly male institution—the military—to restore it.[43]

The call for compulsory military training was both a pragmatic response by preparedness advocates who feared that the United States was ill-equipped to participate in an international world and an ideological response by nationalists who were concerned over the status of citizenship. Nationalists saw the family and the military as key institutions through which to teach good citizenship and often described the two as intertwined. Not surprisingly, nationalist discussion of women's roles focused on women's responsibility to produce loyal American citizens. For example, although Roosevelt believed that men were primarily responsible for guaranteeing national greatness, he argued that women also played a key role that assured racial fitness. A grudging supporter of women's suffrage, Roosevelt nonetheless admired the female reformers who helped shape progressivism.[44] Roosevelt also believed that such women were ultimately less useful and happy than the "average woman," who fulfilled her patriotic duty to "bear at least three children."[45] Concerned that white Protestant women were not bearing enough children, Roosevelt claimed that a race suicide would result from the women's movement's most excessive demands, such as birth control. Motherhood, Roosevelt maintained, was women's most important duty to the nation and ultimately women's greatest achievement. Women who properly performed their functions as mothers deserved the same honor (and privileges?) as the men who properly performed their roles as soldiers.[46]

By the same token, those individuals who rejected this relationship between soldiering and family life were literally nonmen and nonwomen.[47] Roosevelt suggested that pacifist women belonged in "harems" because their misguided pacifism exposed other women to sexual abuse.[48] He also argued that men who refused military service forfeited their roles as husbands because they exposed their families to violence.[49] Such men, in Roosevelt's estimation, were nonmen—"the white handed or sissy type of pacifist, [who] represents . . . the rotting out of the virile virtues . . . of civilization."[50]

Gender ridicule was a common tactic in American politics; its use underscored the close relationship between the family, citizenship, and the state. In the words of one historian, "good government depended on proper household order; tyranny or anarchy, as threats to the republic, appeared in the guise of sexual sin."[51] Proponents of war defined this sexual sin most clearly as Germany's "rape" of Belgium, which represented not only Germany's disregard of international law but also the degeneracy of the German culture that promoted death and sexual perversion. But their description of pacifists as sexual deviants placed the threats posed by German culture within the nation's doors and suggested that if Americans adopted pacifism they, like the Germans, would choose a depraved culture.

The widespread use of poster art expanded the influence of this atrocity propaganda, and made the murdered and ravished woman a powerful pro-war symbol.[52] On one level the purpose of this propaganda was to convince the nation, in the words of one historian, to "embrace the war as [its] own personal commitment."[53] As victims in atrocity propaganda, women symbolized the German threat to each American family. But women also played a positive role in poster art. As lovers or mothers, wartime propaganda suggested, women could exhort men to go to war.[54] In much of this poster art, it was not enough that women raise sons who were willing to sacrifice for the nation; women also had the responsibility to persuade other women's sons to go to war by using their sexuality to reward men who went to war.[55]

As a product of the emerging consumer culture of the early twentieth century, poster art incorporated aspects of the emerging heterosexual youth culture. For this reason, poster artists stepped outside the Victorian gender roles favored by preparedness advocates. Yet in the end, these posters reinforced the complicated assumptions of nationalists about the relationship between heterosexual gender roles and national greatness as it disciplined women's newfound sexual freedom to the demands of war.

Likewise, poster artists began to represent women in nontraditional work roles as the war crisis required women to perform more public sector tasks. Poster artists most often portrayed these tasks as extensions of motherhood and adapted motherhood to those roles in order to reinforce the primacy of patriotic motherhood.[56] Although they were sometimes contradictory, the images in wartime poster art reinforced the contract inherent within patriotic motherhood—soldiers went to war to protect good mothers, who in turn produced sons and daughters who were loyal to the nation and willing to sacrifice for its defense.

But as historian Nicoletta Gullace argues, this propaganda did more than personalize the war or define appropriate gender roles for women. In her examination of British war propaganda, Gullace concludes that atrocity propaganda shifted the meaning of British foreign policy. As that propaganda replaced its "emphasis on the violation of treaty law [with] a vision of the brutalization of women and children," it "domesticated the meaning of British foreign policy and privileged a set of familial and sexual concerns within the stated military policy of the liberal state."Consequently, Gullace contends, "'national honor,' 'treaty violation,' and 'international law' no longer referred exclusively to travesty against a legally grounded international order based on the immutability of texts but came increasingly to be defined in terms of the family itself." In her words, "those who invoked international law repeatedly grounded their claims to legitimacy in the sanctity of the family and female body ... [which led to a] definition of the liberal state that located the safety of women and the family as the primary issue of the public realm."[57]

As I will argue in the chapters that follow, wartime repression located the"the safety of women and the family as a primary issue of the public realm." At stake in America's efforts to fight and win its war against Germany, and later against Bolshevism, was "the sanctity of the family and the female body,"both of which served as important metaphors for the liberal state's unique claims to Americanism. Although the primary motive of the wartime laws was not to control gender roles, the very fact that arguments over loyalty, patriotism, and Americanism were framed in gendered terms illustrates how closely Americans tied the fate of the liberal state with an ordered gender system. The state's emerging surveillance system incorporated this concern by linking women's subversion with sexual degeneracy and gender perversion.

Although conservative men dominated the preparedness movement and men were the primary image makers of pro-war propaganda, women too joined preparedness efforts and staked their claims to citizenship on their participation in movements that promoted Americanism and nationalism. These women often directly challenged the construction of internationalism and maternalism of pacifist women. For many women who supported preparedness or American participation in the war, women's peace activity posed a threat to their identities as mothers and as citizens. Albeit influenced by nationalist thinkers such as Theodore Roosevelt, they did not share his ambivalence over women's socialization of their sons. Instead, pro-preparedness women believed that members of the WPP perverted motherhood and that the majority of American women were patriotic mothers. As historian Barbara Stein-son argues, women in the preparedness movement "believed that their protective function included concern for the defense of the U.S. and that one duty of mothers was to develop courageous and patriotic sons willing to fight at the call of their country."[58] They saw the war as an opportunity "for service, and through service, recognition and respect."[59]

Women's preparedness work emerged from the many relief organizations that formed at the start of the European war. Especially concerned over Germany's invasion of Belgium, American women founded a number of relief groups that, among other things, organized the ambulance corps in France and helped displaced refugees.[60] The largest and most influential of these relief organizations were those affiliated with either the Woman's Department of the National Civic Federation (WDNCF) or the Women's Sector of the Navy League (WSNL). After the sinking of the *Lusitania* and as the significance of the women's peace movement grew, several key relief agencies shifted their work to preparedness.[61] Preparedness work primarily attracted women of high social status, and, as Steinson points out, for many women preparedness work reinforced that status.[62]

Women in the preparedness movement argued that motherhood should advance nationalism and patriotism. In addition to protecting the United States from invasion, the Woman's Sector of the Navy League—the first women's preparedness organization—listed among its goals arousing patriotism among American women and dispelling the anti-militarist image of women. Women in the preparedness movement warned against joining the WPP because it was led by "visionaries, emotionalists, ethereal fancy people with phantoms of what should be, but is not."[63] Their movement offered women an alternative political course, one grounded in a vision of motherhood that recognized and supported the necessity of the concrete moral action of war and the sacrifices it demanded.

National citizenship, pro-preparedness women argued, required manly men and mothers who were willing to sacrifice for the sake of the manhood of their sons. Women in the preparedness movement contended that peace advocates denied their sons that manliness by protecting their sons' lives at the cost of their virtue.[64] According to Josephine Bates, whose son was killed on the *Lusitania,* "There are worse things than war and a woman must not warp standards." "Warped" standards, Bates argued, would "make a man a coward to duty, or worse, betray him in principles and ideals vastly more precious than his life."[65] Here, Bates defined the essence of patriotic motherhood. It was the duty of women to nurture the character of their sons, to instill in their sons the values of Americanism. Women's duties as patriotic mothers, Bates suggested, demanded that they sacrifice their attachment to their sons' bodies; to do otherwise turned their sons into nonmen who endangered the nation through their cowardice and anarchism. Such women robbed their sons of the heroic transcendence that Bates and other preparedness advocates believed defined manliness. Preparedness women stressed that peace advocates, through their selfishness, dishonored motherhood itself.[66]

Although most organizations in the women's sector of the preparedness movement remained neutral toward women's suffrage, the war emergency encouraged anti-suffragists to renew their attacks on women's political participation. Some of these attacks followed predictable lines as anti-suffragists argued that women's nature required women to fight the war from their homes. As one anti-suffrage preparedness advocate wrote,

> we will play various parts in any war but the great mass of women in America will not be called upon to leave their homes.... The backbone of the army of women will be the homes, and these will be the real foundation for the nation's success.[67]

Other anti-suffragists used the impending war emergency to attack women's political participation. The women's peace movement, they argued, only underscored the dangers of women's political participation. To further highlight the seditious qualities of that participation, anti-suffragists contended that the women's suffrage movement drew strong support from the Socialist Party, a charge that some suffrage leaders proved increasingly anxious to refute.[68] Just as significantly, the war revived arguments that linked soldiering with citizenship. Because women could not be soldiers and consequently could not sacrifice their lives for the state, they were not entitled to the same rights as men.[69] In the context of war, anti-suffragists emphasized that votes for women was a selfish demand, especially when the nation was in need of citizens willing to sacrifice individual desires for the good of the entire national community.

As the prospect of American participation in war increased, suffrage leaders found it increasingly necessary to respond to these critics. They understood that American participation in the war could derail their cause.[70] A failure to unconditionally support the war or continued agitation for suffrage during the war crisis could further harden opposition to suffrage. Although many supporters of suffrage were members of the new peace movement, the leadership of the National American Women's Suffrage Association (NAWSA) pledged their organization's support for Wilson's war programs in January of 1917. Their decision was not solely based on expediency. Patriotism motivated the war work of many members of NAWSA.

If the war was to be an opportunity for suffrage leaders to, in the words of Theodora Youmans, president of the Wisconsin Woman's Suffrage Association, "drive suffrage home to the minds of the people as never before," suffrage leaders argued that they needed to refocus their message to serve the specific needs of the war.[71] In the months before the United States entered the war, suffrage leaders prepared their constituency for a strong pro-war position. As Wisconsin's representative to NAWSA explained: "we stand ready to serve our Country with the zeal and consecration which should ever characterize there [sic] who cherish high ideals of the duty and obligation of citizenship."[72]

As war approached some suffrage leaders tailored their arguments to the war effort. Harriot Stanton Blatch, a leader in the New York suffrage movement, suggested that the war would force women into the workforce, thus ensuring their economic and political freedom. Much to the relief of Roosevelt and other preparedness supporters, Blatch constructed a feminist case for women's support of the war by arguing that German politics and culture were uniquely misogynist. Blatch contended that women had a special stake in fighting the war because "German Kultur fixes an inflexible limit to the aspirations of women, while our goal is complete freedom for the mothers of men."[73] Like that of men, the future political and economic freedom of women was dependent on the triumph of the liberal state.

For many suffrage leaders, war work was the vehicle through which women would prove their loyalty to the public virtues that their male counterparts demonstrated on the battlefields of Europe. Accomplishing this goal, however, required a more far-reaching and tangible role for women than simply providing support for the troops.

Suffrage leaders defined their war work in relation to a domestic battle against disloyalty, but unlike preparedness advocates they used nationalist and countersubversive languages to minimize the differences between men's and women's wartime roles and responsibilities. As war approached, suffrage leaders scrambled to secure positions that would maximize their impact on the war program. Wilson appointed suffrage leaders to the Women's Committee on National Defense, but its leadership expressed frustration over their under-utilization and the committee's emphasis on relief work.[74] To broaden their contribution to the war effort, some suffrage leaders pursued Americanization as their major contribution to the war effort. In doing so they tapped into a movement that was gaining momentum from the entry of the United States into the war.

As war broke out in Europe and concern over securing the loyalty of the immigrant population grew, proponents of Americanization argued that their programs secured loyalty without resorting to legal restrictions on speech and immigration. Americanization had its roots in the efforts of social workers to socialize immigrants. By the second decade of the twentieth century, reformers had redefined Americanization as a citizenship issue. Women's clubs urged their membership to develop programs specifically aimed at immigrant women in order to prepare them for suffrage and to empower them within their own families.[75] Americanizers feared that immigrant women had lost moral authority within the home and consequently could not produce patriotic and well-adjusted citizens.[76]

By July of 1917, the chair of the Americanization Committee of the NAWSA, Grace H. Bagley, had outlined a program for suffrage organizations. "Our national defense must come from within as well as from without.... [T]he woman ... who is the means of converting one alien to become a loyal American citizen ... is in the fighting line as truly as the man who goes to the front."[77] Bagley used the rhetoric of a two-front war to place the wartime contributions of women on the same plane as those of men. By adopting this aspect of countersubversive language rather than, for example, patriotic motherhood, suffrage leaders deconstructed the gender dichotomies that shaped the languages of both the preparedness movement and peace activists. Within a wartime political culture defined by clear gender dichotomies, suffrage leaders constructed women as citizens whose actions derived from the same public virtues as those of men.

Suffrage leaders argued that Americanization both ensured loyalty and avoided the potential hatred that wartime conditions could breed. "We believe that a problem unknown to other lands will become accentuated in the event of war," warned Jessie Hooper of the Wisconsin Woman's Suffrage Association,

> Within our borders are eight millions of aliens, who by birth, tradition and training will find it difficult, if not impossible, to understand the causes which have led to the war. War invariably breeds intolerance and hate, and will tend to arouse antagonisms inimical to the best interests of our nation. With a desire to minimize this certain danger, our association . . . offers [Americanization].[78]

Suffrage leaders expected that Americanization would intercept wartime civil liberties abuses.[79] They self-consciously distinguished themselves from nativist traditions that advocated exclusionary laws and deportation.[80] But wartime Americanization programs reproduced the fundamental assumption of wartime countersubversive thought—that foreignness was somehow indicative of disloyal and criminal behavior. Americanizers were often condescending, especially when discussing immigrant women. "On the whole, [the immigrant woman] is a pathetic figure," argued one Americanizer. "[A]rriving in this country wretched, ignorant, exploited on all sides, she is eager to do her share and become part, with her children, of their new country."[81] Americanizers assumed that immigrant families should adopt middle-class gender roles. They constructed Americanization as the "duty" of middle-class women, reinforcing the values of benevolence and moral uplift that characterized the feminism of Anglo-Saxon women. Like the most restrictive expressions of wartime countersubversion, Americanizers assumed that dissent and difference were diseases that they must cure.[82] And although most Americanization efforts focused on men, increasingly women's organizations used Americanization to scrutinize the mothering practices of immigrant women. As war approached, Americanization became an important avenue by which nationalists examined motherhood for its role in reproducing patriotism and national values.

Not all suffrage organizations supported the war; nor did they postpone their work for suffrage. As I have argued elsewhere, the war sharpened differences within the suffrage movement and between liberal and socialist women. Even within NAWSA, members disagreed over that organization's endorsement of war work. Confronted with a wartime culture that emphasized conformity, many chapters of NAWSA refused to accommodate different positions on the war and gratefully watched dissenting members leave that organization, often for the National Woman's Party (NWP).[83]

Unlike NAWSA, the NWP pressured Wilson to support the suffrage amendment and picketed the White House to point out the contradictions between the ideology that justified the war and women's lack of political rights. This action only fueled the accusations of anti-suffragists that women's political participation would weaken the nation. In part because of such criticisms, members of NAWSA distanced themselves from the NWP and condemned the picketing. Interestingly, members of the NWP were not arrested under the federal wartime laws but rather under local ordinances for disorderly conduct.[84]

The European war focused discussions of the meaning of women's citizenship in an international world. For peace advocates, the war underscored the need for the special skills that women brought to politics, skills that they argued were uniquely suited for building a democratic governance of the world. Members of the preparedness movement criticized such arguments as naive and argued that they demonstrated the dangers posed by women's increasing political participation. But to women in the preparedness movement and, later, to some members of the suffrage movement, the business of war offered a unique opportunity for women to prove that like men, they could sacrifice for the nation and through this sacrifice attain a higher ideal of citizenship.

This chapter outlined how patriotic ideals of motherhood and womanhood emerged just prior to American involvement in World War I. Central to these ideas was the notion of women's primary service to the state through the reproduction of soldiers capable of battling the nation's external and internal enemies. Patriotic motherhood reaffirmed that women's obligations to the state were intimately linked to motherhood. But patriotic motherhood contained maternalism's impact on the political. In its most conservative incarnations, patriotic motherhood restricted the contributions of women to the home and accused the increased political participation of women of creating a softness in national character. But not all proponents of patriotic motherhood sought to eliminate women's growing public role; they saw patriotic motherhood as an expansion of women's public role because it placed mothers at the center of nation's battles against its foreign and domestic enemies. Patriotic motherhood redirected motherhood's relationship to the political and placed it at the center of nationalist discourses that strengthened the state's role as the guardian of the nation's most treasured values.

As historians have argued, World War I helped usher in a new role for the state. In the words of John McClymer, "the state was more than the instrumentality of government; it was, or claimed to be, the symbol of all cultural and civic virtues."[85] Although historians have examined women's contributions to and the role of gender in the construction of the welfare state, we know little of women's role in or how gender affected the formation of the surveillance state. Women's trials under the wartime laws were part of the process by which the state claimed its new role in American society as the guardian of "all cultural and civic virtues." It is to women's encounters with the federal wartime laws that I now turn.

2

⚭

Motherhood and Subversion

THE CASE OF KATE RICHARDS O'HARE

In June 1917, Kate Richards O'Hare delivered an anti-war speech to a small audience that consisted primarily of women and children. Afterward, she attended a reception hosted by the founders of the Nonpartisan League of Bowman, North Dakota.[1] A few days later, acting on a tip from opponents of the Nonpartisan League, federal authorities arrested O'Hare, charging that she had made seditious remarks during her speech. Stunned, O'Hare noted that she had given the same speech on well over one hundred occasions, some of which were attended by Justice Department officials. Nonetheless, relying principally on the testimony of a local banker, Jim Phalan, the government indicted her for intending to interfere with the draft, a violation of the Espionage Act.[2]

The Justice Department based its charges on remarks that O'Hare allegedly made about the effects of the war on women, remarks that formed only a brief portion of a two-hour speech that primarily focused on how the war benefited capitalism. What O'Hare actually said was disputed. O'Hare's indictment accused her of calling American mothers "brood sows" and American soldiers "fertilizer":

> any person who enlisted in the Army of the United States for service in France would be fertilizer, and that was all that he was good for, and that the women of the United States were nothing more than brood sows to raise children to get into the Army and made into fertilizer.[3]

O'Hare denied making these remarks. She instead offered the following version of the disputed paragraph:

> When the governments of Europe and the clergy of Europe demanded of the women that they give themselves in marriage, or out, in order that men might "breed before they die," that was not the crime of maddened passion, it was the cold blooded crime of brutal selfishness, and by that crime the women of Europe were reduced to the status of breeding animals on a stock farm.[4]

The specific wording seemed important. Unlike the government's version, O'Hare's passage avoided the direct criticism of the American war effort that was forbidden by the Espionage Act. As the courts interpreted the Espionage Act, however, prosecutors did not have to prove that O'Hare actually criticized the war effort but only that she intended her remarks to interfere with the draft.[5]

O'Hare's guilt rested on a broad understanding of the "bad tendency doctrine" that defined speech as seditious if it simply had a "bad tendency to cause unrest in an impressionable public."[6] The presiding judge, Martin J. Wade, used this broad understanding of the bad tendency doctrine throughout O'Hare's trial. He instructed the jury that if her remarks even potentially interfered with the draft, they violated the Espionage Act. "You have the right to take into consideration," he instructed the jury,

> the general purpose of and feeling of the great majority of the American people that this war must be won; that no other result would be tolerated. You have a right to take into consideration the general knowledge which you must have, as everyone else, that there is only one way to win a war, and that is to have soldiers.[7]

Because of Wade's instructions, historians argue that O'Hare's case "helped set the tone of conservative expectations for espionage prosecutions."[8] They define its importance exclusively in terms of its impact on civil liberties and anti-socialist politics.[9] Yet these interpretations neglect the very issue that makes O'Hare's case fascinating. Although anti-socialism played a role in her conviction, the charges against O'Hare did not ultimately focus on her argument that the war served the interests of capitalism. Instead, the Justice Department indicted her for alleging that the war corrupted motherhood.

O'Hare's remarks and the reaction they engendered underscore the importance of patriotic motherhood to the war effort. As Judge Wade instructed the jury, "the only way to win a war [is] to have soldiers." As patriotic mothers it was the responsibility of women to produce citizen-soldiers. O'Hare's remarks explicitly challenged this understanding of the wartime role of women. O'Hare argued that the experience of war alienated women from motherhood because it reduced women to vehicles for the reproduction of soldiers who in turn killed and were killed for the state. O'Hare defined patriotic motherhood as a labor contract by which women produced surplus value in return for the protection of soldiers. She rejected this contract because it alienated women from their labor, reduced motherhood to its basest reproductive capacities, and denied the essential role that O'Hare believed mothers played in defining character and social morality. In essence, O'Hare contended, patriotic motherhood epitomized the corruption of motherhood that occurred under capitalism and militarism.[10]

Kate Richards O'Hare was born in Ottowa County, Kansas, in 1876 to a homesteading family. After an economic bust in 1887, O'Hare's father moved his family to Kansas City, where he found work as a machinist and later opened a machine shop. Influenced by the poverty she saw in Kansas City and her family's religious values, O'Hare considered a career as a missionary. Like many politically active white women of the late nineteenth century, O'Hare joined the temperance and settlement house movements. Unlike many of the middle-class reformers who participated in these movements, O'Hare worked in her father's machine shop and participated in labor union politics. After meeting Mother Jones, O'Hare converted to socialism and joined the Socialist Party in 1901. With her husband, Frank O'Hare, O'Hare stumped the Midwest and Southeast. Particularly popular among farmers, the O'Hares helped establish the Socialist Party as a major political force, especially in Oklahoma. Like many socialist women of her generation, O'Hare adapted her socialist message to moral reform principles, and often defined socialism as a moral crusade.[11]

As O'Hare's biographer Sally Miller argues, O'Hare's ability to blend a public life dedicated to political change with a conventional private life distinguished her from many of the public women of her time.[12] A central component of O'Hare's socialist crusade was her maternalism. Seldom pictured without her family, O'Hare consciously portrayed herself as the ideal socialist mother. Her book *Sorrows of Cupid* reaffirmed the glories of motherhood; she condemned capitalism because it destroyed the family.[13] In part because of her own investment in maternalism, O'Hare's case contained the most explicit debate about the meaning of motherhood and its relationship to loyalty and patriotism among the trials of women who were charged under the federal wartime laws. O'Hare's popularity in the socialist movement guaranteed that this debate would gain a national audience.

Political disputes that resulted from the strength of the Nonpartisan League in North Dakota motivated O'Hare's arrest. Founded by former socialist organizers, the Nonpartisan League demanded government ownership of commercial enterprises that affected farmers. The Nonpartisan League was especially strong in North Dakota, where it captured several local and state offices. In Bowman, the local leaders of the Nonpartisan League, Edward P. Totten and Lillian Totten, the postmistress, were under attack by the league's opponents. Apparently those who opposed the Nonpartisan League and the Tottens believed that they could discredit the league, which had sponsored O'Hare's talk, if they could indict O'Hare under the Espionage Act.[14]

At the same time, the prosecution focused most intently on proving that O'Hare had called mothers "brood sows" and that draft-aged men had attended her talk. This strategy highlighted O'Hare's violation of patriotic motherhood and the ways in which that violation could disrupt the production of soldiers. Prosecutors argued that O'Hare intended her comments to dissuade draft-aged men from complying with the Selective Service Act. Although there was no evidence that O'Hare's remarks convinced men to resist conscription, the prosecution argued that they could have had that effect if draft-aged men or their mothers had heard them. The defense produced evidence that disputed much of the prosecution's case, yet the jury took only thirty minutes to convict O'Hare.[15]

Even though she did not believe that her remarks had violated the law, O'Hare was not surprised by the jury's verdict. Expecting to receive a six-month jail term, O'Hare was unprepared for Judge Wade's sentence—five years in a federal prison. By all measures, Wade's sentence was harsh. O'Hare's standing in the socialist movement influenced Wade's decision; he made no secret of his hatred of socialism. Wade had been assigned to the case because of the desire of his superiors to use O'Hare as an example to weaken the Nonpartisan League and discourage protests against the war. Before trying her case, Wade had apparently received a letter from the regional office of the Justice Department that urged him to enact a harsh sentence.[16] It is therefore important not to underestimate the importance of anti-socialism in O'Hare's conviction and sentence. At the same time, anti-socialism alone does not explain why her indictment, the press coverage surrounding her case, and ultimately O'Hare's defenders focused on the implications her case held for the meaning of motherhood and its relationship to women's participation in public culture.[17]

Mindful that the severity of his sentence as well as the attention O'Hare's celebrity would call to his actions, Wade carefully detailed the meaning that he hoped his sentence would convey. In a twenty-six–page speech, Wade clarified how he understood O'Hare's subversion and the role that he believed the state should play in controlling it. He began by identifying the criteria by which he had determined the seriousness of O'Hare's crime. He told the court that he had not based his sentence on her precise utterances, for they could be excused as an emotional reaction against war, but rather on "what was in her heart." Wade concluded that O'Hare's long-standing commitment to socialism revealed a fundamental corruption of character and an uncanny ability to infect others with her ideas. These factors, Wade concluded, established the "bad tendency" of her utterances.[18]

O'Hare's commitment to socialism particularly offended Wade, who understood socialism as a uniquely dangerous and anti-American philosophy. "If [socialism's] gospel is the gospel of hate," Wade admonished O'Hare,

> of contempt of religion and charity, it has not any place on the American soil either in times of war or times of peace. The worst poison you can

instill in the hearts of men is a conscious feeling that they are being deprived of their just earnings by some invisible power.[19]

Wade argued that socialism undercut the free labor contract that promised that individual men could exchange their labor for a just wage and economic opportunity. It was this contract, the defenders of American industrial capitalism argued, that guaranteed to each man his freedom. Socialism's worst sin, Wade argued, was its challenge to this most basic of American values. Stripped of their faith in the free labor contract, Wade feared that men would be susceptible to the moral decay that socialism brought upon its adherents.

As Wade framed his anti-socialist statements, they were not specific to O'Hare. According to Wade's criteria, any effective socialist could disrupt the faith in American democracy of otherwise loyal citizens.[20] But as Wade continued his evaluation of O'Hare's crime, he considered the danger posed by O'Hare's specific remarks. In doing so, he defined O'Hare as part of a larger conspiracy that corrupted citizenship by attacking the family, a family that Wade argued was held together by patriotic motherhood.

Wade carefully reminded the court that O'Hare's sedition rested, in essence, in her efforts to undermine the sacrifices made by patriotic mothers. "This is a nation of free speech," he admonished O'Hare, "but this is a time of sacrifice, when mothers are sacrificing their sons, when all men and women who are not at heart traitors are sacrificing their time and hard-earned money for defense of the flag."[21] Without mothers who were willing to sacrifice their sons for the state the nation could not wage war. Just as fundamentally, Wade reiterated that motherhood itself required the act of this sacrifice.

Wade cast himself as protector of the family bonds and gender roles of patriotic motherhood. "American sons are not going to allow their mothers to be linked unto brood sows," he promised O'Hare, "and American fathers and mothers are not going to submit to having their sons assigned to no more glorious destiny than that of fertilizer."[22] Wade's words cast O'Hare's understanding of motherhood outside constructions of the American family and reconfirmed the bonds of loyalty and citizenship that ultimately tied patriotic mothers to their sons.

At the same time, Wade understood his own role as that of a citizen-soldier. Perhaps uncertain of the the ability of the American family to withstand O'Hare's challenge to patriotic motherhood, Wade designed his sentence to reassure the public that the state would protect Americanism from those who wished to corrupt it:

> This defendant does not take pride in her country. She abhors it. She is the apostle of despair and carries only a message of hate and defiance. She is sowing the seeds of discontent. She preaches defiance of authority. . . .

She proclaims that if she is punished, her followers will assert themselves and that the cause she represents will gain in strength and power. Let them assert themselves—they will find that while this nation is kind and generous she is also powerful, and that when the loyal people of the country are fully aroused, traitors will receive the reward of their teaching.[23]

Wade felt that it was his role to interrupt and, ultimately, to silence O'Hare's unnatural construction of motherhood.[24] It was O'Hare's ability to produce subversives from loyal sons that he feared most and that his five-year sentence sought to contain.[25] Wade argued that unless the state intervened and asserted its own understanding of motherhood, O'Hare would literally implant in the heartland of the nation the seeds of its own destruction. He defined O'Hare's subversion as an unnatural reproduction of motherhood itself.

At her trial O'Hare and her supporters emphasized the partisan politics that they believed had motivated her indictment. They argued that Bowman officials lied about the content of her talk in order to discredit the leaders of the Nonpartisan League who had sponsored her visit. Unable to persuade the jury or judge, O'Hare's defenders pressed this interpretation in the socialist press. They represented her conviction as a benchmark in the socialist struggle and argued that her trial underscored the desperation of the Wilson administration as it attempted to impose an unpopular war on workers. "This case," O'Hare wrote, "is but the first pangs of the birth of the new order. There is a story back of this that constitutes a large part of our American life."[26] Increasingly, O'Hare used her conviction as a forum for telling her version of that story and for redefining her legacy within American politics.

Convicted and sentenced in December of 1917, O'Hare toured the country to rally support for her case until her eventual imprisonment on April 15, 1919, six weeks after the Supreme Court upheld her conviction. During this time, O'Hare and her supporters began to shift the meaning of her case. Although they continued to argue that partisan politics and anti-socialism motivated her conviction, O'Hare and her defenders reconstructed her case as a contest over the meaning of women's political identity in general and of motherhood in particular. New York's leading socialist newspaper, the *New York Call*, attributed her conviction to her status as "a dangerous woman, a thinking woman . . . that stirrth [*sic*] up the people."[27] For her part, O'Hare compared her trial to the Salem witch-hunts:

I sat there in the courtroom and watched the comedy of the United States' federal court in 1918 go back to the days of the witchcraft trials in Salem. I was charged with having an intention—not having done so—to cast the evil eye on the younger generation of North Dakota and cause the young men to resist the draft.[28]

O'Hare's words were ironic because they emphasized both the hysteria and the logic of the state's prosecution of her. The Salem witch trials conjured memories of another time in which women stood trial for speaking heretically. O'Hare suggested that, like the actions of the accused witches of Salem, her actions had cut at the core of an oppressive society because they exposed that society as intolerant and incapable of incorporating dissenting points of view.[29]

Similarly, O'Hare's defenders in the Socialist Party's women's sector constructed her case as a moral crusade in which O'Hare reclaimed social motherhood and women's moral authority. The Kate Richards O'Hare Defense Committee upheld O'Hare as the ideal socialist mother in their efforts to further involve women in civil liberties work.[30] "Mrs. O'Hare is not only an able propagandist; she is also a happy wife and mother," wrote Anita Block, the editor of the *New York Call*'s woman's page.

> Her large family of little O'Hares have always figured delightfully in her speeches. The thought that this warm mother, this socially useful woman, is to pay the price of five long years of agony and loneliness in prison for her rare courage and vision seems too horrible to be true.[31]

Like many of the leaders of the Socialist Party's women's sector, Block linked the character of women's politics to their roles as mothers.[32] O'Hare's mothering, Block asserted, proved the morality and purity of her public role.

Socialist women also stressed that O'Hare's conviction underscored a greater threat to motherhood by further removing control of motherhood from women and placing it in the hands of the capitalist state. Theresa Malkiel, a leader in New York's socialist movement, argued that O'Hare had "claimed for [mothers] the right to protect the life of their sons." O'Hare's crime, Malkiel asserted, was that she had "urged the women to use their economic power, their moral influence, their political weapon, in order to restore once more 'Peace on earth, good will among men.'" Malkiel depicted O'Hare as one who represented and acted on behalf of those mothers who rejected patriotic motherhood.[33]

O'Hare further developed this argument in letters that she wrote during her imprisonment, which lasted from April of 1919 to May of 1920, when President Wilson commuted her sentence. Although they were addressed to her children, O'Hare's "Dear Sweetheart" letters were widely distributed and reprinted in the socialist press. Because these letters were propaganda and subject to prison censorship, they cannot be read as literal descriptions of her prison experiences. Instead, they reveal O'Hare's attempts to define the meaning and a purpose for her imprisonment.

O'Hare's letters constructed her conviction as an integral part of the fight against capitalism and as a direct assault on the family. She described prison as a microcosm of capitalist society, and she characterized her own role as that of a regenerator of the prison community through her leadership of a spiritual and political revival.

As "the only mother" imprisoned under the wartime laws, O'Hare constructed her case as the most extreme outrage committed under the wartime laws, but one that mirrored and revealed a larger concern—the state's failure to protect and value motherhood.[34] "It would be far better," she wrote in one of her most cutting passages, "for one to be an enemy spy at the mercy of German Army officers than to be an American mother at the tender mercy of the Wilson administration."[35] O'Hare used powerful pro-war symbols—the German execution of Edith Carvell and alleged German atrocities toward mothers and their children—to underscore the hypocrisy of the Wilson administration's wartime conduct. In the process, she also defined her imprisonment as a violation of the same definitions of womanhood that the Wilson administration's wartime propaganda claimed to protect.[36]

By writing her letters to her children, O'Hare provided her readership with concrete examples of how the Wilson administration's policies destroyed families. Her children were motherless, she continuously reminded her readers, because Wilson had chosen that fate for them. At the same time, O'Hare argued that the exploitation of capitalist society necessitated her imprisonment. "You should only feel that you have loaned me for a time," she wrote her children, "to those who need me far more bitterly than you do."[37]

O'Hare described her stay in prison as a mission consistent with her duty as a Christian and as a mother. "I can feed her and encourage her and pet her," O'Hare wrote of her relationship with an imprisoned drug addict, "and I think if Jesus were consulted on the matter, he would prefer that I should be here this Easter day rather than in some magnificent church."[38] It was by the sacrifices of women and their children that society would purify itself, a theme O'Hare would later revive in the centerpiece of her amnesty campaign—the Children's Crusade.

It would be unfair to simply attribute O'Hare's words to mere propaganda. By all accounts, O'Hare found her imprisonment difficult, and her letters reflected her need to find meaning in what she understood as a personal catastrophe. She discovered that meaning in prison reform, which combined her commitment to maternalism with her growing interest in social science. "I hope that you are not worried about me, for I am having a most interesting time," O'Hare reassured herself as much as her family.

> In Emma Goldman, and the dear little Italian girl, I have intellectual comradeship, and in my little 'dope fiend' someone to mother; in the management of the institution very interesting study, and in the inmates, a wonderful array of interesting fellow-beings.[39]

In spite of her dedication to and success in improving prison conditions, O'Hare bemoaned the distance she often felt between herself and those she wanted to serve. "I want to come close to these women," she lamented, "I want to serve them but I am conscious of the fact that they feel that I am apart from them."[40] O'Hare created this distance. Her language was often condescending as she defined the other inmates as subjects for her study or as victims of a capitalist society rather than as potential colleagues.

Yet, O'Hare retained a strong faith that maternalism could breech the social and political gaps that threatened the socialist movement. As evidence, O'Hare pointed to her growing friendship with Emma Goldman, who had been convicted of violating the Selective Service Act in July of 1917. Goldman served with O'Hare until her release in September of 1919, twenty months after her original imprisonment. Recognizing that their relationship could raise eyebrows among her socialist colleagues, O'Hare reassured them that their differences were in reality rather small. Discounting and even occasionally ridiculing Goldman's anarchism, O'Hare attributed Goldman's influence to her "passionate maternal spirit" and "not her anarchist principles."[41] It was the common base established by each woman's commitment to maternalism that O'Hare believed had enabled her to form a political alliance with Goldman that brought concrete change to the prison. Mindful of the divisions within the Socialist Party, O'Hare used her friendship with Goldman to scold socialists and remind them of their common enemy.

For her part, Goldman respected and liked O'Hare but found her naive. Although she used maternalism to frame some of her anti-war work, Goldman argued that her commitment to anarchism and previous record of arrest had better prepared her for the penalties the state imposed during the war. "Kate Richards O'Hare still had the childlike faith of most Americans that certain things cannot happen," Goldman recalled,

> and that certain things our government will not do so. She said to me "I don't believe for a minute that the Supreme Court, the highest court, will sustain the sentence, and I don't believe for a minute that I will have to go to prison." It was really pathetic to me, in a way, because you see I am a hardened criminal.[42]

Goldman was less willing than O'Hare to understate their differences. Unlike O'Hare, Goldman relished her marginalized status. She saw herself as a realist who scorned middle-class morality. Goldman's own political identity required that she ultimately distinguish herself from O'Hare's brand of politics even as she counted her as a political and personal ally.[43]

O'Hare's construction of her arrest as an attack on motherhood particularly annoyed her detractors. They battled O'Hare over the meaning of motherhood, her claim to maternal politics, and the relationship of both to the war effort. After the war ended in 1918, the Wilson administration began commuting the sentences of wartime prisoners. O'Hare's supporters hoped that Wilson would commute her sentence before she went to prison or soon after. Those closest to her case—Judge Martin Wade and other North Dakota officials—pressured Wilson to uphold O'Hare's sentence. A series of petitions sent to the attorney general by the American Legion illustrates the strategy these interests used. They described any reduction in O'Hare's sentence as a "direct insult to the mothers of all boys and girls who so gladly offered to sacrifice their lives that the world would be made safe for democracy" and a "vile slander upon American womanhood."[44] Commuting O'Hare's sentence, petitioners argued, would not restore the integrity of motherhood, as O'Hare's supporters argued; instead, it would degrade those mothers who had acted patriotically. The petitioners asked Wilson to uphold the values of patriotic motherhood by keeping O'Hare in prison. Their actions demonstrate that even after O'Hare's trial and conviction, her critique of patriotic motherhood remained central to the case against her.

O'Hare's opponents argued that her continued criticism of the government contradicted her moral claims. O'Hare "seems to have glorified in her conviction," wrote North Dakota Attorney General Melvin Hildeth, "and to have used it as an asset to further her financial interests and spread propaganda dangerous to the institutions of our common country. . . . [She has] created discord amongst the laboring classes."[45] This characterization of O'Hare as a bitter yet opportunistic revolutionist resonated throughout the appeals to keep her in prison.

The prosecution convicted O'Hare by preventing the defense from focusing on the political motivations that might have influenced the charges against her. Instead, the prosecution and the presiding judge focused on O'Hare's character to determine her intentions. In their letters to Washington, they worked to maintain this focus and avoid the peculiarities of the politics of wartime.[46] The following memo that recommends against commuting O'Hare's sentence suggests that their efforts had some success:

> Mrs O'Hare's inconsistency is, of course, manifest from this review of the record. She stated at the time of her sentence in a very resigned Christian-like spirit that she would accept the sentence without bitterness or prejudice. Immediately thereafter, however, in a campaign of public speaking she directly, and indirectly through friends, began to go to the edge of her legal rights in criticizing the courts, denouncing the sentence, and her latest from prison shows that she still entertains the same biased opinion of her convictions expressing the view in the solemnly written article (apparently authentic) that she was imprisoned because she differed from the political party in power.[47]

This argument sought to render politics itself illegitimate for women. By acting as a citizen and asserting her political and legal rights, O'Hare proved her own guilt. Although the author of this memo found offense in the particulars of O'Hare's views, his criticism focused on the very fact that she continued to participate in public life. As a good Christian, O'Hare should have accepted her sentence and eschewed her political rights and obligations. Such arguments placed O'Hare in an inescapable bind and effectively negated her rights as a citizen. By treating O'Hare's political disagreements as a moral conflict, the prosecutor and judge had criminalized O'Hare's citizenship.[48] She could not participate in public life without corrupting it.

There is an irony in these comments. The moral standard they accused O'Hare of violating was her own. O'Hare, like her critics, turned politics into a moral crusade. O'Hare sought to preserve women's moral authority in both the home and in public life. She criticized militarism for stripping motherhood of its moral function—of reducing it to the mere production of expendable goods. O'Hare oscillated between claiming a public identity as a citizen and claiming one as a mother. She saw little contradiction between these roles. Yet, as historian Michael Rogin has argued, this construction of politics was not wholly incompatible with the treatment of conflicts over policy as issues of personal moral failure.[49] O'Hare's own politics linked participation in public life with personal morality. O'Hare sought to both protect the link between morality and politics and to preempt the state from defining its terms. She continued to develop these themes in her amnesty campaigns.

Even before O'Hare went to prison, she expressed dissatisfaction with the Socialist Party's handling of her case. According to Sally Miller, these tensions embittered the O'Hares, who were exhausted from constant touring and were under financial strain.[50] Soon after her conviction, her husband, Frank O'Hare, wrote an angry letter to Eugene Debs that accused party leaders of ignoring O'Hare because she was a woman. "I almost believe that Kate is right," he wrote Eugene Debs. "[F]or years she has told me of the snubs and scorn and jealousy of the [comrade] leaders toward her as a WOMAN. I have laughed it away—but why laugh facts away."[51] He demanded that Debs intervene in the case by finding out "from the so-called leaders of the party just what in hell they are going to do and report to me."[52]

Debs responded angrily to O'Hare's letter. He reprimanded O'Hare for his charges against the party and summarily dismissed his accusations of sexism as "bosh."[53] "I do not blame you for feeling as you do," he wrote O'Hare, "but you will have to get it out of your head that Kate is the only martyr in the revolutionary movement."[54] Unlike other wartime prisoners, Debs pointed out, O'Hare had not suffered the indignities of public beatings, and she had a large national following working on her behalf. He recommended that the O'Hares accept Kate's imprisonment as a sacrifice. "Is it not a privilege to serve, even to go to jail, when a million hearts turn to you in love and gratefulness?" he asked. Revealingly, Debs concluded his letter by dismissing the possibility that O'Hare would "go to Jefferson City for an hour." At war's end, he argued, "the higher courts will reverse the lower one or there will be a pardon granted."[55]

Although Frank O'Hare apologized to Debs for the spirit of his correspondence, their exchange revealed fundamental differences between the perception of the O'Hares of their case and that of prominent socialist men.[56] The O'Hares grew increasingly dissatisfied with the party leadership; party leaders resented the tactics the O'Hares used to publicize their case and later amnesty activities.

After her imprisonment, O'Hare continued to clash with Socialist Party leaders, who did not want to reopen her case. O'Hare chided the party's national office, suggesting to one concerned follower that sexism played a role in the party's amnesty focus. "I don't mind really," O'Hare wrote, noting the lack of attention the party gave her case; "they did not overlook Flora Foreman or me because they were bad or unfriendly, but solely because it is the psychology of the male."[57]

Although flip, O'Hare's remark illustrates her growing frustration with the devaluation of women's work and roles by party leaders. She believed that a male party leadership would inevitably neglect those women convicted under the wartime emergency laws. Ultimately, this frustration with the national office led her to design an amnesty campaign that represented a final moment for the blend of social purity and maternalist politics that was so typical of her generation.

O'Hare's bitterness over the party's handling of her case permeated her letters to her close friend Otto Branstetter, the executive secretary of the Socialist Party. O'Hare wrote these letters to convince Branstetter to reconsider the party's refusal to reopen her case. She accused the national office of mismanaging her case, and she threatened to leave the party. Informing Branstetter that she was "deeply hurt" by his handling of her case, she warned that continued inaction would jeopardize the party's credibility with the "rank and file."[58]

O'Hare wanted the national office to send a lawyer to Bowman to gather evidence that witnesses perjured themselves during her trial. She argued that because her case rested on such faulty evidence, a good lawyer could easily gather the evidence necessary to overturn her conviction. If it could demonstrate that her conviction rested on perjured testimony that was obtained to discredit the Nonpartisan League, O'Hare believed that the party could prove that espionage convictions were an attack on progressive political movements rather than a necessary response to the wartime emergency. O'Hare argued that as "one of the most flagrant" and "dramatic" examples of the Wilson administration's misuse of power, her case provided concrete evidence that wartime prisoners were "political prisoners."[59]

Branstetter did not want to reopen O'Hare's case. There were several reasons for his decision, sexism perhaps being one of them. In fairness to Branstetter, he was in a difficult position. Although its membership had increased during the war, the Socialist Party and its ability to forge an effective amnesty campaign had been hurt by the wartime laws. In addition, the party itself was split. A left wing revitalized by the Bolshevik revolution challenged the leadership of party moderates such as Otto Branstetter. The party hoped that a vigorous amnesty campaign could reunite and strengthen it. But the Socialist Party could not establish an effective amnesty strategy until 1921 when Harriot Stanton Blatch took over its amnesty campaign.[60] Short on money and facing increasing public censure, the national office could not devote the resources that O'Hare felt were necessary to her case.

Branstetter rebuked O'Hare for her criticism of the national office and her threat to leave the party.[61] He informed her that the national office lacked sufficient funds to reopen her case, and denied "most emphatically that you have been shamefully or unjustly treated by the National Office."[62] He did promise O'Hare that the national office would do everything in its power to meet her request for legal representation.

O'Hare responded to Branstetter's scolding with her accustomed irony. "My dear man what a case of nerves you have developed," she wrote, "if this letter is a fair sample of what has been going out of the N.O. for the last year no wonder the Party had a brainstorm last summer and proceeded to do the Kilkinney cats act. Be calm for Heaven's sake and get down to normal."[63] She dismissed Branstetter's anger as "emotional stress" induced by his job, an ironic gesture considering that hysteria was a charge generally offered against women. She designed her letter to annoy Branstetter and underscore that it was he who acted irrationally.

Behind O'Hare's anger with the national office was a more fundamental feeling of betrayal. "I am a socialist, a veteran member of the Party and to save its own self respect the Party must stand by me." Furthermore, she warned Branstetter that

> some day I will be released, naturally I will be back on the job, and we will have some job of harmonizing the squabbling factions and getting back into working trim. When that time comes I want to be able to go to the comrades and work for harmony without being forced to spend two thirds of my energy thinking up convincing lies to tell to explain how it all happened. Now when it comes to thinking of lies to protect friends I am some artist. I have had such an awful lot of practice.[64]

O'Hare understood that internal divisions threatened the party's survival. Her stance toward Branstetter was strategic. She gambled that

Branstetter could not survive her defection and warned that the party's failure to take decisive action in her case would deeply affect her "relationship with the Party in the future."[65]

Exasperated and unable to appease O'Hare, Branstetter asked Frank O'Hare to intervene. Frank reassured Branstetter that O'Hare's accusations resulted from prison-induced hysteria:[66]

> I have had a lot of trouble with the N O and other folks since Kate's indictment for they could not realize that she is not calm and cool and efficient and normal. At the present moment I do not even know how long she will be able to hold herself together. This thing of spinsters and men going to prison is one thing. Of mothers of young children is another. The nerve specialists to whom I have taken Kate for treatment during the past two years have all told me the same thing: Her trial and conviction was a tremendous shock. The shock acts peculiarly on her. I will not go into it now. I would prefer talking it over with you.[67]

It is doubtful that hysteria motivated O'Hare. She was ill during her imprisonment and did not have access to all the information about her case. But O'Hare's misreading of the facts surrounding her case was not caused by this illness. Frank withheld information from her. He specifically instructed O'Hare's friends not to write about such stressful topics as her defense and to keep their letters as "cheerful" as possible. Frank's efforts to protect her frustrated O'Hare and perhaps led her to make demands that appeared unreasonable to Branstetter. Even within the Socialist Party, women's political transgressions were linked to hysteria.

Frank's accusations of hysteria were convenient. Since O'Hare's conviction, their marriage had been strained. They would separate in 1924 and divorce four years later. O'Hare used her conviction to propel herself into a new political career. After her release O'Hare helped shape the post-war amnesty campaigns. But her increasing conflicts with party leaders and her frustrations with divisions in the socialist movement drove her out of the party. After she left the party, O'Hare concentrated on prison reform.[68]

His own reasonableness reconfirmed, Branstetter assured Frank that he would "cooperate with [him] to the greatest possible extent," and offered to send a lawyer to Bowman, North Dakota, who would reopen O'Hare's case. He later told O'Hare that he had turned over her case to the Washington office, which would lobby the president on her behalf.[69] These efforts ultimately proved successful; Wilson commuted her sentence after she had served eighteen months.[70]

Not satisfied with the party's efforts, O'Hare and other socialist women formed an independent defense committee, a decision resented by the party leadership. "I think these free-lance self-advertising movements are an unmitigated nuisance," wrote Morris Hillquit about the Kate Richards O'Hare Defense Committee:

and I shall try my best to put my foot down on O'Hare's movement here. I also believe you ought to write Frank O'Hare (care of the Rand school) to desist from his activities, and if he fails to do so, issue a public statement to the effect that there are at this time many comrades in the same position as Kate O'Hare, that the National Office is trying to take care of all of them equally, and that any attempt to single out a particular case for special propaganda would necessarily result in weakening the Party's resources for the defense of other comrades.[71]

Despite his annoyance, Hillquit represented O'Hare.[72] Whether the party ignored O'Hare is unclear; certainly financial restrictions prevented the party from reopening espionage cases. But O'Hare's popularity, as well as her ability to reach the public with her complaints, led some party leaders to take steps to discredit her.

O'Hare's wartime struggles with Branstetter were part of an ongoing conflict between party moderates and O'Hare, who Hillquit wrongly called an "impossibilist." When party members chose O'Hare as a representative to the International Bureau in 1912, Victor Berger complained that O'Hare would make the American party look "ridiculous" because of her extreme views.[73] Hillquit was angry when St. Louis convention delegates elected her to head the committee that wrote the party's anti-war declaration and accused O'Hare's followers of stacking the election.[74] In 1919, O'Hare further alienated party leaders when she challenged Hillquit for party office.[75] When she won that election, the national office voided the results, fearing a left-wing takeover of the party.[76] Throughout her career, O'Hare had a rocky relationship with the national office. She rarely participated in party affairs, and party officials viewed her as a potentially annoying outsider capable of both recruiting a large membership and of undercutting the pragmatic agenda of the national office.

It is not clear why party leaders associated O'Hare with socialism's left wing. She did not support revolutionary tactics; she preferred evolutionary socialism instead. And although she occasionally chastised the party's male leadership for its sexism, her participation in the socialist women's movement was only marginal and she was skeptical of its socialist-feminist analysis.[77] Why did party moderates fear O'Hare and her influence?

Historian David Shannon offers a plausible answer. He argues that the "dignified" Berger and the "debonair" Hillquit were "embarrassed by the presence in the American party of such wild-eyed socialist evangelists as Kate Richards O'Hare."[78] Both her constituency and her political training in the temperance and social purity movements influenced O'Hare's politics. O'Hare was basically a stump speaker. In contrast to the urban centers where party leaders had constant contact with their potential constituents, O'Hare's territory was the isolated small towns of the nation, among which she migrated. She built her reputation as a charismatic speaker rather than as a party functionary. O'Hare's humor, irony, charisma, and style, which blended nicely with the rural socialism of the Southeast and Midwest, disconcerted and perhaps intimidated the more "respectable" socialist leaders such as Hillquit and Berger.[79]

These differences affected O'Hare's construction of amnesty and its rejection by party leaders. In 1922, she organized the Children's Crusade to highlight the poverty inflicted on midwestern families by wartime arrests.[80] O'Hare originally planned the crusade after meeting Dorothy Clark, whose husband was in prison for collecting money for prisoners who were members of the Industrial Workers of the World (IWW). The unwillingness of Washington officials to meet with Clark convinced O'Hare that only a dramatic gesture could call attention to the social costs of wartime imprisonments.[81]

O'Hare recruited thirty-three families to visit various midwestern and eastern cities. Hosted by a women's committee formed by Elizabeth Gurley Flynn and Mary Heaton Vorse, among others, the children paraded in New York and Washington. Their placards emphasized the hardships placed on their families by the imprisonment of their fathers.[82] Although the president refused to meet the children, their supporters argued that the crusade's publicity increased pressure for a general amnesty.[83]

It is difficult to determine what effect, if any, the crusade had on the amnesty campaign. For our purposes the crusade was important for what it revealed about O'Hare's political style and her post-war relationship with the Socialist Party. The crusade underscored the differences in style, goals, and ideology between O'Hare and Party officials.

The Children's Crusade reflected the "wild-eyed evangelism" that Shannon believed characterized perceptions of O'Hare's socialism.[84] But Shannon does not address the intricate relationship between O'Hare's evangelical socialism and gender. Like many socialist women of her generation, O'Hare's socialism embraced moral reform.[85] She viewed socialism as a moral crusade that protected the embattled family from capitalism's intrusion.[86]

O'Hare's crusade evoked moral reform to shame the public. Its name derived from the twelfth-century crusades in which European children joined the Christian armies sent by the Pope to fight the Muslims in eastern Byzantium. Like the Europeans, O'Hare suggested that American society condemned its children because of a marked failure of adult responsibility.[87] As a spectacle rather than a political program, the crusade's symbolism suggested a moral regeneration.[88]

The crusade's portrayal of women and children as the "innocent" victims of public sector corruption revived the separate spheres ideology of the nineteenth century's middle class to underscore the social

consequences of the state's usurpation of women's role as moral arbiters. The crusade emphasized that the purification of society was still
contingent on a moral code protected by women. O'Hare designed the
crusade to highlight the blatant disregard of the effects of the wartime
laws on the family.

O'Hare originally proposed the Children's Crusade as part of a united
amnesty campaign of the Socialist Party, the IWW, and the Civil Liberties Union. None of those organizations officially lent their support, but
individual members participated. When approached by the O'Hares,
the Socialist Party rejected the plan as too costly. Branstetter noted that
the party had sent Bertha Hale White to investigate the cases of Oklahoma families, and that she had instructions to lobby President Harding
on their behalf.[89]

When questioned about his refusal to endorse the crusade, Branstetter argued that Kate and Frank O'Hare used the Crusade solely to
benefit their newspaper, the *National Rip-Saw*. He charged Frank O'Hare
with misusing funds previously donated for Oklahoma families and
called O'Hare's plan "ill-timed" and "launched without proper preparation." He further objected to the fundraising methods of the O'Hares,
announcing that "what prospect there was for general co-operation and
support of other organizations was spoiled by the subscription fea-
tures of their first announcement, giving it all the appearance of a sub-
getting rather than an Amnesty campaign."[90] In spite of his reservations, Branstetter furnished the O'Hares with the names of the families
of the prisoners and offered them advice about Washington contacts.
"While I do not see my way clear to co-operate with you under the circumstances," he wrote, "I would be very glad to see you carry the matter
through to a successful conclusion."[91]

At the time of the crusade, White, fresh from her fact-finding mission
in Oklahoma, met with President Harding, who apparently agreed to
reopen the cases. She too believed that the crusade would jeopardize
this work:

> As a publicity stunt, Comrade O'Hare, the Children's Crusade is a peach.
> If we want to keep all men in prison until we can get a proclamation of
> general amnesty, it is a good thing. But if we want the President and the
> Department of Justice to release the men from Oklahoma and Texas with-
> out waiting for general amnesty, I feel it is unfortunate.[92]

White argued that the best strategy for releasing particular prisoners
was quiet diplomacy. Dramatic public events, she feared, would only
harden Washington's opposition to amnesty.

In addition to Branstetter's accusations that the O'Hares were using
the Children's Crusade to bolster their newspaper, he also opposed
the plan because it interfered with the Socialist Party's strategy. By
1921, the Socialist Party had focused its amnesty campaign on two
strategies: freeing Eugene Debs and lobbying President Harding.[93] Bran-

stetter did not want the Socialist Party's amnesty campaign connected to the IWW or to more controversial methods of other civil liberties groups. Branstetter considered Dorothy Clark and her husband to be of questionable reputation, noting their affiliation with the IWW and previous accusations that Stanley Clark, a long-time opponent of Bransetter, had mishandled funds.[94]

Because of O'Hare's reputation and concerns for the families of wartime prisoners, a coalition of left-liberal women helped her. They welcomed the crusade to their cities and wrote about how the spectacle of impoverished children marching for their father's release underscored the cruelty of wartime arrests. It is possible that the children jarred the conscience of Washington and made it more difficult for amnesty opponents to stereotype wartime prisoners as dangerous subversives. The crusade also appeared dated. Representative of what historian Mari Jo Buhle, identifies as the first generation of socialist women's politics, O'Hare's moral reform was destined to clash with the politics of the second generation of "revolutionary new women" of the left.[95]

O'Hare constructed defenses of women who were convicted under the wartime emergency laws in much the same manner as she conducted the Children's Crusade—as a moral crusade that protected true womanhood from the state. She took a particular interest in Mollie Steimer, who O'Hare had met in prison. To illustrate the absurdity of Steimer's conviction, O'Hare compared Steimer to Clara Smith, an adulteress accused of murdering her lover:

> Was Mollie Steimer a harlot who had wrecked a home, ruined a woman's life, brought disgrace to innocent children, lived in open adultery and murdered her partner in crime? Oh not at all: Mollie was prudish a little Puritan that ever lived, whose ideals of love and marriage was as pure and sweet as apple blossom. Mollie had never sold her sex for a libertine's luxury; she had never wronged a wife or blackened innocent childrens' lives with vulgar scandal. Mollie even refused to eat meat because she thought the slaughter of animals for food brutal. . . .
>
> Clara Smith the concubine, who killed her partner, is free to spread her vileness over the movie screens of the nation. Mollie Steimer, the idealist, who sought to protect the integrity of the constitution of the United States is in prison. IS THIS THE STATUS OF WOMANHOOD IN THE UNITED STATES?[96]

O'Hare applied a standard of moral purity to determine the social value and danger posed by Smith's and Steimer's crimes. Steimer, O'Hare suggested, could not spread social pollution because of her own purity—her adherence to gender-appropriate behavior and idealism. To O'Hare, the legal system's hypocrisy—its unwillingness to stop Smith and its conviction of Steimer—underscored that chaos was likely to occur when the state appointed itself the moral arbiter of society.

Given the legal interpretation of the Sedition Act, O'Hare's construction of Steimer's defense made sense. Congress had passed the Sedition

Act to allow prosecutions of individuals who had not directly criticized the war, but whose political utterances potentially undermined the authority of the government and hence compromised its ability to wage war. When it was broadly applied, the Sedition Act forbade any criticism of the Wilson administration. Supporters of the Sedition Act assumed that disparaging remarks about the American government polluted the minds of the population and weakened the public's resolve in the war.[97]

Steimer's indictment used a broad understanding of the Sedition Act. Steimer and three of her colleagues were convicted under the act for distributing leaflets that criticized the Wilson administration's intervention in the Russian Civil War. Steimer's attorney, Harry Weinberger, argued that because these activities were not directed against the war, they did not violate the law. The courts disagreed; they ruled that if the leaflets only potentially undermined the authority of the American government, they violated the Sedition Act. Steimer's conviction was based on her potential to cause social pollution.[98]

As with other women charged under the wartime laws, prosecutors defined Steimer's potential to spread social pollution as a sexual and gender transgression. Court officials questioned her relationship with her male colleagues and required her to defend her views on marriage, free love, and sex.[99] They portrayed Steimer as an alarming anarchist whose sexual license endangered political and social morality. O'Hare reversed the terms of this argument.

To prove Steimer's innocence her defenders did not stress her political ideas but instead emphasized her "immaturity." Her attorney consistently called her "this little girl" to refer to both her age and physical appearance. Even less sympathetic amnesty workers constructed Steimer as a mischievous child in order to dismiss arguments that she posed a social danger. For example, when asked during a congressional hearing whether a general amnesty could free "such dangerous criminals" as Steimer, Lucy Robins, the coordinator of the American Federation of Labor's amnesty campaign, replied:

> I do not know details of the trial but this will show how extensive a propaganda movement she carried on or could carry on, or how dangerous an "animal" she was. She tried to distribute circulars on the streets in protest of intervention upon Russia, and found that people would not take them or read them; she then got up to the roof and threw them down. The janitor drove her away several times. He told her that if she did not stop that, he would have her arrested. That shows how much influence she had. These were mere children.[100]

An irrational fear of the anarchist threat encouraged prosecutions of ideological anarchists regardless of whether or not they committed a crime. Within this context efforts to distinguish between the danger of ideas and the danger individuals posed made sense. As constructed,

7

however, all of these strategies were limited. No one understood these limitations better than Steimer.

Steimer resisted any efforts that diminished her seriousness as a revolutionist. By refusing to rise in the courtroom or to answer questions that implicated anyone other than herself, she distinguished herself as the most defiant of the Abrams defendants. But even more revealing was the stance she took toward her defenders. When Weinberger addressed her in court by her first name, she steadfastly refused to answer his questions until he extended her the courtesy of a formal address.[101] Steimer insisted that her defenders treat her as they would any wartime prisoner; she explains why in the following letter to Agnes Smedley:[102]

> To my amazement, I got some information that there are people working for my release alone, disregarding, not only all class war prisoners, but even those who have been convicted under the same charge.
>
> This sounds inconceivable. For if the existing powers consider it a crime to protest against the Russian intervention, I am just as guilty of that crime as are my comrades who are now in Atlanta.
>
> On what grounds, then, are those people working? Are they trying to appeal to the emotions of the government officials, or ask for pity? That I resent from the depth of my heart. I want justice, but *not* pity, and if it is unjust to have imposed such a penalty on me it is equally so with Lipman, Lachowsky, and Abrams.
>
> People mention my youth. What about Lipman who is only 22 and who is almost getting blind there? What about Lachowsky who is sick and consequently subjected to more severe suffering than I am.
>
> That woman spoke of importance. I believe that outside of the exploiting class, each individual is of importance in one way or another. Especially among political prisoners. There should be no distinction whatever. . . .
>
> Whoever those people who work for my release are I appeal to them in the name of *real* justice to: either work for the release of *all* or *non* [sic].[103]

When defense workers emphasized the qualities of individuals, Steimer argued, they lost sight of the politics of amnesty. At issue was not her individual guilt or personal morality but how the "exploiting classes" used the legal system to deny citizenship to particular groups. To Steimer justice did not mean her own release but the dismantling of the emerging surveillance state.[104]

Steimer believed that she was just as "guilty"(and dangerous) as her male counterparts. Rejecting the potential "pity" that might lead to her pardon, Steimer noted that her male colleagues were younger and more fragile than herself. Her refusal to allow defense workers to either single her out or to diminish her guilt with appeals to "emotion"stemmed from both her commitment to the class struggle and her self-definition as a revolutionary. The latter concern, in particular, required constant vigilance against efforts to construct her as an idealistic child rather than as a serious political actor.

Unlike Robins, O'Hare did take her seriously. She constructed Steimer as an effective political actor whose integrity served as a model for
"American womanhood." Their differences stemmed from their back-
grounds. Steimer was the "revolutionary new woman"; the immigrant
subcultures in New York City had shaped her experiences.[105] As historians have shown, this culture emerged from the structure of working-
class neighborhoods and the factory experience. It constructed very
different relationships between men and women than those learned by
native-born white women in the late nineteenth century.[106] The combi-
nation of anarchist beliefs about women's freedom and the heterosocial
nexus of East Harlem's working-class neighborhoods produced a different idea of womanhood and its relationship to politics than that imag-
ined by O'Hare.[107]

Of all the federal wartime cases, O'Hare's case most explicitly raised
questions about the meaning of motherhood and its role in constructing
women's political identities. Her case focused on her explicit challenge
to patriotic motherhood and the social cost that her challenge could
bring. Through their prosecution of O'Hare, federal authorities defined
this challenge as seditious, thus protecting and giving statutory power to
the state's right to require of women the production of loyal citizens.

O'Hare agreed with federal officials that her case raised questions
about the role of motherhood in politics. Yet, O'Hare argued that patriotic motherhood threatened the social and moral fabric of the nation.
Patriotic motherhood, O'Hare and her supporters feared, placed motherhood in the service of a militarist state and denied to women their
traditional roles as moral educators. The state's usurpation of motherhood, they believed, degraded women and corrupted motherhood because it alienated women from their primary labor by forcing them to
produce sons for the state to sacrifice in war.

In their arguments both O'Hare and federal authorities legitimized
their positions by claiming public morality for themselves. Since the
mid-nineteenth century, middle-class women had expanded their political roles by emphasizing their responsibilities as arbiters of personal
and public morality.[108] O'Hare understood that the demands of war,
which emphasized experiences and moral traits unique to men, potentially threatened women's claims to this moral discourse. She intended
that her case raise questions about the state's role in shaping the moral
discourses underlying citizenship, and underscored the dangers that
she believed capitalist and militarist state-building posed to the public
virtues that shaped Americanism. But O'Hare's construction of maternal politics clashed with immigrant and working-class women's understanding of their role in radical politics. To further clarify this understanding, we will now turn to the case of Emma Goldman.

3

⚜

Liberty with Strings

THE CASE OF EMMA GOLDMAN

In the months before Congress declared war, Emma Goldman had slipped into a depression. Emotionally and physically exhausted by her political commitments and failing personal relationship with Ben Reitman, she contemplated returning to Russia. "Democracy is an illusion and snare," she told her friend Agnes Inglis,

> Expulsion of teachers from colleges who refuse to sign a pledge. Punishment of children who distribute anti-military literature. Poisoning the minds and hearts of the school-children by thrusting Patriotism and the Flag down their throat. All this in a country that boasts of being free. It is enough to break one's heart.[1]

In spite of her apparent resignation, Goldman had not committed herself to the political sidelines. On the contrary, she expected that the war would be a "physical test" for radicals, who she anticipated would stand alone once the United States officially entered the fray. "One must keep oneself together," she wearily but resolutely told Inglis, "for now is the time to do work more energetically than ever."[2]

It was no surprise that the event of war led Goldman into her most dramatic and ultimately her final confrontation with the United States government. Since the turn of the century, federal authorities had anticipated convicting Goldman of a crime serious enough to deport her.[3] Her arrest in June of 1917 for conspiring to interfere with the draft shocked no one; both her supporters and detractors considered her conviction a foregone conclusion.[4]

Goldman's case was arguably the Justice Department's most important wartime prosecution. By the turn of the century, Goldman had established herself as the "queen" of American anarchism, lecturing on such diverse topics as women's sexual emancipation, free speech, birth control, the labor movement, and anti-militarism. Her involvement in anarchist politics, her probable participation in the attempted assassination of Henry Frick, her ability as a public speaker, her popularity among new immigrants and workers, and her influence on feminist thought had convinced many that she was among the nation's most dangerous subversives.[5]

Goldman's wartime experiences embroiled her not only in a battle over free speech but also in a contest over her own legacy and its place in United States politics and culture. Historian Richard Gid Powers argues that Goldman's wartime legal troubles solidified her status as the quintessential symbol of the alien subversive. According to Powers, Goldman's case had a lasting effect on the career of J. Edger Hoover, who was responsible for writing the briefs that secured Goldman's deportation. Hoover, Powers asserts, transformed Goldman into a symbol of the threats that he and other men of his class and race believed accompanied the entrance of workers and immigrants into public life. With Goldman, Powers contends, Hoover had "provid[ed] the nation with dramatic representations of those threats, a menacing crowd led by well-known individuals." Powers continues,

> Hoover had identified the source of evil as those who were different in appearance, culture, and belief—groups who were alienated from the old truths and pieties of nostalgic America; he then drove those despised aliens from the community in a demonstration of the power of the state and the powerlessness of its enemies, a purgative ritual of national solidarity.[6]

In short, Goldman's trial and eventual deportation reassured the middle class of the state's ability to defend its moral hegemony and its understanding of Americanism.[7]

Historians have not accounted for the importance of gender in this "purgative ritual of national solidarity" in general or in Goldman's case in particular. Goldman's trial contained little explicit discussion of her feminist critiques of class privilege. But her rejection of middle-class gender roles played a key role in her trial. It was the figure of Emma Goldman that most interested federal authorities. Goldman's wartime trial and deportation hearing provided the most dramatic forum the nation had yet seen for clarifying the threat posed by the unchecked influence on public life of immigrant women.

As soon as Congress declared war, law enforcement officials lobbied to arrest Goldman. Her arrest, they argued, would demonstrate the government's willingness to engage the enemy on the domestic front. "If the government assumes a tolerant attitude, it will be construed as an indication of weakness and lack of desire to face an ugly situation," wrote Thomas McCarthy, the federal marshal who eventually arrested Goldman:

> I feel that those who contemplate supporting the draft, and who are in the great majority, should have the encouragement of a rigorous enforcement of the law against all those who for selfish or for other reasons see fit to

frustrate the plan of the government. I believe that an exhibition of force at the outset will have a salutary effect upon all those who contemplate resistance, and the ensuing moral support of law-abiding citizens that will be gained will be of an inestimable value.[8]

McCarthy's comments, made at the onset of the government's anti-radical crusades, illustrate the expectations those of Hoover's ilk held for the wartime laws. McCarthy hoped that vigorous use of the wartime laws would reassure the public of the government's will to fight and win the domestic war. Goldman was the ideal candidate for this war's first and defining battle.

Goldman's arrest ostensibly stemmed from her activity in the No-Conscription League, under whose auspices she gave several anti-conscription speeches. Goldman had founded the No-Conscription League in May 1917 "for the purpose of encouraging conscientious objectors to affirm their liberty of conscience and to translate their objection to human slaughter by refusing to participate in the war."[9] Its organizers claimed that they did not actively dissuade men from registering for the draft; instead, they offered advice to those who had chosen not to register.

The No-Conscription League held several meetings in May and June of 1917 that rallied anti-draft sentiment among immigrants living in New York City's Lower East Side. Violence quickly erupted at these meetings when soldiers and police officers harassed speakers and members of the audience. Disturbed by this escalating violence and concerned that the police might use these meetings to identify unregistered men, Goldman decided to stop holding public rallies. Goldman planned the No-Conscription League's final public meeting for June 14th.[10]

The day after this meeting, federal marshals arrested Goldman and her companion Alexander Berkman, charging each with conspiracy to interfere with the draft, a violation of the Selective Service Act that had been enacted five days before.[11] Federal marshals carefully staged Goldman's arrest. They broke into her offices, ransacked her files, and refused Goldman's request to examine the arrest warrant. When Goldman asked for permission to collect her personal effects, marshals allowed her only enough time to quickly change her dress and grab a copy of *Ulysses*. The marshals then herded Goldman and Berkman into a waiting car and in Goldman's words, "fled throughout the congested streets, frightening people . . . and sending them in all directions."[12]

Federal marshals designed their actions to accentuate the menace that Goldman posed. By breaking into her offices, speeding through the crowded streets of New York City, and denying Goldman sufficient time to collect her personal effects, their actions defined Goldman as unusually dangerous and particularly elusive.[13]

The *New York Times*, which provided the most extensive coverage of Goldman's arrest and conviction, helped sell this perception. Its coverage emphasized Goldman's role in fomenting the dangerous atmosphere that surrounded her arrest, as illustrated by its coverage of even the most benign details such as the dress that Goldman wore to prison.[14] Under the headline, "Arrayed in Royal Purple," the *Times* described the moments prior to Goldman's trip to prison. "Miss Goldman asked if she could have time to put on a more presentable gown," the *Times* reported, "permission was given, and she disappeared upstairs, to return a few minute later in a purple dress."[15] The juxtaposition of the *Times* headline and its explanation suggested that Goldman chose a dress that indicated her status as the queen of the gathering crowd that, according to the *Times*, continuously menaced federal marshals as they arrested Goldman.[16]

The *Times* defined Goldman's crime as her influence over that crowd. To drive this message home to its readers, the *Times* linked Goldman's arrest to two riots that occurred later that night at anti-conscription rallies. "Rioting of thousands of persons at anti-conscription meetings last night," wrote a *Times* reporter, "marked the efforts by police and soldiers to round up conscription slackers, giving to the draft situation the most sinister tinge it has taken in New York City."[17] Although the *Times* reported these riots in a story that directly followed its coverage of Goldman's arrest, it combined the headlines that announced the riots with those that reported her arrest. The positioning of these headlines established a link between the "rioters menac[ing] soldiers" and the events of Goldman's arrest.[18]

According to the *Times*, these riots began after a speech given by a "yiddish woman" that protested Goldman's arrest. After her speech, the *Times* reported that the crowd then rushed out into the street, overwhelming soldiers and police officers. A careful reading of the story belies the interpretation suggested by its headlines. The *Times* acknowledged that the meeting itself "was rather tame" until soldiers began requesting draft registration cards from its participants. Apparently, the crowd went to the aid of colleagues who were being arrested at a similar meeting down the street. The violence ensued when women interfered with these arrests and demanded that the police release their sons and husbands. As the *Times* story indicates, the crowd's violence stemmed from women's concerns that their families could not survive conscription rather than from Goldman's "sinister" influence.[19]

Significantly, these riots had occurred at a meeting held to organize immigrant women against conscription. Working-class women opposed conscription because they could not afford to lose the economic support of husbands and sons. Many eastern European immigrants had fled mandatory military service. Yet, the dictates of patriotic motherhood required women to sacrifice their husbands and sons to the war effort. According to these dictates, the women who attempted to prevent police from arresting husbands and sons violated true womanhood. Goldman provided a framework for reinterpreting the behavior of working-class and immigrant women who viewed this sacrifice as injurious to their families. Within this framework, the family concerns of such women were understood as a danger to Americanism.

Ultimately prosecutors hoped to convince the jury that Goldman intended her actions to have the effects that were reported in the *Times* story—to implant within her audience a disdain equal to her own for the nation's legal, social, and political institutions. To convict her, prosecuting attorney Harold A. Content did not have to prove that Goldman had instructed men not to register or that she advocated violence; he only had to show that Goldman's offer to help men who did not register had a "bad tendency to create social disorder."[20] Given this narrow legal parameter, much of Goldman's defense and the prosecution's case was irrelevant. For this reason, the course of Goldman's trial is especially revealing.

Prosecutors argued that Goldman had advised men not to register for the draft, a clear violation of the Selective Service Act. Although the prosecution's evidence included copies of Goldman's periodical *Mother Earth* and No-Conscription League pamphlets, Goldman's public speeches provided their most explosive evidence. In particular, Content noted one passage from police transcripts of Goldman's speeches that reported that she had instructed her audience to resist the Selective Service Act:

> You say that it is Law. I defy your law! The only Law that I recognize is the Law which ministers to the need of humanity, which makes men and women fonder and better and more humane, the kind of a Law which teaches children that human life is sacred, and that those who organize for the purpose of taking human life are going to be called before the bar of human justice, and not in the wretched little court which is called your Law of the United States.[21]

This use of police transcripts posed potential problems for prosecutors because their accuracy was disputed. Prosecutors emphasized Goldman's public speeches rather than her written words because they allowed prosecutors to portray Goldman as hysterical and avoid the complexities of Goldman's ideas. At the same time, Goldman's public speeches reached the audience that prosecutors feared could be persuaded by her attacks on the government—immigrants and workers. It was on the podium that Goldman established a relationship with her followers, and it was this relationship, prosecutors argued, that most threatened the public order.

Content paid special attention to this relationship in his closing statement. There he carefully defined how he wanted the jury to remember Goldman as they began their deliberations. Significantly, he argued that Goldman did not simply influence her hearers to act, but rather reproduced herself among their ranks. "You have at those mass meetings a very different Emma Goldman," Content told the jury,

> for example than the Emma Goldman who in this court says "thank you" to witnesses. You have there the emotional Emma Goldman, something as you have heard today, with all that fiery oratory that makes her so dangerous to the peace and security of the United States. Anybody who underestimates Emma Goldman's intellectual qualities is a fool. She is all that. She is the best speaker you have perhaps ever heard. And that is why her influence is so pernicious. These people were held spellbound. But Emma Goldman who said for example in Forward Hall: "you say there is a law. I defy your law!"...That is the Emma Goldman that speaks at crowded mass meetings on the east side. That is the Emma Goldman who takes her powerful personality and impresses it upon the minds of ignorant, weaker, and emotional people of the type that you have seen called as witnesses in these proceedings. Is it any wonder that those dolts, those susceptible to influences of a stronger mind, under her guidance though perhaps not under the use of specific words as to registration shall go out and commit crimes and defy the laws of the United States and the laws of organized society? That is the Emma Goldman of the mass meetings, not the Emma Goldman you have seen in court.[22]

Even as Content gestured toward Goldman's "intellectual qualities," he skillfully shifted the court's attention from the content of her arguments to the ways that she affected her audience. Content's maneuver was critical to anti-radicalism as it developed in the early twentieth century. At issue was not Goldman's ideas—her objection to and understanding of specific policy decisions—but rather her personality, and how that personality transformed her followers into a potential revolutionary army.

Content's maneuver fits nicely into Michael Rogin's description of countersubversive thought. "The countersubversive response," Rogin argues, "transformed interest conflicts into psychologically based anxieties over national security and American identity."[23] According to Rogin, countersubversive thought developed from nineteenth-century racial conflicts and culminated in the "criminalization of dissent" by the national security state of the Cold War. At the heart of the countersubversive tradition was "the creation of monsters as a continuing feature of American politics by inflation, stigmatization, and dehumanization"—the politics of demonology. Rogin continues,

> American demonology has both a form and content. The demonologist splits the world in two, attributing magical, pervasive power to a conspiratorial center of evil. Fearing chaos and secret penetration, the countersubversive interprets local initiatives as signs of alien power. Discrete individuals and groups become, in the countersubversive imagination, members of a single political body directed by its head.[24]

In Content's mind, Emma Goldman was this head. By attributing the policy disagreements of the crowd to the personality of Goldman, Content erased politics, focusing instead on issues of character and personality. Adherence to radical politics, Content argued, was itself a flaw of character.

Yet, Content's words add an interesting twist to Rogin's analysis. Goldman, Content charged, held her audience "spellbound" while she "impressed" on them her "powerful personality"; his language conjures images of witchcraft. As historian Carol Karlsen argues, "witchcraft confronts us with ideas about women, with fears about women, with the place of women in society, and women themselves."[25] Witchcraft gave specific meaning to the behavior of women who "failed to, or refused to, abide by the behavioral norms of their society."[26] By defining subversion as a form of witchcraft, Content subtly shifted the dominant nativist paradigm that was used to describe how subversive ideas flourished in the population. Content rejected the disease model in favor of one that emphasized women's connection to the reproduction of citizens to characterize Goldman's influence. Goldman's crime consisted not only in her engagement in this act of unnatural reproduction—in her creation of disloyal citizens—but also, and more significantly, in the misuse of reproduction itself.[27]

Goldman's critics used her relationship with Alexander Berkman to further clarify how Goldman corrupted gender roles. They defined Berkman as an example of how anarchism in general and Goldman in particular perverted male gender identity. Although Goldman and Berkman stood trial together and both conducted their own defense, the prosecutor and press continuously reminded the public that Berkman "was not nearly so brave and defiant as his female comrade."[28] In contrast to Goldman, who seemed exhilarated and regenerated by their trial, Berkman appeared defeated and weak, propped up only by Goldman's "guiding hand."

By subverting his will to Goldman, Content emphasized, Berkman had sacrificed essential qualities of manhood—independence and rationality. "And the Alexander Berkman you have seen here," Content warned the jury,

> and who controlled himself so skillfully under the guiding hand of Miss Goldman—can't you hear him say that he hoped these people *did* prepare that bomb for Rockfeller? How he has controlled himself in court! But you got a taste once of his other self; and that was when he lost control of himself, this Berkman who under Miss Goldman's clever influence has controlled himself.[29]

The prosecutor's comments did more than reassure the public that Goldman's and Berkman's rational appearances were mere performances; they clarified the nature of Goldman's relationship with Berkman. Ironically, Content's comments inadvertently credited Goldman with instructing Berkman in rational citizenship, a role that was consistent with the expectations of patriotic motherhood. But as Content emphasized, Goldman's instructions merely masked Berkman's incapacity to act as a man. Through her possession of him, Goldman had appropriated and perverted Berkman's gender identity, thus reducing him to a nonman who was governed by his passions.[30]

Her relationship with Berkman, Content suggested, was a miniature of her relationship with the crowd. If the jury failed to convict her, the nation would be faced with a crowd of her kind; that is, nonmen and nonwomen who were controlled by their passions and were unwilling to sacrifice for the nation's best interest.

Goldman approached her trial as if her conviction was inevitable. "We did not believe," wrote Goldman,

> in the law and its machinery, and we knew that we could expect no justice. We would therefore completely ignore what was to us a mere farce; we would refuse to participate in the court proceedings. . . . [S]hould this method prove impractical, we would plead our own case, not in order to defend ourselves, but to give public utterance to our ideas.[31]

Goldman described what was known in radical circles as a "revolutionary trial"; that is, a trial that did not seek acquittal but instead served as a forum for the defendant's ideas. Her defense challenged both the prosecutor's versions of her anti-conscription speeches and, more significantly, charges that she manipulated her followers. She defined her dissent as part of a long-standing and cherished American protest tradition. In contrast, she argued, censorship and conscription violated the principles of a democratic society. Doubtful that a jury would acquit her, Goldman worked to shift the ground on which her ideas stood. By evoking history and logic, she challenged arguments that she appealed to the base emotions of her followers.

Although she insisted that her trial was a "mere farce," Goldman mounted a traditional defense that attempted to discredit the prosecution's case against her. Goldman based this part of her defense on practical and philosophical evidence. Arguing that her habit of talking fast prevented anyone from transcribing her speeches verbatim, she challenged state witnesses who claimed that she either advocated violence or told men not to register. Because the prosecution could not establish Goldman's precise utterances, Goldman contended that it lacked the necessary evidence to convict her.[32]

Because neither Goldman nor the prosecution could prove what Goldman actually said in her anti-conscription speeches, each focused on what she would have said, given her political philosophy. Goldman emphasized that her personal experiences and her commitment to anarchism prevented her from dissuading men from registering. "I took the position," she later stated in her autobiography,

> as a woman and therefore myself not subject to military service, [that] I could not advise people on the matter. Whether or not one is led to lend oneself as a tool for the business of killing should properly be left to the individual conscience. As an anarchist I could not presume to decide the fate of others, I wrote. But I could say to those who refused to be coerced into military service that I would plead their cause and stand by their act against all odds.[33]

Goldman's defense challenged the popular image of anarchism by grounding it in individual experience rather than in abstract rhetoric. Her politics, Goldman stressed, reflected only what her experiences and ideology allowed. Dissuading men from registering for the draft would have violated her anarchist principles; consequently, she only offered support to men who had chosen to resist the draft.

Goldman's final address to the jury reiterated these themes. It highlighted the logic of her arguments and their grounding in a distinctly American protest tradition. In her address, Goldman mocked assertions that she had incited disorderly behavior and focused the jury's attention on the behavior of law enforcement officials, suggesting that it was their repression of dissent that had instigated public disorder. "Imagine if you can," she said as she reminded the jury of her arrest,

> a dozen stalwart warriors rushing up two flights of stairs to find the defendants Alexander Berkman and Emma Goldman, in their separate offices quietly seated at their desks, wielding not the gun or the bomb or the club or the sword, but only such a simple and insignificant thing as a pen.[34]

Goldman's account of her arrest inverted the images portrayed in the *Times*. She presented herself as an intellectual who was quietly at work, producing ideas rather than bombs. Yet, Goldman's words were ironic. If her words had acted as bombs, Goldman sarcastically reminded her audience, it was because they exploded the tenuous ground on which militarism and capitalism stood. She was dangerous because she told the truth.

Goldman also challenged prosecution arguments that she headed a secret conspiracy. "At no time," Goldman insisted, "did we keep in hiding under the bed. We have always frankly and squarely faced the issue."[35] In contrast to her own willingness to openly discuss her ideas, Goldman reminded the jury that the Wilson administration forbade frank discussion of its wartime policies. The very existence of the wartime laws, Goldman subtly suggested, implicated the government in a conspiracy. Goldman insinuated that the Wilson administration would not fear public debate over its policies if it truly intended the war to advance democracy. Goldman hoped to redirect the public's readiness to accept the existence of secret conspiracies into a critique of the Wilson administration.

Goldman's response to charges that she advocated violence in her anti-conscription speeches is particularly revealing. The police transcripts that the prosecution used were inaccurate, she explained to the jury, because to have advocated violence would have "merely made the whole speech nonsensical, it would have dragged in something which was irrelevant to the body of the speech or the material used."[36]

Goldman dismissed the prosecution's version of her speech because it was illogical rather than because it was untrue. She claimed to reject violence for the very same reasons that the prosecution claimed that it rejected violence—because its use was irrational. By doing so, Goldman preempted the prosecution's efforts to portray her as a disaffected alien driven by a fervid hatred of Americanism. Goldman did not expect that her words would sway the jury. But she did reclaim the status her trial threatened to deny her—that of a rational citizen.

Goldman claimed this status by placing her actions within a protest tradition that she defined as distinctly American. Although Goldman acknowledged her challenge to the legitimacy of the American state, she identified with a protest tradition that she argued had flourished in the United States—each individual's responsibility to her or his conscience and to an obligation to combat unjust laws. Goldman carefully crafted a history lesson that placed philosophical anarchism within the context of the ideals of the American Revolution that had established a tradition of rejecting unjust and undemocratic laws.

In contrast, she defined conscription and the government's repression of dissent as anti-American. "The kind of patriotism that we represent," Goldman told the jury, "is the kind of patriotism that loves America with open eyes."[37] Blind acceptance of any governmental policy, Goldman asserted, violated the fundamental values of this uniquely American tradition. The Selective Service Act, Goldman reminded the jury, stripped Americans of their capacities as rational citizens to decide for themselves the validity of conscription and American participation in the war.

The prosecution's case not only defined Goldman and her followers as aliens but also reserved rational citizenship and Americanism for those who endorsed the war. By claiming rational citizenship for herself, Goldman also claimed it for the crowd—new immigrants, women, and workers—that Goldman's opponents portrayed as alien by nature. Goldman provided a framework by which the actions of this crowd could be viewed as rational and as consistent with American ideals of citizenship.

Goldman's critics interpreted her conviction as an unmasking and as confirmation of the state's ability to protect the community from dangerous and elusive subversives. As the jury read its verdict, the *Times* reported that "Emma Goldman, her face red with anger and disappointment was immediately on her feet. She never made a more defiant picture."[38] The *Times* coverage ridiculed and belittled Goldman. Its headlines referred to Goldman as "the woman," and its main story described her reaction as a tantrum. By convicting her, the *Times* seemed to be saying, the jury exposed Goldman and stripped her of her most potent weapon—her veil of rationality. Once stripped of this veil, Goldman literally lost her identity as an individual human being.

Yet not everyone was convinced that merely imprisoning Goldman would protect the crowd from her influence. Goldman's ability to masquerade behind this veil of rationality and responsible citizenship continued to worry her critics even after the jury read its verdict. "There is a curious irrelevance in the fact that this purveyor of social bombs is a dress maker and a trained nurse," wrote a reporter for the *Literary Digest*; "[S]he is described in the *Nation* as a small, wiry woman, about fifty years old, who might be passed anywhere in the crowd without notice." The *Literary Digest* used this description of Goldman in its endorsement of her impending deportation:

> Her sharp eyes, intense expression . . . become more significant with familiarity, and her eye-glasses, framed in part by sharply marked brows, give her an air of active mentality which is lacking in some others of her general type. Her face is too symmetrical to be classed as that of a natural "crank," but you have only to talk with her for five minutes in order to discover how strong an appeal the theatrical side of social chaos makes to her. Smiles she reserves mostly for sneering purposes.[39]

Underneath Goldman's rational appearance, the *Literary Digest* warned, was an underside that was visible only to the attentive observer. When stripped of her mask, Goldman revealed the disorder that potentially accompanied any person of her "type"—radical, woman, or immigrant. Within the context of a wartime political culture desirous of securing absolute conformity of opinion, few were willing to trust the ability of a neighbor to see through Goldman's performance. Only by deporting her would the state protect communities from being tricked into believing the false promises she offered.

Goldman was given the maximum penalty allowed under the Selective Service Act—two years in federal prison—which she served, minus four months for good behavior, in Jefferson City, Missouri.[40] Her legal troubles did not end with her prison term. As admitted anarchists and as noncitizens, Goldman and Berkman faced deportation as soon as they stepped outside federal prison.[41]

By the time Goldman left prison in September of 1919, the Justice Department had already begun its deportation campaign. The Justice Department had detained hundreds of aliens who were subject to deportation under the Immigration Act of 1918.[42] Deportation was an efficient way to control radicalism. As an administrative rather than legal procedure, deportation did not require judicial trials. During 1919 and 1920, the Justice Department used deportation in its campaign to eliminate domestic subversion; that policy rid the nation of what the department considered to be the best audience for subversive organizations—new immigrants.[43]

Goldman and Berkman were perfect candidates for deportation. Unlike most of the deportees, they were prominent figures whose names conjured the exact images that Justice Department officials hoped to associate with the deportees. In the words of historian Richard Powers, "Hoover could capitalize on the popular impression that Goldman was the leader of a radical movement to transform the anonymous mass of the deportees—a disorganized helpless rabble—into the image of a revolutionary army."[44] According to Powers, Hoover took personal offense to Goldman's claim that her ideas were rooted in a distinctly American protest tradition. Hoover believed that Goldman's deportation would purge her influence from the nation and discredit her claim to Americanism.[45]

As Goldman sat in prison, Hoover prepared his case against her. He argued that Goldman's past history of violent deeds as well as her philosophical commitment to anarchism proved that she posed a continued threat to the nation.[46] He based much of his case on an old and unproven accusation that Goldman had engineered the assassination of President McKinley. Because Goldman freely acknowledged her commitment to anarchism, proving that her politics justified her deportation was not the most difficult problem facing Hoover. To deport her, immigration officials had to successfully challenge Goldman's claim that she was an American citizen.

Ironically, Hoover's success ultimately rested on the class and gender biases embedded in immigration and marriage laws. Goldman argued that she had acquired citizenship when she married Jacob Kershner in 1887, who she divorced one year later.[47] But immigration officials had revoked Kershner's citizenship in 1909 for falsifying his original application. Hoover argued that under immigration law, women held the citizenship status of their husbands. If a husband's citizenship was revoked, Hoover contended, than so was that of the wife. Immigration officials, Hoover further asserted, had no responsibility to inform the wife of their actions or bring formal proceedings against her. According to this principle, Hoover argued that Goldman had lost her citizenship at the same time that Kershner lost his. "In her [Goldman's] case," a Justice Department brief contended,

> she acquired her status not by any act of her own but merely by grant from the government. This grant was based on the condition that she married a citizen. In the eyes of the law it may be said [that] her husband's certificate

of naturalization was obtained by fraud[:] *he was never a citizen* and therefore his wife acquired no such rights of citizenship. As pointed out above, the preceding being one in *rem* it is not necessary to join the wife in order for her to obtain the citizenship of her husband in naturalization proceedings. Consequently, it would follow that it would be unnecessary to join the wife in a suit to set aside the husband's citizenship in order to affect her citizenship.[48]

The Justice Department based its reading on the tradition of *feme covert*, by which a wife's legal status was essentially "covered" by that of her husband.[49] Coverture assumed that women lacked the rational capacities to form independent contracts. The courts protected coverture by insisting that a woman's responsibilities within the family were more important than her rights and responsibilities as a citizen. Although Hoover used coverture because it was pragmatic to do so, the argument also denied her the rationality she worked so hard to claim at her trial.

Harry Weinberger, Goldman and Berkman's lawyer, did not challenge Hoover's interpretation of immigration law. Instead, he attempted to prove that Kershner had died before immigration officials revoked his citizenship. Hoover outflanked Weinberger, however, by producing evidence that Kershner had died in 1919, after the revocation of his citizenship. Immigration officials upheld Hoover's argument and ordered Goldman deported.[50] Not wanting to be separated from Berkman, Goldman refused to further appeal her case.[51]

It is difficult to escape the ironies of Goldman's deportation. Throughout her career, Goldman had criticized the social, economic, and legal policies that enforced women's dependence. The law by which Goldman received and was ultimately disqualified for citizenship exemplified this dependence on men. By arguing that the citizenship status of a woman was contingent on that of her husband, immigration law essentially stripped immigrant women of their legal rights as persons and tied their political status to the status of their husbands. The war and deportation delirium that followed only further reinforced the already perilous position of immigrant women. Immigration officials refused to transport the families of deportees or to recognize that the economic hardships caused by conscription might provide a rational reason for their protests against war.[52]

The conditions of war sealed Goldman's fate. Armed with tougher laws and backed by a public that was desperate for unity, federal authorities finally succeeded in both symbolically and literally casting her from American shores. As Goldman stood on the deck of the "Soviet Ark," exchanging barbs with Hoover, she remained outwardly defiant. But the event was tragic. As Goldman conceded, it was in the United States that her political ideas bore the most fruit, and like many of those who were deported, she left its soil unwillingly.

At stake in Goldman's trial was not her individual crime but an understanding of Americanism that marginalized the values and concerns of immigrant women. That understanding of Americanism required women to accept their roles as patriotic mothers. Goldman's trial defined her as the quintessential disorderly woman, one who used her influence to discourage immigrant men and women from fulfilling their duties as patriotic men and women.

Goldman continued to serve as a symbol of the subversion of alien women throughout the war's anti-radical crusades. Her name was evoked in the cases of other women who were charged with disrupting the war effort. When Seattle authorities arrested Seattle's leading socialist speaker, Kate Sadler, for allegedly calling President Wilson a traitor, Justice Department spies urged Washington to consider charging her under the Espionage Act.[53] "Perhaps, the most rabid of the woman speakers in Seattle," they wrote of Sadler, "she is an anarchist in views and aspires to the position held by Emma Goldman. She is the alleged wife of Sam Sadler . . . although it is reported that she is not legally married to him."[54] When Louise Olivereau, a secretary for the Industrial Workers of the World, stood trial for violating the Espionage Act, prosecutors and press reports portrayed her as a disciple of Goldman.[55] Although the public and Washington officials might not have appreciated the nature of Sadler or Olivereau's threat to the public order, they certainly understood Goldman's. Such comparisons to Goldman placed Sadler and Olivereau at the threshold of Goldman's "inner circle" and defined their actions as a potent threat to the social order; they also extended Goldman's own reach into the hearts and minds of the populace.[56]

The Justice Department also investigated those women associated with Goldman for their possible participation in plots against the government. After her conviction, the Justice Department tracked the "Guillotine Club," a group of five women that they suspected Goldman had directed to assassinate public officials.[57] Because Justice Department spies failed to prove the existence of an actual political conspiracy, they focused on Goldman's influence over the personal lives of her colleagues. They reveled in gossip that Goldman broke into jealous rages over the romantic relationships of her associates, and that her friend and colleague Eleanor Fitzgerald had stolen Alexander Berkman from her.[58] Such reports depicted Goldman as the matriarch of a perverse family that was united not by their affection for each other but rather by their common hatred of Americanism. If allowed to move beyond the confines of her inner circle, Goldman's perverse and alien family values could "infect" the crowd as they had those immigrant women who protested the conscription of their sons and husbands.

Although state authorities and press reports did not accuse Goldman of directly attacking patriotic motherhood, as they did O'Hare, they understood her political interventions as a threat to the gender and sex roles fundamental to middle-class society. As the quintessential disorderly woman, Goldman symbolized the consequences of women's unchecked entrance into the public. Without the state's intervention, her critics charged, Goldman would reproduce herself into a revolutionary army of nonmen and nonwomen capable of carrying out her conspiracy against Americanism. Her trial and deportation served to reassure the public that the state could control those individuals who were alien to the political and family values of the nation.

4

⚭

The Venom of a Bolshevik Woman

THE CASE OF ROSE PASTOR STOKES

The relationships among patriotism, Americanism, and ideas about true womanhood that shaped the trials of Kate Richards O'Hare and Emma Goldman also shaped anti-Bolshevism. After October of 1917, federal officials, prosecutors, and the pro-war press used the Bolshevik Revolution as an example of the disorder that would result from unchecked criticisms of the war. Increasingly, Bolshevism symbolized all that was outside the legitimate parameters of Americanism. Definitions of gender were central to these constructions of anti-Bolshevism.

It is clear that Americans felt betrayed by the Bolshevik peace with Germany, a peace that only supported arguments that the Bolsheviks had received German support for their revolution and that leading Bolsheviks were in fact German agents. The pragmatic and very real problems that Russia's withdrawal from the war posed for the Allies also contributed to anti-Bolshevik sentiment. Without Russia on the eastern front, Germany could divert more troops to face American soldiers on the western front. That troop diversion, Allied strategists feared, would not only endanger American lives but also could tip the standoff in Germany's favor.[1]

In addition to these basic strategic concerns, Bolshevism provided a plausible alternative to progressive internationalism. The Bolshevik peace plan called for an end to the war with no indemnities and no annexations, a plan that was similar to the one promoted by American socialists and members of the liberal peace movement. Wilson disarmed some of this potential support for the Bolshevik peace program in January of 1918 in a speech to Congress, when he announced his vision for the post-war world. Wilson hoped his Fourteen Points would strengthen progressive internationalism and the American role in guaranteeing the peace, justice, and prosperity obtained through the principles of democratic government, negotiated settlements, and international cooperation.[2] Given Wilson's new promise of post-war international democracy, many Americans saw only disorder in Bolshevism and viewed support of the Bolshevik revolution as sabotage of the war itself.

Some members of the left expected that the Bolshevik Revolution would reinvigorate American socialism and perhaps provide a model for social reform in the United States.[3] Rose Pastor Stokes was one such individual. Although Stokes initially endorsed American intervention in the war and joined pro-war socialists in their belief that the war could facilitate democratic socialism, her support for the Bolshevik Revolution eventually led to charges that she had violated the Sedition Act. Her trial illustrates the ways in which anti-Bolshevism grafted itself onto wartime definitions of patriotic motherhood. With the exception of Kate Richards O'Hare, Stokes was the best-known socialist woman convicted under the wartime emergency laws.[4] Her fame generated a highly publicized trial that served as a public forum for exploring Bolshevism's corruption of women's political influence.

Born in Poland in 1879, Stokes immigrated to the United States as a child. While she lived in Cleveland, Stokes worked in a cigar factory to help her parents raise her six younger brothers and sisters. In 1903 Stokes migrated to New York City where she helped edit a Yiddish newspaper while she worked in settlement houses. There she met and married the "millionaire socialist," Graham Stokes. In the years before the war, Stokes continued to work for the labor movement, participating in strikes and raising funds for the defense of workers. At the same time, her marriage to Graham Stokes integrated her into a circle of socialist intellectuals living in Greenwich, Connecticut, that included William English Walling, Anna Strunsky Walling, and Helen Stokes.[5]

In 1916, Stokes asserted her independence from Graham and other members of this circle by expanding her role in the birth control movement. That year she "deliberately broke the law" and informed supporters that she was "willing to go to jail" for distributing birth control materials at a meeting held in Emma Goldman's honor.[6] Although Goldman applauded Stokes's actions, other birth control activists urged Stokes to temper her activity, pointing out that she was more useful out of jail.[7] Stokes's closest colleagues attributed this activity to her growing personal independence and her desire to prove herself a leader in left-wing politics.[8] Ultimately, however, it was the war that transformed her political and personal life. Her trial and conviction for violating the Sedition Act pushed Stokes's politics to the left. After her conviction Stokes divorced not only evolutionary socialism but also her husband; she joined the Communist Party in 1920.[9]

Early in 1917, Stokes was an unlikely candidate for arrest. Three weeks before the United States entered the war, Stokes resigned from the New York Woman's Peace Party. "I love peace but I am not a pacifist," she explained; "[I]f the United States were to become involved in war I would place myself at the service of my country."[10] With her husband, Stokes left the Socialist Party and criticized its anti-war stance. "I am a socialist, and of course an internationalist,"Stokes confessed, "but I have misconceived in the past both my socialism and my internationalism, as tens of thousands of socialists in this country are doing to-day."[11]

Stokes was disappointed with the Socialist Party's official position on the war conceived at the St. Louis Convention, held in April of 1917. The majority resolution endorsed active interference with the war effort, a move that Stokes felt was imprudent and unnecessarily belligerent. Although most socialists eschewed such interference, Stokes nonetheless feared that the language of the majority resolution exposed the Socialist Party to repression and encouraged violent confrontations between anti-war protesters and government officials.[12] Perhaps most importantly, Stokes believed that Germany was a threat to democratic nations and that its defeat would promote international stability. At least initially, Stokes believed that Wilson had entered the war to promote international democracy; she argued that "America . . . stands among the free nations of the world, eager to follow where Liberty beckons."[13] Unlike other pro-war socialists, however, Stokes did not condemn anti-war socialists and she maintained close friendships with anti-war socialists such as Eugene Debs and Helen Stokes.[14]

Stokes's break from socialist politics was brief. In late 1917 she worked for Morris Hilliquit's New York City mayoral campaign; she officially rejoined the Socialist Party in early 1918.[15] Why Stokes returned to the Socialist Party is unclear. Stokes attributed her return to a growing disillusionment with Wilson's peace program and his intervention in the Russian Civil War. "I want to come back," Stokes wrote in February of 1918,

> because I see no hope of functioning 100 per cent for the common people except through the Socialist Party. I left because I considered dangerous the Party's attitude toward America's participation in the war; but the crisis created by the St. Louis resolution is past, and the present immediate danger is an imperialist peace, which I believe only a unified and strengthened internationalist socialist movement can prevent.[16]

Although still supporting Germany's defeat, Stokes argued that the war must "precipitate the social revolution."[17] She explained that she no longer believed that the Wilson administration's policies furthered international democracy and social justice. She concluded that the Socialist Party and, perhaps more significantly, the Bolshevik peace program best ensured international democracy. It was this argument—that Bolshevism presented a viable and preferable alternative to Wilson's progressive internationalism—that marked her as a dangerous subversive.

Stokes's decision to rejoin the Socialist Party represented an important break in her personal and political affiliations with the "millionaire socialists" of Greenwich, Connecticut. Graham Stokes opposed her decision and actively discouraged her participation in wartime socialist politics. Yet these family tensions were not solely the product of wartime politics. Even before the war, Stokes's participation in birth control and labor politics had embarrassed Graham and alienated her from his family.[18]

Stokes's politics led at least one member of Graham's family to inform the Justice Department of her potential disloyalty. Only two weeks before Stokes gave her fateful speech at the Kansas City Woman's Club, W. E. D Stokes, Graham's uncle, wrote a letter to the Justice Department that expressed concern over Graham's relationship with Stokes. Calling his nephew a "good man," W. E. D. nonetheless warned that

> he is married to a woman who was born under a cloud with a grievance, and she is dangerous. You will find her so, and I have tried to use my influence to break him away from the influence of this misalliance, and I think to a certain extent, I have succeeded.[19]

Perhaps concerned that his nephew could become a target for the Justice Department, the elder Stokes moved to protect his family's reputation by simultaneously asserting his own patriotism—he also urged that the government shoot all German spies—and focusing the government's attention on an in-law. His letter speaks to the passion of anti-radicalism and its capacity to disrupt family relations.[20]

Stokes's legal troubles began soon after she rejoined the Socialist Party. In March 1918 Stokes addressed a women's club in Kansas City. After hearing that her talk had offended some members of the audience, a reporter for the *Kansas City Star* asked Stokes to clarify her position on the war. He reported under the headline "Mrs. Stokes for the Government and Against the War at the Same Time" that Stokes had urged Americans to support the Wilson administration's war effort. "I believe that the government of the United States," the reporter quoted Stokes as saying, "should have the unqualified support of every citizen in its war aims."[21] Angry that the reporter's story had misrepresented her position, Stokes clarified her remarks in what she later characterized as a hastily written letter. "I made no such statements," she wrote to the *Star*'s editor, "and I believe in no such thing. No government which is *For* the profiteers can also be *For* the people and I am for the people while the government is for the profiteers."[22] Following the *Star*'s publication of her letter, the Justice Department indicted Stokes for making "false reports and false statements with intent to interfere with the operation and success of the military and naval forces of the United States."[23] Although she was initially convicted and sentenced to ten years in prison, the Supreme Court overturned her conviction before she served any prison time.

At issue in Stokes's trial was whether she had intended to criticize the war, and whether her remarks potentially interfered with the recruit-ment of soldiers. Throughout her defense, Stokes claimed that she had intended to criticize only specific Wilson administration policies. Stokes contended that in her haste she had failed to emphasize that her re-marks applied only to those policies. She argued that she never opposed the war and that she continued to support Germany's defeat.[24]

In contrast, prosecutors Elmer B. Silvers and Francis Wilson argued that Stokes intended her remarks to foment a Bolshevik-style revolution in the United States. They charged that Stokes was organizing a con-spiracy that could lead American soldiers to abandon the war as had the Bolsheviks in Russia. "She is an open and deliberate advocate of the Bol-sheviki form of government or principles in this country," prosecutors charged, and "that is enough to convict her of the intent charged in the indictment."[25] Prosecutors represented Stokes's support of Bolshevism as a criminal act that in itself was equivalent to obstructing the war ef-fort. But to convict Stokes under the Sedition Act, prosecutors had to demonstrate that she had conspired to obstruct the war effort. To accom-plish that end, prosecutors depicted Stokes as a sinister and calculating revolutionary bent on turning American soldiers into Bolsheviks.

Prosecutors began their case with the stenographer Stokes had used when she wrote her letter to, in the prosecutions's words, "prove . . . beyond a shadow of doubt, that she in a cool state of the blood, wrote what she did to the *Star*."[26] Stokes's letter, prosecutors emphasized, was part of a premeditated conspiracy to discredit the American govern-ment. Although they hoped to depict Stokes's words as irrational, pros-ecutors wanted the jury to see Stokes herself as a rational political actor who carefully conceived every aspect of her plan. Prosecutors further developed this argument as they outlined their version of Stokes's talk to the Kansas City Woman's Club.

Stokes's reputation as a socialist and feminist speaker had raised concerns among some members of the Kansas City Woman's Club even before she actually spoke. Those members had objected to inviting Stokes, causing Blanch Rienke, the club's president, to defend Stokes's presentation as the "biggest thing [the] club ever did." Press reports were divided over what Stokes had said at her talk, and how the audi-ence had responded to her remarks. The press attended her talk hoping to determine if rumors of Stokes's return to socialism were true. Several news stories confirmed that Stokes had indeed returned to socialism, noting that members of the audience had walked out in protest. But news stories disagreed over the number of audience members Stokes offended or whether she had made disloyal remarks.[27] For some, Stokes's talk confirmed her commitment to socialism, thus raising the specter of disloyalty. Other members of the audience, however, expressed dis-appointment that her address contained little of the fiery rhetoric that they had expected, given her reputation.

Even if objections to Stokes's presentation were confined to a minority, the prosecution was able to produce witnesses such as Maude Flowers to confirm Stokes's disloyalty.[28] Flowers testified that Stokes had claimed that soldiers would quickly learn that they had been duped in their belief that the war was a war for democracy, and that this discontent would lead to a social revolution much as it had in Russia. A second witness for the prosecution, Florence E. Gebhart, testified that Stokes had upheld Russia as an example of a free society, stating that American "boys" were not fighting for democracy. Prosecution witnesses also claimed that Stokes had called herself pro-German and had recommended withdrawing support for the Red Cross.[29]

It is unlikely that Stokes had supported Germany in her remarks, but it is also likely that she expressed sympathy with the Bolshevik revolution and even presented it as a model for political reform. Stokes claimed that her remarks had either been misunderstood or misrepresented, reminding the court that "no evidence [was] produced to prove that I oppose the war."[30] She also denied denigrating the Red Cross, pointing to her own service in that organization as well as her brother's military service as evidence of her loyalty. Stokes also clarified her position on a possible social revolution in the United States. "I never said that our men were befooled," she told the court,

> I said our men answered the call for democracy, believing that they were fighting for democracy and when they came home, when—if they found the things they fought for were not gained, that undoubtedly we should have both an individual and social revolution in the country.[31]

Stokes acknowledged that she had hoped that her speaking tour would foster critical discussion of the war by "stir[ring] up the people to consider the question of democracy[;] we were doing our part to fight for the very thing our boys have gone to fight for."[32] At the same time, Stokes claimed that her protest only sought to reinvent the democratic principles originally outlined in Wilson's war message.

By defining the Bolshevik Revolution as a plausible alternative to progressive internationalism, Stokes committed an unforgivable heresy. If only implicitly, Stokes's remarks, or at least the prosecutor's version of those remarks, threatened the domain claimed by Wilson's progressive internationalism. It was that domain that the prosecution asked the jury to defend. "Do you want to discourage her doctrines?" he asked the jury,

> And do you want to endorse her ideas that Bolshevik government is pure democracy? If you do, as her socialist lawyer says for you to do, and acquit her, I want to say to you, under the evidence in this case, that you will regret it to the last moment of your lives, and an unworthy heritage, the shame [of] it[,]will descend to your children.[33]

The prosecution appealed to the jury as the protectors of the nation, emphasizing that their verdict revealed both their individual character and their vision for the country. As in other wartime trials, prosecutors defined only one loyal course of action for the jury; jurors would not simply decide Stokes's fate but would also define the heritage that they would leave for their children.

Of course such rhetorical devices were not unique to Stokes's trial; both prosecuting and defense attorneys recruited wartime juries into apocalyptic battles for the nation's soul. The forms that these battles took, however, were part of the intricate web through which the participants in wartime trials spun the meanings that those trials acquired. In Stokes's case prosecutors constructed this battle as a contest over the meaning of true womanhood. Specifically, they asked jury members to defend patriotic motherhood.

Prosecutors emphasized that, unlike Stokes, most American women not only accepted but also defended their roles as patriotic mothers. Quite simply, Stokes was the wrong type of woman. "We want strong, loyal women," the prosecutor reminded the jury,

> like those we saw marching in the streets here one day after we had been arguing a motion in the case. Women who are loyal unto death for their country. The working women Madam of this city, for whom you create an idea when they live ideals, now under the American flag which flutters to every social breeze that bears to them the gladsome tidings that they are social equals to queens.... Those are the kind of women who have gone out to fight for the Red Cross, which she figuratively spat on.[34]

Prosecutors were referring to a parade held during Stokes's trial by Kansas City women in support of Stokes's prosecution. Like those women who passed petitions asking President Wilson to keep O'Hare in prison, those who marched in the Kansas City parade believed that Stokes threatened their identities as patriotic mothers.[35] They hoped that their parade would aid prosecution efforts to cast Stokes outside the parameters of Americanism.

Prosecutors argued that the parade confirmed the investment of most women in a uniquely American approach to class and ethnic differences. Stokes's politics, prosecutors emphasized, found little support even among the working-class women that socialists such as Stokes charged were most victimized by capitalism. "There are women who work in factories in this city who are [happy] and contented," prosecutors reminded the jury,

> who have raised families, who are taking part in the great economic machinery of this country without complaint; because they know that ... every remedy that she could give them from what she terms her ideals are now obtainable under the constitution of this country. But where are young women attempting to foment and disturb the country at a time like this? If you will find me one good woman in the country or in the city, whether they are rich or poor, who is not imbued with patriotism or the

right sort of patriotism in times like these, for every one of them I will show you a thousand good women who are activated by entirely different motives.[36]

Although prosecutors conceded that "good women" might have legitimate criticisms of the government, the "right kind of patriotism" demanded that they look to the American legal system for their remedies, not to foreign governments. In times of war, "good women" did not question the basic foundations of their country's political decision making regardless of their class or ethnic identities. Stokes's crime, the prosecutor insinuated, was partly attributed to her failure to Americanize; that is, to master the duties and responsibilities of patriotic motherhood.

Prosecutors specifically marked Stokes as a foreigner during their discussion of Stokes's position on the Red Cross.[37] "Before America went into this war she was for the Red Cross," Wilson reminded the jury, "and since then she has not done Red Cross work, [which illustrates] more vividly the venom that is in the heart of this foreign-born woman."[38] Pragmatically, prosecutors hoped to further discredit Stokes by showing that she had lied about her work for the Red Cross. As significantly, prosecutors constructed a specific meaning for Stokes's disloyalty, one that tied her denigration of patriotic motherhood to her status as a "foreign-born woman."

It is not surprising that Stokes's alleged denigration of the Red Cross played a role in her trial. As historian John F. Hutchinson argues, by the time that the United States entered World War I "Red Cross patriotism" was an important part of Wilson's war plans. In Hutchinson's words, "once devotion to the nation became conflated with devotion to the Red Cross, the patriotism of civilians would be measured by how much work they did for, and how much money they gave to[,] the National Red Cross Society."[39] By withdrawing support for the Red Cross, prosecutors insinuated, Stokes had deserted the war effort in much the same manner as had the Bolsheviks.[40]

As Hutchinson notes, gender shaped Red Cross patriotism, which promoted service to the nation based on middle-class ideals of womanhood—care, nurturance, and devotion. Often contrasted with the selfishness of the women's rights movement, the "real feminism" of Red Cross patriotism required that women, like men, fulfill their obligations to a military state.[41] Support of and participation in the Red Cross was a woman's most tangible expression of patriotic womanhood.

Prosecutors both exploited and refined this link between Red Cross service and patriotic womanhood. They noted how Stokes's own withdrawal of her labor from the Red Cross paralleled her descent into Bolshevism. According to prosecutors, the danger of this descent was

not confined to the loss of Stokes's individual labor; even more perniciously, Stokes subverted motherhood by reproducing subversive ideas
in her audience.

Prosecutors accused Stokes of recruiting and teaching other wom-
en the art of unnatural reproduction. Although prosecutors emphasized that "loyal, strong women," like those who marched in support of
Stokes's prosecution, would reject Stokes's maleficium, naive women,
such as those who had invited her to speak in Kansas City, might suc-
cumb to Stokes's sorcery. "Ah, she (Mrs. Stokes) did not tell them fairly
and squarely what she should have done," the prosecutor explained to
the jury in an attempt to paraphrase Stokes's supposed intent;

> that I intend to inject poison into this multitude so that it can be spread as
> a pestilence to do those very things which the indictment charges. Why
> did she keep it locked in her heart then, if the heart was not bad? If it was
> not vicious, and if she had not conceived and born anew a hatred for Am-
> erica? [If she did not seek] the renunciation of America, which she once
> bore here. She did not want to tell them. The poison [was] to be injected so
> skillfully that [she] might stand at arm's length as she is today. In my
> opinion [she is] the most vicious German propagandist in the USA now at
> large. [42]

As the prosecutor did in Goldman's case, prosecutors described Stokes
as the head of a larger conspiracy. They argued that Stokes's goal was to
reproduce herself within the crowd, thereby creating her own inner
circle of followers who could then go out and further spread her ideas.
Here prosecutors gendered nativism. They described how a disorderly
woman such as Stokes spread her "poison" through an act of unnatural reproduction. According to the prosecutor, Stokes polluted the populace as she "conceived" and "bore" a "hatred for America." Essential to
the unnaturalness of this act was that Stokes had usurped the male
reproductive role in order "to inject" her diseased offspring into the
women of the Kansas City Woman's Club. The product of this unnatural reproduction was a bastard child—Bolshevism. Only by reestablish-
ing the patriarchal authority of law could the jury protect American
women and their sons from the effects of Stokes's unnatural reproduction. [43]

Like the many judges presiding over wartime cases, Abra S. Van
Valkenburg influenced the jury's verdict. He instructed the jury that the
remarks that were attributed to Stokes had violated the law. Their
responsibility, he emphasized, was to determine if Stokes had made
those remarks. Because Stokes admitted writing the letter that was
reprinted in the Star, the jury's task was simple. They quickly convicted
her, and Van Valkenburg sentenced her to ten years in prison. [44]

Stokes's conviction and sentence received mixed reviews. The Literary
Digest reported that Van Valkenburg's sentence is

taken generally by the press as a proof that the new Espionage law has teeth in it, and is a timely warning "to the whole tribe of pacifists and obstructionists," yet there are many regrets that the first notable victim should not have been a more dangerous enemy of the commonwealth.[45]

Conservative newspapers, the *Literary Digest* noted, concurred with this reasoning, arguing that Stokes's actions were part of "a systematic program to create discontent with the war." For this reason, Stokes's sentence would remind others that "this is not the right season to spread disloyalty."[46]

Stokes's former pro-war socialist colleagues protested her sentence, suggesting the jury had misunderstood her position. Although pro-war socialists did not object to espionage prosecutions per se, they urged the state to focus on those who had actually obstructed the war effort. John Spargo, for example, noted that Stokes's utterances were "foolish and petulant" but contended that Stokes was not pro-German or a traitor but instead a "misguided idealist." Graham Stokes, although privately dismayed by her return to socialism and by her behavior, protested her sentence, arguing that Stokes supported the war.[47] For her part, Stokes reiterated that she did oppose the Wilson administration's motives for and manner of waging war but had never opposed the war itself.[48]

Pro-war socialist and feminist author Charlotte Perkins Gilman echoed the arguments of progressives and liberals who contended that the severity of the sentence made the government appear arbitrary. "This particular weight of sentence on one ill-advised woman who used her tongue unwisely seems almost Prussian in its ruthlessness," wrote Gilman to Attorney General Thomas Gregory:

> Our government needs to be strong and stern against all pro-German pacifism, Bolshevism, and untimely demands for privileges or even rights not allowable in time of war, but any punishment savoring of cruelty or injustice arouses widespread protest, and tends to promote the very spirit it endeavors to suppress.[49]

Gilman feared that the prosecution of domestic dissent had gone too far. Rigid enforcement of the Espionage and Sedition Acts, she argued, only strengthened anti-war sentiment and, perhaps even more perniciously, eroded democracy itself by sanctioning reactionary efforts to suppress legitimate disagreements.

In trying to distinguish between dangerous subversives and Stokes, pro-war socialists like Gilman and Spargo typecast her as an idealist whose utterances betrayed an immature political development, a position consistent with the civil liberties discourse that took shape during the war. In pragmatic terms, the purpose of such statements was to portray the government's prosecution of wartime dissent as hysterical or, at the very least, as misplaced. In doing so, Stokes's supporters often characterized her as naive and without sincere political conviction.

Ironically, it was Stokes's staunchest critics who took her political views seriously.

Anti-war socialists, not surprisingly, painted a different picture of Stokes's conviction. They argued that her conviction and harsh sentence testified to her lifelong commitment to working-class politics. Writing under the pen name "Pippa," Meta Stern portrayed Stokes as a genuine working-class hero, attributing her politics to both her class background and, in an ironic twist on patriotic motherhood, to her mother's tutelage.[50] Eugene Debs, a close friend of Stokes, also criticized Stokes's and O'Hare's convictions as an assault on critical thought and working-class movements. Like Stern, Debs also contended that Stokes's commitment to working people explained the vindictiveness of Van Valkenburg's sentence. The Justice Department charged that Debs's spirited defense of O'Hare and Stokes obstructed the war effort. He was later convicted of violating the Espionage Act for his remarks and sentenced to ten years in prison.[51]

Her conviction had a profound effect on Stokes's personal and political life. It caused Stokes to abandon pragmatic politics and her faith that American political institutions were fundamentally sound. Always searching for an identity apart from Graham and his circle of intellectuals, Stokes believed that her conviction heightened her status as a working-class leader. In a language that might have further convinced Gilman and Spargo of her naivete and idealism, Stokes described her newfound status. "Ten years is a long time, at my time of life. I shall come out as an old woman," she wrote to her friend, Anna Strunsky Walling:

> But if I find a young social-democracy I know that it will make me young again. The prosecuting attorney could not understand my calm, quiet manner, my glad smile, my personal unconcern, all through the trial. The whole force of the government hurled itself against me, but I was stronger than itself.... I did not shed one tear for myself, or have an extra heartbeat. I felt all the immovable power of the organized proletariat of the world in me. These courts and these governments of the master-class were hurling their power against me but I was a cliff—an immovable cliff. God *had* made me to be that cliff.[52]

Although prosecutors argued that Stokes's criticisms of the war revived her status as a "foreign-born woman," Stokes contended that her conviction represented a return to her working-class and immigrant roots, roots temporarily hidden by her marriage to Graham Stokes and the comfortable lifestyle that marriage had given her. Not surprisingly, Stokes completed her personal transformation by divorcing Graham Stokes. "Since the war," she later wrote about her relationship with Graham, "we have been only friendly enemies. Our profound political differences tended to develop situations domestic and personal that caused both of us intense suffering."[53] Apparently bitter over these differences, Graham refused to grant her a divorce based on mutual incompatibility. He instead accused her of infidelity.[54] After their divorce Stokes expressed relief over her separation from both Graham and his family.[55]

Once convicted, Stokes embarked on a speaking tour during which she framed her case not only as an attack on free speech but also as a calculated effort to reprimand her for her participation in socialist and labor politics. Stokes produced a letter allegedly written in November of 1917 by an unnamed member of Congress that predicted her trial and conviction. The letter was addressed to an unnamed senator and threatened "punishment" for Stokes's "lifelong work for the cause of socialism."[56] How or if Stokes ever obtained such a letter is unknown. It is certainly possible that patriotic societies and their sympathizers wanted to see Stokes tried under the wartime laws. Regardless of its authenticity, Stokes used this letter as part of a dramatic performance that defined her conviction as part of a general assault on the labor and socialist movements.

Throughout this tour Stokes reiterated that she supported the defeat of the German imperial government "as all socialists do," but argued that capitalist interests and profiteers had taken over the war effort.[57] She confirmed her support for the Bolshevik revolution, arguing that it posed a legitimate alternative to those capitalist interests that dictated American policy. Her conviction, Stokes contended, was an attempt to prevent American workers from understanding the ideas and promises of the Bolshevik revolution.[58]

After the Supreme Court reversed Stokes's conviction in 1920, the Justice Department had to decide whether to retry her. As in O'Hare's case, those directly involved in her trial argued most vigorously for a retrial. "Mr Wilson [the prosecuting attorney] thinks this case should be retried," wrote an assistant attorney general; "[T]here is nothing to differentiate it from the ordinary espionage case except that this woman has a powerful personality, extensive influence, and is one of the leading spirits in radical movements."[59] Such charges were ironic, given Stokes's critique of wealth and privilege. It is certainly possible that her wealth shielded her from retrial although there is no direct evidence to support such claims. A better explanation lies in the changing perceptions of Stokes specifically and wartime dissenters generally once the war ended.

Although federal officials never explained why they did not retry Stokes, many in Washington feared that they could not obtain a conviction once the war ended. Despite "personal feelings" to the contrary, an assistant district attorney decided "that in view of this fact [that her offense had happened during wartime] and in view of the character of the evidence, and in view of the defendant being a woman, the probability of conviction would not be great."[60] Furthermore, he argued that an acquittal would damage the current government efforts to control subversion.

Some federal officials questioned whether some women's reputations as dangerous subversives had been exaggerated. In a memo to the solicitor general that recommended clemency for Kate Richards O'Hare, John Lord O'Brian, director of the War Emergency Division of the Justice Department, ridiculed Stokes and O'Hare, suggesting that neither had ever posed a real danger to the government. "In regards to Mrs. Kate Richards O'Hare—I have always considered in her case, and in that of Mrs. Stokes," he wrote,

> that they were largely two ill-advised brilliant women, with highly emo-
> tional natures and a great lack of saving grace or common sense (wouldn't
> they be mad to hear this?), who were disposed to regard themselves as
> martyrs in the holy cause of liberty, and whose incarceration was justi-
> fied more on the idea of keeping them [from] doing harm than in any other
> way.[61]

By May of 1919, when O'Brian wrote this memo, federal officials were increasingly concerned about pursuing wartime cases, especially those that involved high-profile defendants such as Stokes. They were more likely to dismiss a defendant's threat to the public order than to highlight it. Yet the fact that federal officials dismissed their politics as emotional responses only underscores their continuing investment in depicting disorderly women as irrational political actors.

Although the government debated whether or not to retry Stokes, public support for her conviction remained strong in part because of Stokes's post-war speaking tour. Some who supported retrying Stokes wrote to the Justice Department to express their dismay that she had not been re-arrested. The most vitriolic of these letters were written by one F. Guyon. "Here is a miserable, wretched woman, a bitter enemy of the state," Guyon wrote in December of 1919. A month later, Guyon's frustration was still evident; he wrote that "it is a sham that this loud mouthed woman anarchist should be allowed to go around NY today mingling with parlor bolsheviki at their meetings and at the same time making public speeches denouncing this government." Guyon argued that an organized conspiracy was intimidating the Justice Department and blocking the deportation of Goldman as well as the imprisonment of Stokes. "What rotten political influence is it that protected this Stokes woman," Guyon asserted, "and also stops the deportation of Emma Goldman one of the worst wretches we have seen in this country[?]"[62] Although there is little evidence that Justice Department officials paid attention to Guyon's letters, Guyon's characterization of Stokes's gender identity provides some evidence, albeit limited, of the public's acceptance that Stokes and Goldman led a conspiracy of disorderly women. Guyon's argument reflected the confluence of anarchism, Bolshevism, and gender disorder that the state used to deflect class, ethnic, and gender conflicts in an attempt to reinforce the idea that consensus was the essence of loyal citizenship and Americanism.

In her initial enthusiasm for the goals outlined in Wilson's war message to Congress, Stokes claimed that for the first time in her "twenty-seven years [since migrating to] America [she had] stood upon any platform as an American." [63] At least for a brief period, Stokes argued that Wilson's war program had Americanized her. Ultimately the war was a personal odyssey for Stokes, but it did not lead her to permanently embrace a newfound status as an American. Instead, Stokes's trial and conviction led her to embrace an identity as an alien who was exiled by the narrowness of American nationalism. To play this role, Stokes once again reconstructed her identity to serve, in the words of one historian, "as the Communist image of revolutionary womanhood."[64]

Stokes did not link this odyssey to gender. She based her support of the war, her criticisms of particular Wilson administration policies, and her support of the Bolshevik Revolution on her responsibilities as an international citizen. To the degree that Americanism fostered this role, Stokes supported American nationalism. But when American nationalism threatened principles that she defined as fundamental to internationalism—specifically the Wilson administration's efforts to destroy Bolshevism—then she rejected it.

Yet gender did shape her wartime experiences. Prosecutors used wartime understandings of patriotic motherhood to explain the nature of Stokes's threat and to alienate her from American society. They recast Stokes as a "foreign-born woman" whose ideas and actions were fundamentally incompatible with American womanhood. In their courtroom characterizations, when Stokes spoke, she spoke as a foreign-born woman who was capable of transforming American-born sons into Bolsheviks.

Stokes's case ultimately employed a fine distinction—the difference between criticizing the policies of a president and condemning American democracy. The Sedition Act blurred such distinctions and had the practical effect of linking the fighting of the war with Wilson's increasing animosity toward and desire to overthrow the Bolshevik revolution.[65] By positing Bolshevism as a more democratic alternative to Wilsonian democracy, Stokes had tapped into fears that Bolshevism could compete with Anglo-American conceptions of the ideals of freedom, justice, and democratic processes. Such concerns would crystallize in the years following the war as anti-communism became an essential component of Americanism.[66] Stokes's trial demonstrates that gender disorder was a key trope used by state authorities to define why Americans needed to purge Bolshevism and Bolsheviks from the body politic.

We have explored how gender influenced and shaped the meanings produced in the trials of the three most public leftist women who were charged and convicted under the federal wartime emergency laws. How typical were the constructions of gender that emerged from their encounters with the wartime legal system? To better understand how the wartime constructions of subversion affected women's experiences and understanding of their roles as citizens, we need to broaden our analysis. To accomplish this task, we must now turn to the cases of women who were charged with subversion who were not national celebrities or influential political actors.

5

⚕

Disorderly Conduct

SUBVERSION AND THE POLITICAL WOMAN

On August 16, 1917, Seattle's leading socialist stump speaker, Kate Sadler, addressed an anti-war rally. Harvey O'Connor, Sadler's friend and colleague, described what had happened when the police attempted to arrest her for disorderly conduct:

> While Kate Sadler was speaking, the police thought they heard her refer to Wilson as a "traitor." After her speech, they nabbed her and led her away from the platform. The astonished crowd, seeing what was happening to Seattle's best-beloved radical orator, closed in and rescued her. The police sought safety in flight and Kate returned to the rostrum in triumph.[1]

O'Connor attributed the crowd's response to Sadler's status as a prominent working-class leader, a status Sadler had earned through a long history of labor organizing. Born in Scotland, Sadler emigrated to Seattle after working as a domestic on the East Coast. She married Sam Sadler, a longshoreman and socialist, and quickly established herself as one of the most colorful socialist leaders in the Northwest. In 1913 she helped organize Seattle's free speech fights, where she obtained legendary status after she wrested the Socialist Party's roll book from the hands of a would-be thief by stabbing him with a hatpin.[2] Sadler's propensity for "disorderly conduct"—her noncompliance with middle-class expectations of gender-appropriate behavior—only further legitimized her role and helped forge her identity as a working-class leader.[3]

Agents observing Sadler's speech for the Justice Department had a different interpretation of her behavior and its effects on the crowd. They emphasized the disorder bred by Sadler's actions and described the scene that accompanied Sadler's attempted arrest as an "ideal time and place for a Haymarket massacre of police."[4] In particular, the agents blamed Sadler for the crowd's unruliness. "She delivered practically the same kind of speech as the afternoon in the labor temple," they explained in their report:

except that she worked herself into a semi-frenzy of enthusiasm for the "revolution." . . . While Kate was screaming against the existing order, George Swanson (I.W.W. editor of the *Daily Call*) who was sort of a master of ceremony, as in the day meetings, was warned by the M.P. that Sadler would have to moderate her voice; that patients in the hospital nearby were alarmed. Kate squared her shoulders, like a man, grinned and said (almost breathless from her vocal exertions): "Ah I didn't know I was so powerful. Let 'em listen[;] it will do them good." She continued her speech in a loud voice ending with the denunciation of press.[5]

Sadler's encounter with the wartime legal system provides more insights into how federal authorities characterized the women they accused of political subversion. Sadler functioned in the agent's description, as she did in O'Connor's, as a disorderly woman. But as Sadler "grinned . . . almost breathless" and "squared her shoulders like a man," she resembled the witches and spinsters of fairy tales rather than the heroic labor leader that O'Connor described. The agents characterized Sadler's insistence on talking as an unnatural appropriation of a male subject position, and contrasted her behavior with the reasonable requests of state authorities to temper her remarks. In doing so, the agents transformed Sadler's assertion of her right to talk—her disagreement with a specific policy—into an indictment of her gender identity.

If the agents had not been obsessed with Sadler, we would know little about her wartime experiences. Although she was a colorful and popular local leader, Sadler was not a national figure nor did her various conflicts with state authorities garner attention from the national press. Yet in the minds of the agents, Sadler was part of a national conspiracy that attacked the political order by subverting gender roles. "Perhaps the most rabid of the woman speakers in Seattle, she is an anarchist in views and aspires to the position held by Emma Goldman," they wrote of Sadler. "[S]he is the alleged wife of Sam Sadler . . . but it is reported that she is not legally married to him."[6] Like Goldman, Sadler's disorder extended from the political to the family. Her rejection of marriage was indistinguishable from her rejection of the "existing order."

The agents' comparison of Sadler to Goldman was off the mark. Sadler was a socialist who had little patience for national organizations or conspiracies, preferring instead to concentrate her efforts on Seattle's Skid Road.[7] Although she may have known Goldman, there is no evidence that Sadler sought to extend her influence much beyond the Northwest. But by early 1917 the name Emma Goldman lent credibility to rumors of a radical conspiracy that threatened not only the war effort but also the foundations of American society itself.

The threat of such conspiracies legitimized the prosecutions of individuals whose wartime actions posed a limited threat to the war effort. This is not to say that those who accused and prosecuted those individuals were lying about the existence of such conspiracies, even if we acknowledge that such highly organized conspiracies simply did not exist. Those who enforced the wartime laws believed in the threats posed by labor radicalism, pacifism, feminism, anarchism, and, later, Bolshevism to the public order; prosecutions under the wartime laws provided the necessary theater to further clarify the extent and danger of political subversion.

This chapter further explores the meaning women's political subversion acquired as state authorities continued to charge women with violations under the wartime laws. It clarifies the interconnections drawn between gender, ethnicity, and subversion in the cases of women whose anti-war politics brought them to the attention of federal authorities. Unlike Kate Richards O'Hare, Rose Pastor Stokes, or Emma Goldman, the women described in this chapter were not national leaders. Their cases, however, provide important insights into how and when gender entered into discourses of political subversion, and how women who were accused of subversion understood their political identities, their actions, and the charges against them.

Also speaking at the labor temple on the day of Sadler's arrest was Louise Olivereau, who within six months of Wilson's war declaration would herself stand accused of violating the Espionage Act. Unlike Sadler, Olivereau lacked strong roots in the Seattle labor community. After attending college in Illinois, Olivereau lived a transient life and made her way west by supporting herself as a stenographer. By 1909 Olivereau had converted to socialism. She settled in Portland, Oregon, and became involved in the modern school movement.[8] While in Portland, Olivereau met Minnie Parkhurst, a socialist and birth control activist. They soon became close friends; when Parkhurst moved to Seattle, Olivereau soon followed. There, after reading the works of Alexander Berkman and Emma Goldman, Olivereau converted to anarchism.[9] By 1917 Olivereau was also holding regular study sessions in her home that attracted a small group of local radicals that may have included Anna Louise Strong, Minnie Parkhurst, and Adele Parker.[10]

Olivereau's legal troubles began soon after Elihu Root, former secretary of state under Theodore Roosevelt, visited Seattle to promote Wilson's war program.[11] During a public address, Root apparently urged the crowd not to question either the reasons for American involvement in the war or the way that the Wilson administration conducted the war. Olivereau, who read about Root's speech in the newspaper, objected to Root's prohibition against dissent. In protest, Olivereau wrote, printed, and financed two circulars that encouraged men to resist conscription. She then mailed her circulars to men whose names she had gleaned from the newspaper lists of recent draftees.[12]

At the same time that Olivereau was writing and mailing her circulars, the Justice Department was preparing a campaign against the IWW in

Seattle. The Minute Men, founded by veterans of the Spanish-American War, emerged as a powerful vigilante, pro-war organization. The organization was associated with the American Protective League and supported by anti-labor conservative business leaders and law enforcement agencies and tracked disloyal behavior among labor organizers, socialists, and members of the IWW. By the summer of 1917, their accusations had the ear of President Wilson, who expressed concern over the radical "influences proceeding from Seattle."[13]

The "influences proceeding from Seattle" were the result of a decade of acrimonious labor disputes; battles between progressives and conservative business interests; and the perceived strength of the IWW and socialists. As in other communities, the war polarized political divisions between radicals and progressives, leaving conservative organizations such as the Minute Men to define the parameters of loyal behavior. The result was, in the words of one historian, the "transform[ation of] longstanding economic conflicts into political concerns." Groups such as the Minute Men defined disputes between workers and their employers as part of a German and, later, a Bolshevik conspiracy to destabilize American democracy.[14]

By the fall of 1917, the stage was set for a series of Justice Department raids on the IWW, an easy target. Although it officially urged its members to do nothing illegal to protest the war, IWW rhetoric that encouraged the disruption of industrial production through sabotage led countersubversives to brand anyone associated with the IWW as disloyal.[15]

When the Justice Department raided IWW offices in September of 1917, Olivereau was working as the office secretary. Soon after the raid, Olivereau called Howard P. Wright, the local representative of the Justice Department, and requested the return of her "personal property," which included books published by the IWW and the circulars she had mailed to draftees. When she arrived at Wright's office, Assistant District Attorney Clay Adams and Seattle's postal inspector, C.W. Perkins, met Olivereau and questioned her about her two anti-conscription circulars. Olivereau explains what happened next:

> Mr. Allen said he didn't know if I was harmless, sentimental, or dangerous. A Mr. Perkins said I was a very dangerous woman and after a conference, I was arrested. They asked if I had more circulars and I said yes. We went to the house and I gave them over; also a copy of a letter to a lady explaining that I had the desire to dissuade any one who had seriously thought it his duty to enlist.[16]

Olivereau represented the agents as confused by her quiet demeanor and candid answers to their questions. However, in interviews following her arrest, Allen argued that federal agents had little doubt about Olivereau's danger, having "been on her trail for some weeks" following her mailing of her anti-war circulars.[17] In any case, it was her confession that finally forced the agent's hand; Olivereau's acknowledge-ment of her purpose in writing the circulars placed her actions in clear violation of the Espionage Act. At the same time, public perceptions of the IWW and anarchism shaped the meanings attributed to her trial and its outcome.[18] Olivereau's trial and conviction reassured a wary public that the state could control dangerous foreign elements and preserve the homogeneous understanding of Americanism demanded by war-time nationalism.[19]

The major focus of Olivereau's trial was on her self-identity as an anarchist rather than her IWW affiliations, although many did not dis-tinguish between the philosophy of the IWW and anarchism. Several newspapers reported that once Olivereau stated her support of anar-chism potential jurors rose as if to indicate that they could not objec-tively judge an anarchist.[20] One newspaper focused its coverage solely on Olivereau's connections to Goldman, suggesting that Olivereau was an agent of Goldman. Olivereau's support for Goldman's ideas, such reports implied, provided concrete evidence that her actions were part of a sinister conspiracy to disrupt the war effort. Other newspapers, not satisfied with portraying Olivereau as simply a pawn of Goldman, dubbed Olivereau as "one of the most widely known anarchist leaders in the United States."[21] In part because of these biases, Olivereau spent much of her defense explaining the meaning of anarchism and its rela-tionship to military service.[22]

Olivereau's defense mirrored that of Goldman. Like Goldman, Oli-vereau argued that she never told people to resist the draft, but instead "call[ed] attention to the fact that they are asked, or rather ordered, to resign their right to think for themselves."[23] At issue in her case, Olive-reau claimed, were basic civil liberties issues, specifically whether "citi-zens of these United States [have] the right to confer together on the subject of war, and upon closely related subjects."[24]

Although at least one historian characterizes Olivereau's protest as naive and a reflection of a hyperactive personality, both her circulars and her speech to the jury display a lucid understanding of conscientious objection and its challenge to nationalism and militarism.[25] Her circulars also laid the groundwork for a manly opposition to military service. They encouraged men to reject the definitions of manhood associated with that service. Specifically, Olivereau urged draft-aged men to subvert wartime rhetoric that linked manhood with fighting and to attack terms of gender ridicule such as "slacker" and "coward."

"Slackers" in the true sense we shall only be, if we have not the courage to go forward, steadily and firmly refusing to be drawn aside from the path marked out by our own deep-rooted principles and convictions. "Cow-ards" no one but a fool will call us, since we know that by refusing to be tools for the attainment of ends opposed to our deepest beliefs, we shall lay ourselves open to imprisonment and torture such as has been the lot of conscientious objectors in Europe.[26]

Olivereau's circulars attacked the characterization of conscientious objection as a "feminine" act. They redefined courage as the willingness to act in accordance with principles dictated by individual conscience rather than the directives of the state, actions that challenged pro-war definitions of manhood that tied rational and manly citizenship to military service. As historian Frances Early argues, this reconstruction of conscientious objection as a manly act of citizenship was an integral part of women's civil liberties politics.[27]

Believing that no lawyer would represent her views, Olivereau conducted her own defense. Like Goldman, she staged a "revolutionary trial" to expose the legal system's bias against radicals and to provide a forum for her own ideas. She took advantage of her closing statement to carefully outline her political views. In a statement that well known defense attorney Charles Erskine Scott Wood called "fine, clear, [and] logical" if not "calculated to bring a verdict of guilty," Olivereau criticized the wartime emergency laws and outlined how the experience of war exploited workers.[28]

Olivereau's statement to the jury attacked nationalism. Like Goldman, Olivereau argued that wartime repression and the fervid nationalism that it protected were inconsistent with long-cherished American ideals. Emphasizing that the United States was unique because of ethnic heterogeneity, Olivereau challenged contemporary visions of Americanization that attacked cultural pluralism as a divisive and weakening presence in the nation. "To America have come the peoples of all the earth; believing it to be the land of equal opportunity," Olivereau contended:

> where the freedom of which they had dreamed was an actuality. America has been aptly called the melting pot of the nations: a place where the various races were to be fused, and out of which was to come an understanding nation—a people unique in the history of the world, whose country should be not like the old countries.[29]

Olivereau argued that each nation as well as each culture depended on the other and rejected the ethnocentrism that she believed characterized pro-war nationalism. As a nation of immigrants, Olivereau argued, the United States could take the lead in forging a new ideal of citizenship based on international rather than national ideals. She argued that nationalism was an outmoded and dangerous idea. "I am an American citizen, and I love this country," she told the jury, "but I do not and can not love it to the exclusion of other countries from my affections."[30] Olivereau held herself up as an example of this internationalism, explaining that although she was the daughter of immigrants, she had received her intellectual training from the homegrown radicalism of Henry David Thoreau and Robert La Follette.

Olivereau concluded her address by reiterating the primary theme in her circular: the responsibility of each individual to her or his conscience. This responsibility, Olivereau told the jury, superseded law. "And regardless of what your decision with regard to me may be, the principles for which I stand, the ideas which I have in every limited way advocated," Olivereau stated:

> the work which I have tried to further, will be carried on by more and more people with a greater and greater intensity and effectiveness. Will those in power never learn that ideas can never be imprisoned? Will they never learn that on the contrary, a vital idea only grows faster when its suppression is attempted?[31]

Like Goldman, Olivereau stressed that her case was part of a larger struggle, and that her trial only further exposed the contradictions of nationalism and capitalism. It was repression, Olivereau contended, not the principles for which she stood, that posed the greatest threat to democracy.

The prosecutor portrayed Olivereau's ideas as wholly inconsistent with Americanism. He reminded the jury that their task was to "protect the very life of the nation," a task that required a guilty verdict. If they failed to convict Olivereau, the prosecutor warned that they would "sow the seeds of mutiny and disloyalty" and would encourage "the evil fruits ... which we know would be similar to those terrible acts now transpiring in Russia."[32] The issue, the prosecutor emphasized, was not whether Olivereau violated a specific law but whether her ideas were compatible with Americanism. The prosecutor cast the jury as the last line of defense; their decision would either strengthen Americanism by purging it of the "foreign" ideals espoused by Olivereau or emasculate Americanism by diluting it with the ethnic heterogeneity and anarchy that Olivereau claimed characterized Americanism.

In his final instructions, Judge Neterer defined the jury's task as quite simple. The only acceptable verdict, Neterer implied, was the one requested by the state. "The time for a discussion of the merits of the war is past," Neterer reminded the jury; "[T]here are two sides to the war. One side is in favor of the United States; the other side is in favor of the enemies of this country."[33] Olivereau was convicted in less than thirty minutes and sentenced to ten years in prison. She served twenty-eight months at a federal prison in Canon City, Colorado.[34]

Olivereau's courtroom defense received mixed reviews. Mainstream press reports defined her politics as irrational, suggesting that her support of anarchism alone merited a conviction. The *Seattle Post Intelligencer* offered the most detailed analysis of Olivereau's case. Like other press reports, the *Post Intelligencer* began its coverage with Olivereau's confession that she was an anarchist.

The *Post Intelligencer*'s coverage mixed brief discussions of Olivereau's ideas with depictions of her courtroom activities and physical appearance. "Miss Olivereau is a sturdy figure, foreign in appearance," wrote the *Post Intelligencer*:

> She said in her argument yesterday that her parents were born in France. She is tall and heavy, with a mass of brown hair, plainly arranged, and she wears thick spectacles. She wore yesterday a loose belted dark brown dress, with white sailor collar, fastened in front with a dull gold pin, and white cuffs. She thrusts her head forward when she walks, and when she talks she says "conscientious objector" through her teeth.[35]

The *Post Intelligencer* emphasized but did not directly explain what was "foreign" about her appearance. But their description provides important clues as to how the *Post Intelligencer* defined her "foreign appearance." The picture painted by the *Post Intelligencer* was that of an ordinary spinster whose "sturdy" but plain appearance belied an angry underside that was exposed each time Olivereau uttered the words "conscientious objector." This picture was strikingly similar to the *Nation*'s description of Goldman. Both portrayals depicted their subjects as masquerading behind an appearance that was carefully crafted to display intellect and order. But ultimately, a sneer betrayed each when their trials exposed them as disorderly women who were contemptuous of Americanism and outside the authority of men.

To further discredit her ideas, the *Post Intelligencer* characterized Olivereau's courtroom behavior as childish and emotional. It depicted Olivereau as an individual who courted celebrity and described her cross-examination of witnesses as "superficial," noting that Olivereau "displayed the ability to express herself dramatically."[36]

The *Post Intelligencer*'s coverage did paraphrase the constitutional arguments Olivereau used in her defense. It highlighted the danger those arguments posed by sprinkling its story with inflammatory direct quotations such as, "'the rights of the individual before the protection of the country,'" and, perhaps most damaging, "'I have no desire to maintain my citizenship in America if I must relinquish my citizenship in the world.'"[37] Both statements were consistent with Olivereau's views; however, the *Post Intelligencer*'s selective reporting of Olivereau's most inflammatory statements underscored that Olivereau's support of internationalism and ethnic heterogeneity threatened Americanism. The *Post Intelligencer*'s coverage suggested that Olivereau's goal was to bring foreign ideals and affiliations into the nation.

Of particular concern to the *Post Intelligencer* and other newspapers that covered Olivereau's trial were the groups of women who attended Olivereau's trial to offer her support. The *Post Intelligencer* used these relationships to both belittle Olivereau and define the extent of her danger. "When she wasn't listening to witnesses," the *Post Intelligencer* wrote, or occupied with cross-examining them she would swing about in her chair and smile at them, and during recesses she was here and there about the room, chatting and laughing with small groups of them.[38]

This description portrayed Olivereau as delighting in the attention she received from her trial. Her actions, the *Post Intelligencer* implied, further discredited her ideas. But the press attributed particular significance to Olivereau's supporters because they included embattled school board member Anna Louise Strong.[39] Strong's presence at Olivereau's trial, news reports stressed, belied any suggestions that Olivereau was a harmless idealist. Through Strong, such press reports implied, Olivereau extended her influence into the public schools and into the minds of Seattle's children.[40]

In sharp contrast, Seattle's socialist newspaper, the *Seattle Daily Call*, characterized Olivereau as an uncompromising radical who had cut her political teeth on the western free speech fights and who willingly went to jail to defend her beliefs. "She will plead guilty when arraigned on Sept. 13," the *Call* announced, "and has instructed her friends to attempt to make no defense. She declared that 'she expected to pay the price' and was happy in having done so."[41] The *Call* also quoted from Olivereau's circulars, emphasizing her rejection of government and the role that conscientious objection played in the development of a free citizenry.

Olivereau disagreed with the *Call*'s characterization of her positions. She denied pleading guilty, explaining that "confession implies a con-sciousness of guilt, and I am not aware of being 'guilty' of any crime whatever." Olivereau also noted that although she had supported vari-ous free speech fights she had not actually participated in them. As sig-nificantly, Olivereau objected to the *Call*'s choice of passages from her circulars. "I am somewhat surprised at the passages you selected from my circulars for quotation," Olivereau wrote to the *Call*. "I could wish you had quoted my analysis of a patriot's duty. Perhaps, had you quoted that passage, the *Call* would have been suppressed." Olivereau further clarified her reasons for asking socialists not to fund her defense. Al-though she requested that socialists provide "truthful publicity" for her case, she also asked that socialists spend their money on "industrial war-fare" rather than in her defense. Her case, Olivereau asserted, was sim-ply part of a larger struggle, a struggle that took precedence over the troubles of individuals.[42] The fact that Olivereau so painstakingly clari-fied the *Call*'s story underscored her investment in dictating the mean-ing of her protest.

Olivereau's closest allies also characterized her as a sincere revolu-tionist motivated by an unflagging commitment to individual conscience and workers' movements. Even the cantankerous Goldman praised Olivereau as "among the few truly brave women in this country who is thoroughly free from middle-class psychology and who consecrated her

life to the emancipation of labor."[43] Goldman respected Olivereau's refusal to censor her speech to obtain a shorter prison sentence.[44] Goldman corresponded regularly with Olivereau and publicized her case in
Mother Earth.

One of the most interesting documents to emerge from Olivereau's
case was a defense pamphlet written by her friend Minnie Parkhurst. In
close consultation with Olivereau, Parkhurst wrote her pamphlet after
bureaucratic errors prevented her from filing an appeal on Olivereau's
behalf.[45] Parkhurst's pamphlet placed Olivereau's protest within civil
liberties traditions established by birth control activists. "Consider also
that other women have been jailed," wrote Minnie Parkhurst,[46]

> and similarly treated for advocating that women should have the right of
> voluntary motherhood and for teaching the women of the very poor how
> to lessen their misery and all the misery of the children they already have,
> by limiting the size of their family.[47]

Women's birth control activities were a primary focus for pre-war civil
liberties activity. As war approached, civil liberties workers shifted their
focus to concentrate on the ways in which government restrictions on
speech affected workers' movements. This shift was important; it is
crucial to an understanding of the gender politics of the wartime civil
liberties movement. Parkhurst's pamphlet was one of the few wartime
defense pamphlets that drew a clear connection between the wartime
prosecution of dissenting women and the struggles of women for birth
control.[48]

But at least some of Olivereau's supporters used maternalism to
defend her actions. Jessie Lloyd argued that Olivereau "felt the war as a
personal pain, and could not bear that the youth of our country should
follow Europe into the meat grinder without protest."[49] Lloyd's husband,
Harvey O'Connor, described Olivereau as "a quiet, heavy-set, dark-
eyed motherly kind of woman in whose breast burned an utter loath[ing]
of war."[50] Although they respected Olivereau's sacrifice, Lloyd and
O'Connor sentimentalized her actions, deflecting attention from her
political critiques of the draft and of American nationalism.

Despite their support of Olivereau, some of her colleagues in the
labor movement expressed reservations about her actions. Writing several years after the fact, Strong expressed admiration for Olivereau's
motives, claiming that her opposition to war derived from the fact that
"she heard in her soul the shrieks of each murdered victim and hated
war with emotion." But Strong also called Olivereau's actions "singu-
larly futile" because the "mimeographing was so badly done that one
could hardly read it."[51]

Some of these reservations were motivated by the fact that opponents of labor and the IWW used Olivereau's case to attack Washington's
leftist labor movement. For example, although the *Industrial Worker*,
the IWW newspaper, expressed "ungrudging admiration for the brave

stand she has made of the principles she holds dear," as time went on members of the IWW distanced themselves from Olivereau, apparently angry that the government used its case against her to attack their organization.[52]

Throughout her trial and imprisonment Olivereau remained optimistic that her case somehow advanced free speech and anarchism, but she also complained of isolation and loneliness. She was frustrated by her lack of independence. She disliked relying on others, such as Parkhurst, to do political work on her behalf.[53] After Wilson commuted her sentence in June of 1919, Olivereau worked for amnesty and labor reform in Portland, Oregon. But the feeling of isolation remained. "I've not seen anybody 'in the movement,'" she wrote to a friend, "I don't know are they all alive or dead, nor whether I myself am dead."[54]

Apparently her loneliness only increased over time. Friends later reported that Olivereau married and moved to California. Frustrated with internal divisions and the success of anti-syndicalist laws, Olivereau apparently severed all ties with the Seattle radical movement. "As for my part in the radical movement—that seems to be a good deal of a dream, or a joke, or something," Olivereau later wrote; "[I]n the first place, I can't find any radical movement . . . I am very skeptical as to their accomplishing anything whatever by it."[55] During the 1920s Olivereau resumed a transient life after divorcing her husband. She later became friends with Alice Park, a California peace activist who followed the cases of women convicted under the Espionage Act. Olivereau died in 1963 after collapsing a few blocks from the Golden Gate Bridge.[56]

It is difficult to dispute that Olivereau intended to interfere with the draft or that her actions violated the Espionage Act. There is no evidence, however, that her actions were part of a larger conspiracy that was financed or supported by either German or Bolshevik agents. However, it was the existence of a conspiracy that the prosecutor evoked when he characterized Olivereau's actions as similar to "those terrible acts now transpiring in Russia."[57] The Bolshevik revolution and its specific meaning for American society and foreign policy affected Olivereau's case. As the results of the Bolshevik Revolution became known to Americans, that revolution would play a larger role in how protests against the war were understood.

A confluence between Bolshevism, anti-Americanism, and gender disorder influenced the trial of Mollie Steimer, the most famous of the Abrams defendants.[58] But that confluence also masked the importance of class, ethnic, and gender conflicts in wartime prosecutions. Soon after the passage of the Sedition Act, Justice Department officials arrested Steimer and four associates for protesting American involvement in the Russian Civil War. Their case is most famous for the Supreme Court decision it produced. Although that decision further restricted speech because the majority of Supreme Court Justices applied the bad tendency rule to the case, the dissent of Oliver Wendell Holmes gave civil liberties defenders a weapon in the fight against further limitations on speech. Holmes lay the foundation for a broader interpretation of the "clear and present danger clause" that he had established in *Shenck vs. U.S.* In a new twist that applied laissez-faire economic principles to constitutional law, Holmes's dissent called for a "free trade of ideas" in which truth was determined "in the competition of the market" rather than by government regulation.[59]

In his study *Fighting Faiths: The Abrams Case, the Supreme Court, and Free Speech*, Richard Polenberg makes a convincing case for studying the Abrams case as a "clash of cultures." At stake, Polenberg argues, was not only the constitutional boundaries of free speech but also "rival visions of what the nation had been and was becoming."[60] His work demonstrates the ways in which ethnicity and class shaped the state's role in defining legitimate political discourse and action. Here, I want to highlight how gender helped shape the class and ethnic conflicts Polenberg described.

Steimer and her co-defendants were charged with publishing and distributing pamphlets that were critical of the Wilson administration's intervention in the Russian Civil War. The pamphlets recommended a general strike to protest that intervention. Steimer had allegedly thrown these leaflets from roofs on New York City's Lower East Side. The leaflets, some printed in Yiddish, others in English, caught the attention of local authorities and the city's newspapers. After a brief search, the police discovered the pamphlets in the possession of a worker, Hyman Rosansky, who under police questioning admitted that he was scheduled to meet the pamphlet's distributors later that night. Justice Department officials followed Rosansky to his meeting and arrested Steimer, Jacob Abrams, Samuel Lipman, Jacob Schwartz, and Hyman Lachowsky. The Justice Department argued that the pamphlets could harm the war effort and charged them with violating the Sedition Act.[61]

Because the defendants had confessed to writing, printing, and distributing the pamphlets, the government's case seemed simple. The Sedition Act defined any criticism of the government as potentially harmful to the war effort. To obtain a conviction, the prosecution only had to establish that the pamphlets in question could hurt the credibility of the Wilson administration.

Harry Weinberger, the attorney for the defendants, argued that the pamphlets had not violated the Sedition Act because they contained information that was true. Weinberger asserted that Wilson's interference in the Russian Civil War was in fact illegal and that because the Bolshevik government was not pro-German, the pamphlets raised legitimate concerns about Wilson's policies but did not aid a recognized enemy of the United States. It was not the intent of the Sedition Act, Weinberger continued, to forbid legitimate and fair discussion of the

President's actions.[62] Like Stokes, the defendants made a distinction between challenging the war effort or even criticizing the American government and opposing the programs of the President.

The presiding judge, Henry DeLamar Clayton Jr. ruled that the Sedition Act covered any criticism that potentially hurt the waging of the war even if that criticism raised legitimate questions about policy or contained information that was essentially true.[63] Clayton's ruling derailed Weinberger's defense and virtually assured the conviction of the defendants. As Polenberg notes, however, Clayton's investment in the case extended beyond his legal rulings. Clayton designed his questioning of witnesses to highlight the class, ethnic, and gender identities of the defendants.[64] By doing so, Clayton pushed those defendants further outside the jury's expectations of Americanism.

When Abrams took the witness stand, Clayton interrogated him about, among other things, his choice of work. Clayton seemed unconvinced that Abrams's occupation as a bookbinder was legitimate work. Polenberg attributes Clayton's doubts to his assumptions that work constitutes physical labor, assumptions that were consistent with a rural nineteenth-century work ethic. Clayton's questioning, Polenberg contends, underscored the cultural and political differences between Abrams and the jury and defined his occupational choice as symptomatic of his failure to adopt an American work ethic. Because he lacked this work ethic, Clayton implied, Abrams remained a foreigner, a point that was reinforced by Clayton's outrage over Abrams's reference to "our forefathers" during his testimony. Clayton's questioning demonstrated a predisposition to see cultural difference as subversive.[65]

Clayton's questioning of Steimer likewise underscored the cultural and ethnic differences between Steimer and Clayton's view of Americanism. Yet, the questions he asked her were very different from the ones he asked Abrams. Clayton questioned Steimer about her views on marriage and the family. The always forthright Steimer responded to Clayton's inquiries by criticizing the institution of marriage as an economic agreement, arguing that under patriarchal capitalism love played little role in marriage. Laws governing marriage, Steimer asserted, compelled couples to stay together even when they no longer loved each other. When asked when a marriage should end, Steimer replied that "I believe that two people should combine when they love each other truly, and not because of any law."[66]

By calling herself an anarchist, Steimer had raised the specter of gender disorder. Given the popular stereotypes of anarchists, their knowledge that Steimer was an anarchist could have led the jury to assume that she advocated the destruction of the family and of marriage. Given this context, Clayton may have simply been giving Steimer an opportunity to speak for herself and clarify her views for the jury.

Even if we grant this possibility, the questions Clayton chose are revealing. Although Clayton acknowledged that Steimer's answers had no bearing on her guilt, he designed his questions to expose and vilify Steimer's gender identity. When juxtaposed with his questioning of Abrams, Clayton's specific inquiries show how linked gender, class, and ethnic identity were in countersubversive discourses.

As Polenberg notes, Clayton was especially offended by Abrams's comment that his protests were consistent with those of Christ. Interested in defining Abrams and his colleagues as foreigners, Clayton grew angry at any suggestion that either Christianity or American revolutionary principles supported anarchist ideals. Attacking the gender identities of both Abrams and Steimer was essential to Clayton's construction of them as individuals who were outside the acceptable parameters of Americanism.[67]

Men's engagement in productive work was a fundamental prerequisite of citizenship in the ideology of countersubversive thought. This point was made clear in the trials of both Goldman and O'Hare, when court officials criticized both women for undermining men's independence through their critique of the free labor contract. A man's success in the capitalist marketplace defined his worth—the free labor contract guaranteed to each man that his success or failure within the marketplace was due to his talent and initiative. A man's work not only marked his class position but also his understanding of himself as an individual, rational being capable of full citizenship. Like Judge Wade and the prosecutor in Goldman's case, Clayton implied that anarchism or socialism produced and appealed to men who were incapable of participating in this labor contract or of fulfilling their obligations as citizens. Clayton very subtly pointed out to the jury that in a very fundamental way Abrams failed as a man.[68]

As Polenberg notes, "the fact that [Steimer] was a woman had a great deal to do with the kind of anarchist she became, with her behavior in the courtroom, and with the response she elicited from the judge."[69] Wartime ideologies firmly linked womanhood to motherhood and the family. Although the first decades of the twentieth century offered women choices outside the middle-class family, the fact that some women exercised these choices alarmed professionals and politicians alike, many of whom held working-class women in general and political radicals in particular responsible for the breakdown in middle-class values. As a young, working-class woman with a clearly articulated feminist critique of the family, Steimer not only espoused ideas reprehensible to middle-class men, she also embodied them. But it was not only Steimer who approached the courtroom as a gender renegade. Abrams and the other male defendants approached the courtroom as nonmen. Clayton's line of questioning highlighted the gender disorder that anarchism and participation in a clearly defined immigrant working-class community promised.

Steimer was the most unbending of the Abrams defendants. Her refusal to acknowledge the legitimacy of her trial led her to not only reject courtroom protocol but also to initially refuse to accept a lighter sentence in exchange for an immediate deportation.[70] Federal agents and courtroom officials interpreted this steadfast commitment to her political beliefs as further evidence that she was unassimilable. Federal agents, for example, emphasized Steimer's confession and her refusal to name her colleagues as evidence of her guilt. One report quoted her as gleefully admitting to the distribution of the pamphlets: "Yes, I did it; I am responsible for that circular and stand by every line in it."[71] A second federal agent who described Steimer's activity after her conviction concluded that she "appears to be courting deportation," and he recommended that Steimer be placed under "heavy bond." As evidence of her continued "menace," the agent noted that "I personally, have seen her openly defy the court and refuse to leave her seat when a band outside was playing the national anthem."[72] Like O'Hare, her refusal to be humbled by her conviction was used as further proof that Steimer could never be assimilated into the American political community. As Clayton made clear to Steimer, it was his responsibility to show her in particular that "there is some authority, even over an anarchist woman."[73] The law reestablished patriarchal authority by criminalizing the gender identities of working-class and immigrant women.

This brief reading of the Abrams case suggests that gender played a fundamental role in defining the foreignness of the defendants. The gender identities of both Steimer and Abrams were implicated in their subversion. By tapping into preexisting stereotypes of anarchists as disorderly women and nonmen, government officials only heightened public fears that anarchists would inject foreign influences into the culture of the nation. In the years immediately following the Bolshevik revolution, such abstract concerns increasingly found fertile ground in the communist challenge to the progressive internationalism originally advanced by Wilson.

As historian Michael Hunt argues, the American response to the Bolshevik Revolution was consistent with a long historical tradition. In Hunt's words, "in their efforts to explain what seemed to be the almost invariable tendency of revolutions to self-destruct, Americans looked to the personal failings of foreign leaders and the unfortunate traits of foreign people."[74] Bolshevism came to represent the antithesis of Americanism and provided Americans with a clear marker of what they were not. As outlined in the trials of Olivereau, Stokes, and Steimer, Bolshevism represented a gender as well as a political disorder. In their efforts to explain why there were Bolsheviks in their midst, government officials and the majority of Americans who supported Espionage and Sedition Act prosecutions defined defendants as foreigners who should be expelled from the body politic before they could contaminate it. But the antipathy of Americans toward revolution and their willingness to blame the disorder that often accompanies those revolutions on "the unfortunate traits of foreign peoples" was not limited to the Bolsheviks, even if Bolshevism increasingly came to explain why Americans should support or oppose particular revolutionary movements.

In April 1918, John Preston, the attorney general of California and one of the most active enforcers of the wartime emergency laws, explained the significance of the convictions of twenty-nine Indian nationals for their role in the "Hindu Conspiracy." "This country is now realizing," Preston told a reporter for the *San Francisco Chronicle*, "that we must teach the non-assimilable, parasitic organizations in our midst that while this is a land of liberty, it is not a country of mere license."[75]

Pragmatically, the Justice Department's prosecution of Indians who were involved in anti-colonial activity supported a wartime ally whose effectiveness could be undercut if it had to quell a violent uprising in one of its colonial holdings. For this reason, the Justice Department arrested and charged Indian and Irish anti-colonial activists with violating the wartime laws. But as Preston's comments suggest, some understood the battle against anti-colonial activists in the context of traditional nativist frameworks. For Preston, the convictions signified a triumph for Americanism, a further guarantee that foreign ideas would not penetrate and cripple the nation.

The "Hindu conspiracy" provided a context for Americans to understand the complex relationships between British colonialism and the Allied war effort. Apparently, between 1914 and 1917 Indian nationals living in North America used German agents in Mexico to ship arms to anti-colonial forces in India. This use of German agents violated the neutrality laws that were passed to prevent Americans from aiding either side during the European war. At the same time, British intelligence in-creased its pressure on the Justice Department to investigate Indian nationals living in the United States. By the time the United States entered the war, British intelligence had convinced many in the Justice Department that the Indian anti-colonial movement was part of a German and, later, a Bolshevik conspiracy that threatened Anglo-American values and government.[76]

As aliens, Indian nationals who were arrested for their participation in the "Hindu conspiracy" faced deportation, and as supporters of Indian independence, they faced possible execution if they returned to India. Their case, as well as rumors of previous executions by the British government, galvanized support for Indian independence and against Indian deportations among left-liberal native-born Americans.[77]

Perhaps because of this growing support among native-born Americans, Preston and others in the American law enforcement community saw Indian nationalism as a fundamental threat not only to the war effort but also to Americanism itself. In response, the Justice Department stepped up its surveillance of American citizens who associated with Indian nationals. Their efforts eventually ensnared two women—Agnes Smedley and Marion Wotherspoon—both of whom were eventually indicted but were never tried under the Espionage Act.[78]

There is little biographical information available for Marion Foster Washburne Wotherspoon. Married to W.A. Wotherspoon, a lawyer also indicted for befriending Indian anti-colonialist activists, Wotherspoon was the former school editor for the Chicago *Evening Post*. She first encountered Indian nationalists at the World's Parliament of Religions in 1893. Wotherspoon studied theosophy and opened her home to members of the People's Council as well as to Indian anti-colonialists.[79]

Agnes Smedley is best known for her support of Communist China. Her interest in Asian anti-colonial movements, however, began with the movement for Indian independence. Born in Missouri to a tenant farmer, Smedley taught school in New Mexico before moving to New York City in 1916. While in New York, Smedley attended New York University at night and supported herself as a journalist by day.[80] Her involvement in the Indian independence movement began in March of 1917 after she attended a talk by Lajpat Rai, the founder of the Indian Home Rule League of America. Rai advocated Indian self-rule within the British commonwealth and supported the British war effort. Soon after attending Rai's talk, Smedley began studying Indian history and working as Rai's secretary. By the fall of 1917, Smedley had shifted alliances within the Indian independence movement. Apparently, members of the Ghadar Party convinced Smedley that Rai's position had little support outside of the educated elite in India.[81]

The Ghadar Party, a nationalist group that advocated the violent overthrow of British colonial rule, challenged Rai's leadership within the Indian independence movement. Led in the United States by Taraknath Das and Sarindranath Ghose, among others, the Ghadar Party's main source of support came from Sikh farmers in California and Bengali students. The party's main goal was to use political education to unite Indians who were divided by religious and regional differences. Unlike Rai's Home Rule League, the Ghadar Party solicited and received aid from Germany.[82]

Smedley agreed to help Das and Ghose form the Indian National Party, a government in exile that represented the aspirations of Indian nationalists. She used her connections with the American left to contact Russian revolutionists on behalf of Das and Ghose. Smedley also sent and received mail for the Indian National Party. Under the letterhead of the Indian National Party, Smedley wrote Washington officials to ask them to receive members of the party. Their suspicions already aroused by this activity, Justice Department officials searched Smedley's apartment after postal authorities intercepted a letter to her from Ghose. During their search, Justice Department officials found a letter to Leon

Trotsky from the Indian National Party in Smedley's handwriting. Smedley's letter apparently praised the Russian Revolution and solicited aid from the Bolsheviks.[83]

The discovery of this letter led Justice Department officials to indict Smedley under the Espionage Act. Specifically, they charged her with conspiring with Ghose and others Indian nationals to "falsely assume and pretend to be officials of a foreign government accredited as such by the government of the United States," and passing illegal communications. Because Smedley had sent mail under the letterhead of the Indian National Party, Justice Department officials argued that Smedley had misrepresented herself as a foreign agent. Smedley's indictment also charged her with obstructing the war effort by publishing and distributing Das's anti-colonial pamphlet, "Isolation of Japan in World Politics."[84]

Some press reports also claimed that Smedley had been charged with violating a local ordinance against distributing birth control information. This charge involved Margaret Sanger in Smedley's defense, who along with other liberals and socialists, helped raise Smedley's ten-thousand-dollar bail. Smedley's arrest further solidified her interest in birth control politics. After the war, Smedley worked on Sanger's *Birth Control Review* and helped distribute birth control information while she was in Southeast Asia and Germany.[85]

On June 11, 1918, Smedley, along with Ghose, Das, Marian and William Wotherspoon, Bluma Zalaznek (a Russian immigrant who Preston identified as an anarchist and leader in the Bolshevik conspiracy), and Bhagwan Singh, were indicted in San Francisco. Although Smedley avoided extradition on these charges, she spent several weeks in jail, some in solitary confinement, awaiting trial under the New York indictment. While in jail, Smedley met Mollie Steimer and Kitty Marian, a birth control activist, who nurtured her growing dissatisfaction with reform politics.[86] Smedley continued to integrate her birth control activity with her anti-colonial politics throughout her career. Like Stokes, Smedley's wartime arrest pulled her politics to the left and shaped her future public career.

From the beginning Justice Department officials recognized that their indictment against Smedley was faulty due to an illegal search of her apartment.[87] Perhaps for this reason, Justice Department officials offered to drop their charges against Smedley if she cooperated with their investigation against Das. When Smedley refused, her interrogators allegedly threatened to provide the press with embarrassing information about Smedley's sexual relationships with Indian nationals. Her refusal, Justice Department officials argued, only further demonstrated her guilt. If she had not previously been part of the Hindu conspiracy before her indictment, her unwillingness to help "her country" break up that conspiracy was itself a violation of the Espionage Act. Because it lacked concrete evidence, the Justice Department dropped its San Francisco indictment in October of 1919. It waited until 1923, however, to officially dismiss the New York indictment.[88]

Still this questioning terrified Smedley. She recognized that such accusations could hurt her credibility in the Indian independence movement—a movement to which she was originally drawn because of its sexual conservativeness. At the time of her interrogation, Smedley was emotionally devastated after having been raped by one of Ghose's associates. In her autobiographical novel *Daughter of Earth*, Smedley's character—Marie Rogers—reacts to this rape by attempting suicide and ultimately accepting blame for seducing her rapist. Once this assault is revealed, Rogers's marriage to the head of the National Party ends and she prepares to flee the country because her reputation in Indian politics is ruined. Written ten years after Smedley's arrest, *Daughter of Earth* is a scathing critique of middle-class morality and the dangers it ascribes to women's sexuality. It also shows how, even in leftist political movements, women's political reputations hinge on sexual reputations that are clearly defined through patriarchal expectations and privileges.

The charges against Smedley and the Wotherspoons reflected the Justice Department's concern over the support that Indian nationals received from America's liberals and radicals. Yet, if Justice Department officials were uncertain about their case against Smedley, they were even less sure of the legality of their indictment of the Wotherspoons. In the fall of 1918, Justice Department officials pressured Preston to either produce concrete evidence against the Wotherspoons or to drop the case.

Although Preston acknowledged that "it is possible that Mrs. Wotherspoon, on the account of her sex, might not be convicted," he was fully committed to prosecuting the Wotherspoons and consistently resisted Attorney General Thomas Watt Gregory's orders to dismiss the indictment.[89] Hoping to preserve the indictment against the Wotherspoons, Preston charged that the Wotherspoons had lied about their involvements with Ghose and sympathized with the Bolsheviks. Preston harbored particular animosity for Marian Wotherspoon. "Mrs. Wotherspoon in appearance, is quite a cultured woman but for years she evidently has been feasting on Hindu Indian philosophy and pacifism until she is absolutely un-American and disloyal to the extreme degree," wrote Preston to Gregory:

> She has no regard whatever for the truth and as citations in this report will show, deliberately falsified both to the government agents and on the witness stand. She is one of those fawning creatures. She has been associated with the People's Council, with the Socialists, with Bolshiviski, and is no more in favor of the prosecution of the present war from an American standpoint, than the Kaiser is. Her heart is not in the war, neither is she in favor of her son being in the service.[90]

In an effort to save his indictment, Preston depicted Wotherspoon as a liar and a political subversive for harboring Ghose and members of the People's Council.[91] As significantly, Preston also charged that Wotherspoon was an unpatriotic mother for failing to encourage her son to serve in the military. In a separate memo to Gregory, Preston continued to emphasize her relationship with her son, accusing her of manipulating her son into secretly marrying Bluma Zalazneh "for the purpose of suppressing evidence." For Preston, the marriage emphasized the duplicity of "the red element" and demonstrated conclusively how that element perverted family relationships.[92]

In "deference" to Preston, Attorney General Thomas Gregory did not immediately dismiss the indictments against the Wotherspoons despite claims by members of his own staff that the indictments were a "misuse of power."[93] Gregory's advisors dismissed Preston's arguments that Wotherspoon was a particularly dangerous subversive, but they confirmed Preston's assessment that Ghose and Das had seduced Wotherspoon, implicitly suggesting the possibility of a sexual liaison between Wotherspoon and Ghose. "Mrs. Wotherspoon appears to have been an impressionable woman, who was taken in by the mystery of the east," wrote one advisor to Gregory, "and to have fallen very easily for the attractions of these Hindu gentlemen." Although the Wotherspoons were "keeping bad company," the same advisor argued that "there are not set forth circumstances which would sustain a conviction under the present indictment."[94]

The charges against both Wotherspoon and Smedley stemmed primarily from the participation of each in anti-colonial politics, politics that the Justice Department charged potentially damaged the Allied war effort. To sustain their charges, the Justice Department linked the Indian independence movement with a German and Bolshevik conspiracy to destabilize the American government. As Preston's comments reveal, however, the "Hindu conspiracy" raised classic nativist concerns about racial contamination and foreign infiltration. The Justice Department depicted both Smedley and Wotherspoon as fallen women—women whose flirtations with the East had led them to both political and sexual subversion. Although it was never stated directly, the involvement of native-born, white women in the "Hindu conspiracy" heightened these concerns; the political and personal relationships between Indian nationalists and white women raised the specter of miscegenation. It was this contamination of white women's bodies that federal authorities felt compelled to stop in their prosecution of Smedley and Wotherspoon.

The cases examined here demonstrate the salience of gendered understandings of subversion in the cases of women who were charged under the wartime laws. They also illustrate the investment of defendants in asserting and protecting their understanding of citizenship.

Although the protests of Olivereau and even Steimer may appear to court convictions, those protests underscore the commitment of each woman to a particular political philosophy and their desire to control the meaning of their actions. The defendants described here did not use maternalism to defend their actions; instead they relied on constitutional arguments that defended their freedom to disagree with government policies and advance anarchist or socialist critiques of militarism and capitalism. Although they did not explicitly challenge patriotic motherhood, defendants did criticize the gender system of the middle-class family. The actions of the defendants demonstrate both the varied nature of women's citizenship during World War I and the deep commitment that defendants had to the defense of their rights as American and international citizens.

In addition to their commitment to left-wing politics, the other most consistent characteristic of women charged under the wartime laws was their status as professionals. The next chapter examines what role, if any, this status played in women's encounters with wartime anti-radicalism.

6

⚜

"Conduct Unbecoming"

SUBVERSION AND THE PROFESSIONAL WOMAN

At a Seattle school board meeting in March of 1918, school board members, the PTA, and other interested parties discussed a replacement for Anna Louise Strong, who had recently been recalled from the school board seat she had won only fifteen months before. Strong, the only woman elected to the school board in Seattle, attended the meeting to request that the board name a woman as her successor. Some of those responsible for Strong's recall agreed that a woman should take her place, but they also emphasized that her successor should be a woman unlike Strong. "The woman should be a mother, and preferably one with school-age children," one delegation explained, "whose patriotism is absolutely unquestioned."[1]

Strong arrived in Seattle with impeccable progressive credentials. A Ph.D. from the University of Chicago, Strong had experience as a journalist and had worked with the Children's Bureau. She moved to Seattle somewhat reluctantly, joining her father, Sydney Strong, a pacifist and clergyman. Despite her status as a relative newcomer, leading progressives asked Strong to run for the school board. An unknown at the time, Strong ran as a child advocate. Perhaps assuming that the establishment candidates would win easily, few people voted in the 1916 school board election. Strong won her seat with strong support from progressives and from labor.[2]

Strong was a formidable presence on the school board because she refused to endorse traditional policies. In fact, Strong voted no on measures more often than she voted yes. Along with socialist Richard Winsor, Strong opposed efforts by Seattle's preparedness movement to militarize the schools. Her refusal to endorse the school policies of the business community and her own growing interest in anti-militarist and labor politics reinforced her position as an outsider in school politics.[3]

In the months surrounding American entry into World War I, Strong's participation in anti-militarist and radical labor politics grew. She founded Seattle's chapter of the American Union Against Militarism and affiliated with Seattle's No-Conscription League. The public's perception of Strong changed soon after two socialist members of the No-Conscription League distributed an anti-conscription pamphlet. The Justice Department, arguing that the Socialist Party had funded the pamphlet, arrested several prominent socialists, including Hulet Wells and Sam Sadler. The attorney for the defendants, George Vandeveer, approached Strong and asked her to testify at their trial. He warned Strong that her testimony could erode her support among progressives in Seattle.[4] Strong nonetheless testified. She noted that prominent liberal members of Seattle's anti-war community, not the Socialist Party, had commissioned the pamphlets in question. That testimony, which helped Vandeveer secure a hung jury, caused Seattle's primary loyalty organization, the Minute Men, to petition for her recall.

Although this initial effort failed, the Minute Men's campaign raised suspicions about Strong's loyalty, suspicions that were no doubt fostered by Strong's growing involvement with the *Seattle Daily Call*, a socialist newspaper. The event that ensured Strong's recall, however, was her attendance at the trial of Louise Olivereau. Strong claimed that she befriended Olivereau out of personal sympathy rather than agreement with her politics.[5] News reports emphasized Strong's intimacy with Olivereau; one paper noted that "at noon recess they locked arms and left the courtroom."[6] They also reported that Strong interrupted the judge's sentencing to object to the high bail set after Olivereau's conviction and headlined the fact that "the woman school director, already under attack for recall, had befriended an anarchist."[7] This press coverage tapped into fears that disloyalty had spread to all facets of society, including the education of children.

Once associated with anarchism, Strong's recall was virtually assured. Still, the local labor movement rallied to her defense and the recall vote was surprisingly close. Strong argued that her recall sharpened differences between the labor movement and progressives, exposing the fallacies of liberal reform.[8] The conditions of wartime did undercut coalitions between progressives and the left. At the same time, wartime conditions heightened the uneasiness over Strong's position as an outsider—a new member to the community, an unmarried and childless woman—that had marked her tenure on the school board. This was precisely the type of woman who was easily attracted to anarchism; consequently, as Strong's opponents argued at the school board meeting that was called to find her replacement, it was necessary to ensure that her replacement was the right kind of woman—a loyal mother—who would remain immune to subversive influences.

Strong's recall was one chapter in the story of Seattle's contentious wartime political climate. As in other parts of the country, Seattle's preparedness and loyalty advocates argued that educators played an essential role in producing patriotic citizens. The same forces that led Strong's recall also monitored teachers and encouraged investigations of those whose loyalty came under suspicion. During the war, the Seattle school board fired at least six teachers, including Strong's brother-in-law, Charles Neiderhauser. Countless others were investigated because they kept German language and texts in the curriculum or because they were relatives of those suspected of disloyalty. At issue in these firings and investigations was how the political or perceived political activities and beliefs of educators might influence their students.[9]

Strong's story illustrates how anti-radical crusades intersected with women's increasing participation in and influence over the professions. During the first decades of the twentieth century, women expanded their political roles by claiming professional expertise. As historian Robyn Muncy has argued, middle-class white women constructed a professional space for themselves by defining particular policy areas as the dominion of women. White middle-class women fostered a professional identity that drew from the emerging social sciences. They then used that identity to influence public policy areas such as child welfare and education.[10] Although it is not clear that Strong advocated the vision of female expertise that Muncy describes, she shared the same experiences—training at the University of Chicago and in the settlement houses—as those who constructed a female dominion from their professional expertise. Her recall from the school board challenged the ways in which Strong applied that training to her newfound political role.

School board elections were one area in which women were recognized as having a vested political interest. Some states allowed women to vote in school elections even before they granted women the vote. Still, women made only slow inroads into school politics. Strong was the only woman to run successfully for the Seattle school board despite the efforts of other highly qualified female candidates who, in the words of one historian, could not escape "the board's self-image [as] men running a rapidly expanding business."[11] It was this image that Strong challenged.

Despite women's progress in defining a "female dominion," the meaning of women's professionalism and its relationship to politics remained contested. For example, as I noted in the first chapter of this study, nationalist progressives criticized women's political intervention in wartime as lacking the necessary prerequisites for political engagement, which men saw as primarily experience and rational decision making.[12] The argument that women's politics remained grounded in sentiment reinforced a peripheral role for women in formal politics and gendered anti-war politics as feminine and hence corrupting.[13]

As Muncy notes, some social reformers took advantage of the wartime political climate to relate the health of children to America's new world mission. Only by raising healthy children, they argued, could the United States guarantee for itself an effective fighting force. Such arguments grafted patriotic motherhood onto World War I state-building, giving the state a larger role in producing healthy citizens.[14] In addition, pro-war reformers such as Frances Kellor used the new social science techniques mastered at the University of Chicago to rationalize women's role in nationalist politics.[15] But even if we acknowledge that demands for loyalty did not necessarily destroy this dominion or reduce women's role in social welfare work, we must concede that such demands constricted how women could define the outcome of their professional expertise. Women's professionalism was compatible with Americanism if women used their professional roles to support patriotic motherhood. Although they often did not have experience as mothers, the creators of this female dominion legitimized themselves through their creation of a national citizenry—through scientific motherhood, for example—that was capable of defeating the nation's internal and external enemies.[16]

This chapter examines the ways in which the professional identities of defendants indicted for subversive activity during World War I affected the charges against them, and how both defendants and accusers defined the relationship between those identities and political subversion. Here my study departs from the federal cases to include female teachers and doctors (Ruth Lighthall and Marie Equi) who were accused of disloyal behavior—and charged under the federal laws. I will argue that although the professional status of Lighthall and Equi called attention to their behavior, it was not a primary cause of their arrest and conviction. But each woman was accused of perverting her professional knowledge; that perceived perversion of knowledge formed a context for understanding the nature and danger posed by the subversive activity of the female physicians. In contrast, teachers were charged with subversion because their politics were incompatible with their professional obligations. Their cases brought into sharp relief the incompatibility between anti-war sentiment and their roles and identities as professionals.

In June 1918, Dr. Ruth Lighthall stood trial in Chicago, charged with attempting "to cause insubordination, disloyalty, mutiny, or refusal of duty in the military."[17] Lighthall was arrested after she refused to purchase thrift stamps for the Red Cross that were being sold by neighborhood children. According to her indictment, the children reported to their parents that Lighthall had declined to buy the stamps because she "hoped Germany would win the war." When confronted by the children's parents, Lighthall allegedly reiterated her opposition to the war and directly attacked patriotic motherhood itself by criticizing one mother for letting her son fight in the war. Lighthall's indictment also accused her of calling President Wilson a traitor and a "coward morally and physically."[18]

Lighthall's profession influenced the accusations against her. As a medical doctor, Lighthall held an unconventional and potentially controversial role within her community. According to her indictment, Lighthall provoked these concerns by using her professional expertise to criticize the contributions of her neighbors to the Red Cross. "If you knew as much about the Red Cross as I do, who have studied medicine," Lighthall explained to her neighbors, "you probably would not subscribe to the Red Cross."[19] The press further called attention to Lighthall's profession by reporting accusations that Lighthall had told her neighbors that she would not aid American soldiers injured during battle despite her training as a doctor.[20] These reports contributed to perceptions that Lighthall's medical knowledge was integral to her subversion.

Women charged under the Espionage Act were often accused of criticizing the Red Cross. As volunteers for the Red Cross, women's service to the state received some formal recognition that was analogous to men's service in the military. A woman's Red Cross service marked her not only as a loyal citizen but also as a true woman. By challenging the Red Cross, Lighthall immediately implicated herself as a disorderly woman because patriotic women uniformly supported and participated in Red Cross work. Even more significantly, Lighthall's criticism attacked those women who acted patriotically. When it indicted her, the state defended those women who served in and supported the Red Cross.

Women's Red Cross work increased their participation in the medical profession. Women who volunteered for the Red Cross performed medical tasks that ranged from rolling bandages to nursing. The Red Cross appealed to women's accepted roles as caregivers to recruit nurses and volunteers. These roles placed women in potentially powerful positions over men; injured men literally depended on women for their lives. Some critics contend that the images that were produced to recruit women into Red Cross service reveal both an endorsement of and an ambivalence toward how nursing in particular empowered nurses ("mothers") vis-à-vis soldiers ("sons"). That ambivalence was partly the result of struggles to define the meaning of women's nursing in particular and their roles as professionals in general. The Red Cross firmly situated such roles and, by extension, the knowledge women needed to fulfill them within the confines of maternalist ideology. As such, the Red Cross, and wartime understandings of women's role within that organization, maintained a clear division between women's and men's medical roles, a division that both supported and was supported by gendered understandings of professionalism. The Red Cross defined women's contribution to the war effort as an extension of patriotic motherhood, which ensured that the potentially unconventional roles women might acquire during wartime would not challenge conventional ideals of womanhood.[21]

Lighthall's indictment subtly portrayed her as the antithesis of the Red Cross nurse or the patriotic mother. It paid particular attention to how she represented her home to her neighbors, accusing her of displaying an "American flag of the United States covered with a heavy black cape and veil" that was "visible" to the neighborhood children and their parents.[22] Lighthall intended this display to mourn the death and destruction of the war. Lighthall's indictment turned her critique of the war into a wish for American children to die. Along with press reports that accused her of desiring to withhold medical attention from injured soldiers, Lighthall's indictment associated Lighthall herself with death. These commentaries represented Lighthall as a macabre spinster whose professional knowledge only intensified her threat to the children of the community.

At her trial, Lighthall emphasized that her status as a free-born American rather than her medical knowledge qualified her to speak openly about the war. Partly for this reason, Lighthall did not challenge the accuracy of the charges against her; she instead used her trial to reaffirm her opposition to the war and the laws that governed dissent. She based this opposition on constitutional issues, arguing that the constitution protected her right to "talk" about the war. Lighthall wanted to keep her defense simple; the Espionage Act, she reminded her lawyers, was unconstitutional.

Lighthall's insistence on "talking" angered courtroom officials and provided fodder for reporters, who portrayed Lighthall as hysterical and comic. Press reports focused particular attention on Lighthall's confrontations with Kenesay M. Landis, the presiding judge.[23] Apparently, Landis assumed that Lighthall was foreign born and could not speak English, an assumption that brought an angry rebuttal from Lighthall. She responded to Landis's suggestions by stating that her family had a long history in the United States that dated to the Mayflower. Angered by Lighthall's rebuttal, Landis threatened her with contempt of court if she continued to "talk" out of turn. The press ridiculed Lighthall after this exchange with the headline: "Ruth Insists She is Going to Talk All She Wants."[24] Quoting Lighthall as defiantly telling Landis that she "would talk [her] head off," press reports constructed Lighthall's effort to participate in her own trial as hysterical and disorderly.[25]

Such reports deflected attention from the basis of this exchange—Landis's assumption that Lighthall must be foreign born given her political beliefs. This assumption stemmed from Landis's belief that anti-war politics were alien. Landis had no empirical reason to believe that Lighthall was foreign born. Instead, his assumption that Lighthall could not speak English and his offense at Lighthall's response that her ancestry dated to the earliest white settlement on the continent stemmed from his belief that radicalism was a foreign importation. Lighthall challenged this belief when she claimed status as a native-born woman.

When press reports characterized Lighthall's talking as hysterical they defined her citizenship claims as irrational. They confirmed that her dissent derived from some personal aberration and thus verified her status as an alien within American political culture.[26]

Lighthall's refusal to temper her criticisms of the war worried her defense team. They expressed dismay at Lighthall's insistence that she persist in her confessions of disloyalty throughout her trial. "I do not know what will be done at this time," wrote an exasperated member of her defense team:

> Miss Lighthall has taken the position all the time that she would keep on talking and repeating just what she said and for which she was indicted and this has aggravated the Department of *Justice* very much and I do not doubt but what they will attempt and perhaps succeed in convicting her.[27]

Lighthall's defense team believed that they could prove that her precise utterances did not violate the Espionage Act and they urged her to keep quiet about the war. In doing so, they pursued the defense strategy commonly used in espionage cases that argued that the defendant had not made disloyal statements.

Lighthall rejected this strategy. She argued that her utterances were inconsequential and urged her attorney to challenge the Espionage Act itself. "I am convinced," wrote Lighthall,

> that there is a misunderstanding on the position which I have taken[,] otherwise you would not have advised me to accept Judge Carpenter's bribe and [you would not have stated that] you thought I was taking the wrong attitude or position.[28]

In a detailed ten-page letter to her lawyers written from prison, Lighthall argued that the Espionage Act represented "class legislation" and was "treason to our constitution." She rejected any defense strategy that even implicitly recognized the validity of that law.[29]

Despite Lighthall's wishes, her attorney refused to challenge the Espionage Act itself. "This you will see," he wrote, "does not involve the question as to whether Congress has a right to pass a law prohibiting the obstruction of recruiting or creating insubordination in the army."[30] Instead, Lighthall's attorney argued that the Bill of Rights protected her particular utterances.

Lighthall's disagreements with her defense team illustrate her expectations for her case. She believed that her status as an American entitled her to speak her mind about the war and that the American constitution protected that right. For her, wartime prosecutions of dissent challenged this fundamental principle, and it was this principle that Lighthall wanted defended at her trial. Within this context, her insistence on talking about the war was not hysterical or irrational but rather an effort to define the meaning of her actions. She viewed her action as an act of civil disobedience, an act that challenged both the state's understanding of appropriate wartime conduct and the pragmatism of her defense team.

It was Lighthall's status as a free-born American rather than her professional conduct that the court seemed most invested in challenging. But it was Lighthall's profession that gained the attention of her neighbors and the press; both used that profession to underscore the peril of Lighthall's political subversion. As a doctor Lighthall had the opportunity to sustain life; instead, her accusers argued, she promoted and encouraged death. They understood her as the antithesis of womanhood—a witch who threatened the lives of the community. It was this perversion of womanhood that provided a context for her political and professional identities.

Like Lighthall, Dr. Marie Equi was defiant about her arrest and wartime conviction for calling soldiers "dirty, contemptible scum" during a speech in June of 1918. Yet, even before she allegedly slandered the reputations of American soldiers, Equi was a controversial figure. A medical doctor who performed abortions, Equi supported Margaret Sanger's birth control campaigns. In 1916, Equi organized Sanger's west coast trip. Equi was also a lesbian, a fact that apparently titillated Justice Department officials. They monitored Equi's personal life, including in their reports of her subversive activity the names of women with whom they assumed she was having affairs. Equi's activity on behalf of Sanger's campaign, her medical practice, and her lesbianism provide the context for the state's charges of disloyalty.[31]

Prosecutors took advantage of Equi's pre-war status as a disorderly woman to portray her as a dangerous subversive. As in other espionage cases, prosecutors placed Equi's specific remarks within a larger pattern of disloyal behavior. They produced several witnesses who testified that Equi had made disloyal remarks prior to her June speech. In particular, witnesses noted several incidents when Equi had made public protests against the war. The most famous of these incidents occurred when Equi interrupted a preparedness parade and displayed an anti-war banner. Apparently, police had to intervene to protect Equi from the crowd's wrath.[32]

Because Equi's trial took place the day after World War I ended, prosecutors had to convince jurors that Equi posed a continuing threat to national security. Prosecutors accomplished this task by recruiting the jury into an apocalyptic battle against Bolshevism, warning them that if they failed to convict Equi the red flag will "float over the world." Prosecutors linked Equi's activities with a worldwide Bolshevik conspiracy, drawing on fears that American radicals were foreign agents bent on instigating revolutions at home.[33] Although the United States had defeated the threat of German aggression, the prosecutor reminded the jury that Bolshevism jeopardized American democracy. For this reason, jurors still had a responsibility to act decisively and convict subversives.

But the importance of Equi's status as an abortionist and a lesbian cannot be overlooked. Both held important cultural meanings in the late nineteenth and early twentieth centuries. The abortionist and the lesbian symbolized the excesses of the liberated women. As symbols, the abortionist and the lesbian turned women's rejection of marriage and motherhood into a gender disorder that threatened American men with literal death.[34] In his closing statement, the prosecutor invoked such fears to seal Equi's conviction. He reminded the jury that Equi was an "unsexed woman," suggesting that this "fact" should influence their deliberations. Justice Department reports supported the prosecutor's assessment of Equi. They traced her sexual liaisons and called Equi "an anarchist, a degenerate and an abortionist."[35] In Equi, government officials suggested that they had the embodiment of the liberated woman as monster. Federal authorities called on jurors to reestablish control over such disorderly women.

In her defense, Equi claimed that she never called "working-class" soldiers scum, and like Olivereau and Goldman, used her testimony as an opportunity to air her views on a variety of social topics. Newspaper reporters apparently enjoyed the exchanges between Equi and the prosecuter and argued that "such a battle of wits was on as is seldom seen in a courtroom between a man and a woman." The *Oregon Journal* reported that

> Dr. Equi proved to be a skillful and able witness in her own behalf. Cool, collected and alert, quick to grasp the dramatic possibility and tactical advantage, she piloted her testimony through the even current of her examination in chief and the troubled channels of her cross examination with consummate ease and ability.[36]

According to such reports, Equi denied being an anarchist and noted that she had applied to do Red Cross service in France and had done relief work. These contributions counted for little; newspaper coverage emphasized that Equi had been arrested four previous times and had raised funds for well-known IWW leader Elizabeth Gurley Flynn's west coast speaking tour.

Once convicted, however, Equi seemed to lose this veil of rationality. "White as marble and with flashing eyes Dr. Equi addressed the court upon the delivery of the verdict," wrote the *Oregon Journal*. "[Equi protested] her innocence . . . and demanded an apology from Deputy U.S. District Attorney Barnett Goldstein for remarks made to the jury."[37] Equi was angry with Goldstein for questioning her womanhood during his closing remarks. "There is one thing more," Equi told the Judge:

> Barnett Goldstein who calls himself my friend, referred to me yesterday as an "unsexed woman." When a Russian Jew comes to this country to sit

in judgment upon an American woman and makes such remarks as that about her, I think that the court should require him to make a public apology."[38]

When the judge refused to order an apology, Equi threatened to "shoot" Goldstein, telling the press, "if anyone even questions my loyalty or my virtue there will be the biggest little shooting you ever saw and I don't care what happens to me or who gets hit."[39]

Equi's comments illustrate her investment in defending not only her rights as a native-born citizen but also those as a native-born woman. Equi defended these rights by using nativist arguments similar to those used by women's rights supporters, who contended that universal manhood suffrage unfairly put native-born white women under the rule of African-American and immigrant men. Equi demanded that the court protect her status as a true "American" woman by reprimanding the "Russian Jew," who, according to Equi, should not have the right to "sit in judgment upon an American woman."

But Equi's words were also ironic. Goldstein had defined Equi's threat to national security by claiming her sympathies with Bolshevism by virtue of her sympathy with the IWW. In her anger, Equi turned this argument against the prosecuter, claiming that it was he who embodied and spread foreign (Russian) ideas by questioning her loyalty and virtue. It is impossible to determine if Equi intended her words to convey this meaning; given the parameters of wartime nativism, her words more than likely only encouraged any anti-Semitism felt by her sympathizers.

Despite her threat to use frontier justice to settle her disputes with government officials, Equi did not shoot those who continued to question her virtue or her loyalty. She did, however, violently defend herself and her lover when they got into a scuffle with William Bryon, the Justice Department agent in charge of her case. During this scuffle, Bryon apparently hit Equi and pushed her lover, Harriet Speckart, to the ground. Although Bryon's homophobia led him to believe that Equi was not entitled to the status of a woman and therefore was subject to violence, Equi was no stranger to defending herself and others from physical violence. She welcomed these confrontations as was illustrated by an incident in 1913; while she was defending a woman who was being arrested for speaking at an IWW rally, Equi got into a fistfight with a police officer.[40] Such confrontations, which only contributed to Equi's status among the members of Portland's working class, further marked her as a disorderly woman within the law enforcement community. At the same time, Equi's defense of her "virtue" challenged the negative stereotypes of lesbianism that were becoming a more significant part of criticisms of women's public roles in the first two decades of the twentieth century.

In both Lighthall's and Equi's cases, the fact that they were doctors was not the primary cause of their arrest and conviction. Instead, their professions formed part of the web in which they and their accusers wove their political identity. Lighthall's and Equi's accusers defined their politics in relation to their professions, but they did not explicitly argue that their cases directly implicated their professional identities. They implied instead that Lighthall and Equi had perverted their roles as healers, choosing to use their knowledge to destroy American sons rather than to preserve lives.

It was in the cases of teachers charged with disloyal behavior that accusers and defendants directly confronted the relationship between professionalism and subversion. Secondary and higher education played an important role in Wilson's war plans because schools provided a space in which the state could control how ideas were presented to young people. Even before the war, public education had acquired a citizenship focus that encouraged efficient participation in social and industrial life. Federal and state authorities had instituted Western civilization and history requirements that emphasized citizenship, Americanism, and loyalty. With the outbreak of war in Europe, educators debated the role of schools in preparedness efforts and military training. Although some educators wanted schools to play a larger role in preparedness work, others resisted the military's intrusion into education.[41]

Once Congress declared war, much of this resistance faded. American participation in the war increased demands that education produce loyal and patriotic citizens. For example, Dr. John Tildsley, the associate superintendent of schools in New York City, argued that a teacher's adherence to radical ideas such as Marxism was sufficient grounds for her or his dismissal. "The public schools," he contended, "should be the expression of the country's ideals, the purpose of its institutions, and philosophy of its life and government."[42]

During the war, teaching the country's ideals entailed not only affirming Americanism but also purging anything German, such as German language and history courses. Not satisfied that all teachers would voluntarily conform to these standards, most states passed laws that compelled teachers to take loyalty oaths and to actively support the war. The most famous of these laws, New York State's Lusk Laws, established a regulatory apparatus that ensured a teacher's compliance in teaching patriotism and promoting the war. The Lusk Laws further required that teachers be of good moral character, which the laws defined as "loyal and obedient." Buttressed by the Lusk Laws, New York City led the nation in wartime teacher trials and dismissals.[43]

Discussions over the role of schools in the war effort took place at a time when there was considerable anxiety over the status of the teaching profession. This anxiety was part of a broader conflict in which Americans negotiated how the changes brought by industrialization, centralization, and urbanization affected definitions of masculinity and femininity.[44] By the time the United States entered World War I, teachers had acquired reputations as "immature women and feeble men."[45] The demographics of those who entered the teaching field had changed dramatically. Eighty percent of the public schoolteachers were women, most of whom were single and childless. Numerically, schoolteachers were the women most likely to be affected by formal efforts to enforce loyalty.[46]

Most of the female teachers who were accused of seditious behavior were charged under state laws. The most notable exception was Flora Foreman, whom federal authorities convicted of violating the Espionage Act for allegedly encouraging a female student to leave her boyfriend after he enlisted in the service.[47] Although Foreman's advice directly challenged both the war itself and the image of womanhood that was deemed essential to winning the war, as the cases of New York City teachers accused of disloyalty illustrate, the boundaries of acceptable dissent and sedition were much less apparent in the cases of many teachers who were fired for seditious behavior.

Gertrude Pignol was among those most vulnerable to charges of disloyalty. She had immigrated to the United States from Germany in 1905 and filed her citizenship papers six years later. She taught German at the Manual Training High School in Brooklyn and had received commendations for meritorious teaching. Once the United States entered the war, rumors began about past behavior that favored the Kaiser. In June of 1918, a Brooklyn school board fired Pignol for her refusal to unconditionally endorse the American war effort.[48]

The school board never accused Pignol of teaching disloyalty; it challenged only her personal views about the war. Specifically, the school board leveled four charges against Pignol: she did not believe in the war; she would not do everything in her power to further the policies of the United States; she argued that it was not necessary for the United States to be in the war; and she would not cooperate in every way with the American war effort.[49] School officials had contended that her personal reservations about the war were sufficient grounds for her dismissal. Believing that these charges did not distinguish between a teacher's personal beliefs and her or his professional conduct, lawyers for the Bureau of Legal First Aid agreed to defend Pignol. In fact, they argued that her firing was "perhaps the most important of [its] cases."[50]

The charges against Pignol stemmed from a personal dispute between Pignol and her colleagues. Because Pignol was German and had previously expressed her affection for German culture, her actions were inherently suspect. Under scrutiny from her colleagues and concerned that her reservations about the war might jeopardize her duties as a teacher, Pignol took a leave of absence. When she returned, an unnamed colleague sent a letter to the Justice Department accusing her of disloyalty. Although the Justice Department did not pursue the accusations, the principal of her school began his own investigation. Convinced that her "conscience scruples" about the war could influence her students, Pignol's principal, with the support of several teachers, asked the school board to fire her.[51]

Pignol acknowledged her ambivalence about the war. Because she had family in Germany, Pignol stated that she did not want to see Germany "crushed" during the war. Although she conceded that this concern could dampen her enthusiasm for selling war bonds to her students, Pignol promised to obey the law. "I shall urge the pupils," Pignol told the school board,

> I shall tell them that the school urges them to buy Liberty Bonds, and I shall produce all the arguments favoring Liberty loans which have been suggested and which are in the spirit of that request; though I am afraid they will impede me, for I, myself, might not feel enthusiastic.[52]

Although Pignol's accusers produced no evidence that she attempted to influence her students against the American war effort or in favor of Germany's position, this acknowledgment probably sealed Pignol's fate. Her case rested on the perception of how her admitted lack of enthusiasm for Germany's complete defeat in the war might affect her ability to rouse unconditional loyalty among her students. In firing Pignol the school board reconfirmed that the production of loyal citizens was her primary objective as an educator.

Civil liberties advocates did not use Pignol's case to directly challenge the right of the state to dictate the political position that educators took in the classroom. Instead, Pignol's attorney, Charles Recht, emphasized the separation between Pignol's conduct in the classroom and her rights as a citizen. "Throughout the entire hearing," Recht argued,

> it is to be remembered that the respondent was not questioned so much as to her views and beliefs as a teacher but principally as a citizen. It is contended that the rules of the Board of Education do not require a person to hold beliefs and convictions as a citizen, provided such a person does not teach or propagate those convictions in school and among her pupils.[53]

By firing Pignol, Recht argued, the school board had violated a distinction central to the preservation of civil liberties; that as a citizen a teacher had the right to hold unpopular political views even if the school board also had the right to determine which political views were appropriate for the classroom. Pignol's case, Recht wrote to her supporters, implied a new standard—that "a school teacher must be absolutely loyal and do with her mind what the soldiers do with his body, namely give it without reserve to the government."[54] Recht contended that Pignol's dismissal expanded the reach of countersubversive regulations that subjected teachers to a standard of conduct that was once reserved only for military service.[55] To Pignol's defenders this standard represented a dangerous militarization of society.

In keeping with this defense, Pignol's supporters portrayed her as an innocent victim of arbitrary state authority. The *New York Call* referred to Pignol as a "thin nervous woman with kind blue eyes, very much unlike the picture current in the mind of the people when the word 'pro-Germanism' is mentioned."[56] Similarly, the yearbook of the New York Bureau of Legal Advice argued that "Miss Pignol's greatest offenses are her honesty and inability to play petty politics of a public school of today."[57] Such descriptions of Pignol belied her own understanding of her firing as a challenge to the basic democratic principle—the right of citizens to debate public policy issues. "I do not believe that our government is democratic," Pignol explained to a *Call* reporter, "because it has not endeavored to ascertain the will of the people. The constitutional rights of freedom of speech and press have not been obeyed."[58] As I have argued earlier, defendants in espionage cases often clashed with their supporters about the meaning of their cases. With few exceptions, women who were charged with seditious behavior preferred that their defenses address the civil liberties issues raised by their cases, but their supporters argued that they were incapable of inciting disloyalty. For defendants, addressing such issues was key to their self-identity as professionals and as political actors.

Like Pignol, Mary McDowell was fired for her inability to unconditionally support the war. But unlike Pignol, McDowell's objections to the war stemmed from her political and religious beliefs. A Quaker and member of the Woman's Peace Party, McDowell refused to sign a loyalty pledge, raise money for the war, or teach patriotism in the classroom. Because she taught Latin rather than history or civics, McDowell contended that patriotic education was irrelevant to her subject matter. Although McDowell's actions were more confrontational than Pignol's, like Pignol she was never accused of recruiting her students into the anti-war movement.[59]

After her principal reported her refusal to participate in school programs favoring the war, the New York Board of Superintendents charged her with "conduct unbecoming a teacher." The seven specific charges included McDowell's personal opposition to the war and her refusal to teach patriotism and sell Red Cross thrift stamps. Her superintendent was particularly indignant over her unwillingness to support the Red Cross.[60] Her hearing took place in May of 1918, one month after Pignol's hearing.

McDowell argued that because her objections to the war stemmed from her religious beliefs, the Constitution protected her actions. Her attorney distinguished between McDowell's religious opposition to the war and seditious behavior. "No one has doubted her loyalty or her love of her country," her attorney emphasized, "no seditious thought, much less utterance, has been attributed to her at any time." Her attorney argued that the school board erred when it conflated opposition to the war with sedition. He also asked the school board to consider the consequences of their actions, reminding them that branding McDowell as a subversive "would spell ruin to her career as a teacher. It would mean to her what disbarment means to an attorney, or unfrocking means to a priest."[61]

McDowell, believing that her firing raised fundamental civil liberties issues, appealed her case to the New York State Court of Appeals. The court, however, agreed with school officials who had argued that McDowell's refusal to teach patriotism and sign a loyalty oath set a dangerous example for her students. In upholding her firing, the New York State Court of Appeals wrote that "while the petitioner may be entitled to the greatest respect for her adherence to her faith, she cannot be permitted because of it to act in a manner inconsistent with the peace and safety of the state."[62] With this decision, the court ruled that an essential part of a teacher's role was patriotic conduct, which implied full support of the war.

By the early 1920s, the excitement of the war had dissipated and school officials were able to review McDowell's case in a calmer setting. In 1923, the New York Board of Education reinstated McDowell, noting that the original punishment was "too severe" and a product of "great public hysteria."[63] McDowell continued to work in the liberal peace movement and retired from teaching in 1943.[64]

Although Pignol claimed only to have "conscience scruples" against the war and McDowell defended her actions through her religious views, Jessie Wallace Hughan had an undeniably political motivation for opposing the war. Hughan was a pacifist and a socialist. Her active participation in socialist and anti-war movements brought her into conflict with Brooklyn school officials, who were under increasing pressure to censor her activity.

Hughan had joined the Socialist Party in 1910 while writing her doctoral dissertation at Columbia. She wrote several books and articles on socialist theory.[65] Hughan's politics prevented her from securing a college teaching position, so she taught in the Brooklyn school district until her retirement. When war broke out in Europe, Hughan joined her friends Frances Witherspoon and Tracy Mygatt in forming a variety of peace organizations that linked pacifism, Christianity, and socialist politics.[66]

By the time the United States entered the war, Hughan had developed a sophisticated socialist-pacifist position. In a series of debates with prowar socialist Graham Stokes that was printed in the *Intercollegiant Review*, Hughan dismissed arguments that the Allies were fighting a defensive war against German aggression and should therefore have the support of socialists. "There is no element of attack and defense at all," Hughan wrote, "unless it is the defense of *an aggressive foreign policy*— two dogs quarreling over a bone which neither has a right to possess."[67] The concept of a defensive war, Hughan concluded, was a myth that legitimized aggressive wars to protect American economic and colonial aspirations.

Hughan also rejected the economic determinism that she believed limited the socialist position. She worried that American socialists were unprepared for the possibility that the United States might enter the war. As early as 1915, Hughan urged her socialist colleagues to prepare to fight the war against the war. "In America," Hughan declared sarcastically,

> as in Europe, we Socialists have long and rightfully prided ourselves upon our comprehension of the economic causes of war. War is a byproduct of capitalism, we say, and will pass away with it. Teach the workers their economic interests and they will not fight; destroy capitalism and only then will war be abolished. With these splendid generalizations we scoff at militarist and pacifist alike.[68]

Despite their rhetorical commitment to internationalism, Hughan reminded her colleagues that European workers and socialists had both succumbed to nationalism and supported their country's war effort. "Therefore," Hughan contended, "whatever may be the economic motives of the ruling class in initiating a war, it is hardly practical for us, in analyzing the reasons why men fight, to keep to economic motive."[69]

Hughan aimed her comments at those socialists who dismissed the women's peace movement and pacifists as bourgeois and naive. Hughan feared that because socialists focused exclusively on economics and alienated the pacifist movement, American socialists could not counter the nationalism of the working class. This concern over the narrowness of socialism led Hughan to peace groups and active political lobbying on behalf of nonintervention. She searched for an anti-war ideology and movement that could unite socialists and pacifists as well as organize the working class into an effective anti-war force.

In 1915 Hughan and Frances Witherspoon founded the Anti-Enlistment League. The league asked men and women to sign a pledge that promised absolute resistance to any war. "The anti-enlistment league does not stand for any puny non-resistance," their friend Tracy Mygatt told a reporter,

> it demands moral resistance. The mental and spiritual education of people is a long task; we appeal to the mature sanity in men and women; to the militancy of the spirit.[70]

The goals of the Anti-Enlistment League mirrored those of the Christian socialists with whom Hughan associated. Both appealed to men's and women's moral resolve, challenging pro-war constructions of masculinity and femininity that defined "mature" men and women as active participants in war. The league hoped to gain enough signatures to prove the war's unpopularity and dissuade the Wilson administration from entering the war.

When three of Hughan's students signed an Anti-Enlistment pledge in early 1917, Hughan's anti-war activities came under scrutiny. Under pressure from the public and legislature, the Board of Education considered firing her. "We expect," announced her superintendent Wilcox,

> to bring before the Board of Education a resolution that will put a stop to Miss Hughan's utterances and to those [of] other teachers who have adopted a similar attitude. . . . When a woman takes advantage of her position as a teacher to express such views as Miss Hughan did, she betrays the trust that has been given her.[71]

Wilcox's comments suggest that Hughan used her classroom to criticize the war. At issue, Wilcox implied, was Hughan's failure to separate her political and professional activities. But even her less-than-sympathetic principal, Dr. William Vlyner, admitted that "she has at no time urged her propaganda as a teacher but simply as a private citizen."[72]

Perhaps unintentionally, Wilcox's comments implicated Hughan's gender identity by implicitly suggesting that she had failed to distinguish when she was acting as a woman and when she was acting as a teacher. By March of 1917, when this conflict took place, some people clearly identified peace politics with women and a feminization of American culture.[73] Take, for example, the following letter written by an anonymous patriot to Hughan during her conflict with the school board:

> You are a *traitor* to your country, a contemptible woman & a cowardly pacifist. You disgust all true Americans & it is to be hoped that the Board of Education drives you out of the school, such miserable Female characters as you are, should be driven from the country.[74]

The author's reference to "miserable Female characters" implied that at least some members of the public associated anti-war politics with women and specifically with women who perverted womanhood. By engaging in anti-war work, the author suggested, Hughan had forfeited both her professional rights and her citizenship. State authorities and members of the public expected teachers to act as patriotic professionals who promoted war through citizenship training.

Like Pignol, Hughan argued that as long as she separated her role as a teacher from her actions as a citizen, she could express her position on the war:

> The whole question it seems to me centers not about war or peace, but about the right of an individual to express a personal opinion in public. For this right I am prepared to fight and fight hard. . . . I have never expressed my views in the school in which I teach and have never spoken as

a teacher. So I cannot have been "taking advantage of my position as a teacher."[75]

Unlike Wilcox or the anonymous patriot, Hughan did not mount a defense based on gender issues but instead invoked an argument based on individual rights. Like Pignol's attorney, Charles Recht, Hughan contended that as long as she did not express her views in classroom, her actions as a citizen were separate from her responsibilities as a teacher. But such distinctions were irrelevant to her detractors, who argued that Hughan's professional obligations were intertwined with her political identity, a political identity corrupted by her commitment to peace politics. Although they never fired Hughan for her anti-war activities—perhaps because their disagreement took place before the United States actually entered the war—the school board, the press, and the public harassed her for her activity in the anti-war and socialist movements.[76] In fact, Hughan's case was partly responsible for the legislative activity that enabled New York school boards to fire teachers, such as Pignol and McDowell, who did not fully endorse the war effort.

The consequences of drawing attention to one's politics during the war differed for Pignol and Hughan. Although she retained her freedom, not surprisingly Pignol disappeared from public record soon after she lost her teaching position. Unlike Hughan, she did not choose a political career and was an unwilling participant in the wartime battles over loyalty. For Hughan, however, the war only reconfirmed her commitment to pacifism and the need for socialists to develop a coherent anti-war program.

This link between an individual's political ideals and their character and professional conduct was the most important factor in the wartime dismissals of teachers. For women, these links were complicated by an equally strong belief that women's responsibility in producing, from young men, loyal mature citizens underlay their basic social and professional obligations. In this manner, wartime laws and policies further integrated women's professional identities and obligations with the needs of the state.

Conclusion

When Mollie Steimer refused to address court officials, choosing instead to direct her comments to the gallery, an exasperated Judge Henry DeLamar Clayton Jr. snapped, "you turn around and address the Court. This is one time, Mollie, when you are brought in touch that there is some authority, even over an anarchist woman."[1] Clayton's comments reminded Steimer of the purpose of the court proceedings—to reassert the rule of law over aliens such as herself who mocked the core ideals of Americanism. Although her crime was sedition—undermining the Wilson administration's ability to wage war by questioning its decision to send troops to Russia—in Clayton's mind, Steimer's identity as an "anarchist woman" posed the greatest threat to Americanism. As an anarchist woman, Steimer valued none of the core doctrines of Americanism—patriotism, nationalism, or the middle-class family. As an anarchist woman, Steimer threatened to turn both the gender and the political order on their heads.

Yet the proceedings against Steimer were not a monologue. Instead, they were part of an exchange in which accusers and defendants debated the acceptable rhetorical and legal boundaries of women's citizenship. Like Steimer, the women examined in this study did not define themselves as foreign agents but rather as citizens whose political actions protected cherished democratic ideals. They defended these ideals by drawing on their knowledge of the law, history, and woman's place. With the exception of Kate Richards O'Hare, defendants evoked a historical and legal tradition of individual rights and a vision of international citizenship rather than a maternalist ethic to legitimize their political actions. In the process, defendants resisted efforts to cast them as foreign, claiming instead a distinctly American citizenship that welcomed critical engagement and heterogeneity rather than the conformity demanded by wartime political culture. Furthermore, they resisted efforts by their defenders to diminish their politics by attributing them to immature or reckless actions. Their political beliefs led some defendants to reject the advice of their defense attorneys, choosing instead to conduct their own cases. Although these decisions encouraged convictions, they demonstrated the passionate investment that many defendants had in determining the meanings of their protests.

Like defendants, accusers were also invested in shaping the meanings of women's wartime trials. Most consistently, accusers charged that defendants interfered with the recruitment of soldiers, an argument dictated by interpretations of the Espionage Act. In some cases, defendants intended their actions to undermine conscription, but in many instances how and why the utterances of defendants harmed the recruitment of soldiers were unclear. Accusers suggested that defendants had violated the wartime laws because they either explicitly or implicitly challenged the dictates of patriotic motherhood. Patriotic motherhood required that women produce loyal sons capable of defending the nation against its internal and external enemies. Women could mark themselves as patriotic mothers by performing Red Cross work, selling or buying war bonds, or most impressively, by sacrificing their own sons to the war. Accusers often portrayed women who were charged under the wartime laws as violators of the gender conventions of patriotic motherhood either by their denigration of those women who acted patriotically or, most commonly, by their potential to turn loyal sons into subversives and draft dodgers.

Although O'Hare directly challenged patriotic motherhood and Rose Pastor Stokes and Ruth Lighthall may have directly criticized the Red Cross, the ways in which other defendants denigrated patriotic motherhood were less clear. Yet defining how defendants imperiled patriotic motherhood was an essential if not always an explicit aspect of women's trials. Accusers often used nativist language to describe the specific dangers posed by defendants. Nativism was a language of reproduction. It explained how an idea or character type could reproduce itself and imperil the American body politic. Because nativism described an unnatural reproductive process, it provided a pliable and convenient language by means of which accusers could define the potential dangers that accompanied women's unchecked forays into the public. Furthermore, nativism provided accusers with a framework for linking women's participation in the proliferation and reproduction of subversion with growing ethnic heterogeneity.

Accusers used nativist languages to describe how defendants participated in an act of unnatural reproduction to produce disloyal sons. As "women on top," defendants corrupted the reproductive process by rejecting male authority and usurping men's roles and responsibilities.[2] In the language of accusers, defendants both "planted the seeds" of disloyalty and "conceived and bore" the bastard children that resulted from this act. It was through these bastard children that defendants introduced foreign elements into American society. Although not a literal language, these nativist constructions conjured images of women made too powerful by their control over social reproduction. As historians have noted, this fear that women had too much authority over the character of men was a fundamental part of World War I–era militarist discourses.[3] It is not surprising that this anxiety also influenced anti-radical crusades.

Still, the major function of the Wartime Emergency Laws was to control political behavior; the primary reason that women were accused, tried, and/or convicted under the Wartime Emergency Law was because they disagreed with specific political decisions made by the Wilson administration. The gendered languages used by accusers deflected attention from the political challenges the defendants posed. That language instead described defendant's actions as the result of a character flaw caused in part by a mistake in their gender identity. In the words of historian Michael Rogin, such strategies "turned conflicts of interest into problems of personal and social adjustment."[4] Within this framework, competing political positions took on the form of diseases that threatened the core values of Americanism. For women, these core values included a narrow understanding of motherhood that required them to produce sons willing to sacrifice their bodies in war. Women who failed to internalize this political position were defined as nonwomen and their understanding of motherhood was, through the cases of the women described in this book, defined as subversive.

The wartime laws further encoded an Anglo and middle-class ideal of Americanism by formalizing very specific historical memories, rights and obligations, and relationships between (gendered) individuals and the state. Many defendants laid claim to protest traditions drawn from American conditions and history that were summarily and violently denied within the courtroom. Accusers distinguished between distinctly American forms of citizenship and the "foreign" ideals of Bolshevism, anarchism, and pacifism. In their search for wartime consensus, accusers criminalized heterogeneity and internationalism and defined the adherence of defendants to either ideal as symptomatic of "foreign" influences. As the cases of women who were charged under the wartime laws indicate, accusers clearly linked the importation and spread of these foreign influences to women's misuse of social reproduction and saw the wartime laws as one way to control the outcome of women's role in social reproduction.

Given the investment that accusers had in patriotic motherhood/womanhood, why were not more women charged under the wartime laws? In fact, the federal government specifically chose not to charge those members of the National Women's Party who picketed the White House under the wartime laws, preferring instead to use local ordinances against disorderly conduct. One reason that federal authorities gave was the difficulty they faced in convicting middle-class liberal women under the wartime laws. This decision indicates that we should not underestimate the class politics of the wartime laws.[5] Even in cases when local authorities wanted to charge women under the Espionage Act, federal officials refused to pursue the allegations, arguing in some cases that it was too difficult to convict women.

Despite the relatively small number of women actually charged under the federal Wartime Emergency Laws, wartime measures against subversion affected significant numbers of women. As birth control advocates, labor leaders, and suffragists, women were charged with sedition under state and local ordinances. As teachers, women lost their jobs, and as political activists, women faced harassment and violence at the hands of loyalty leagues.[6] And as wives and mothers of men who were charged with subversion, women had to play a larger role in the family to either protect husbands and sons charged with sedition or to financially support their families. Such families often faced isolation within communities that zealously adhered to wartime demands for loyalty.

The demonization of foreign influences, the threat of deportation, class prejudices, and the many laws that governed citizenship and family relations particularly affected working-class and immigrant women. Some immigrant women faced suspicion based solely on their nationality, which increased the likelihood that they would be targeted by wartime measures. For example, German women faced the humiliation of registering as "enemy aliens." Immigrant women responded in a number of ways to wartime conditions. Some, like those accused of rioting after the arrest of Emma Goldman, tried to protect husbands and sons from arrest and the draft. Others hoped to prove their commitment to their newly adopted country by joining the Red Cross and participating in Americanization ceremonies.

Working-class and immigrant women also faced the loss of sons and husbands to the wartime laws. If charged and convicted under the wartime laws, aliens faced possible deportation, yet few provisions were made for how such deportations could affect the wives and children of male offenders. In addition, the conviction of a husband or a father under the wartime laws endangered the economic survival of the family when the loss of income pushed already economically marginal families into poverty. One such woman, Mrs. G.A. Harris, explained in a letter to Winnie Branstetter of the Socialist Party the needs the loss of wages created and her own efforts to cope with her husband's imprisonment:

> I sure did appreciate the money for I have no way to get help but to work for it and I have to pay house rent and cloth[e] and feed me and my grandchild. She is 5 years old and I am 56 and suffer from a heap with rheumatism, and all help is sincerely appreciated, greatly though I would have worked on and tried to make out on what I could make before I would call on anybody for help. I was used to plenty when Mr. Harris was at home and he knew that I would work when I was not able to work, which I have

done the most of the time[.] [S]ince I have been left we spent all we had and that left me in bad shape, but I won't beg for help but if I can get a little help I sure will appreciate it but I would not suffer if I did not get any help at all[.] [B]ut I would have a hard time trying to live without Mr. Harris, he is a good loving husband and to think we have to be separated, after we lived together for forty years and all for nothing to[o]. [I]t looks like it is more than I can stand some times[.] [T]hen I think it will not do to give up and I will go to work in earnest again.[7]

For many working-class and immigrant women, protesting the draft and arrests of husbands and sons protected their families. Yet federal authorities and the pro-war press defined such protest as antithetical to motherhood and as further evidence of why the state needed to control those women who challenged the war.

It is difficult to trace the general effects of the wartime laws on those women accused of sedition during World War I. For some well-known members of the left, their trials began new political careers. O'Hare, disgusted with the conditions at Jefferson City, turned to prison reform. Rose Pastor Stokes, Anna Louise Strong, and Alice Smedley all turned to communism in the years following the war. But for others, time spent in prison as well as the more conservative political climate that followed World War I proved devastating. Both Emma Goldman and Mollie Steimer were deported, and although they remained symbols of the American left, neither regained their past political influence. The health of Flora Floreman and Dr. Marie Equi never fully recovered from their stays in prison; Louise Olivereau's disenchantment with the postwar left caused her to sever her radical ties.

But it is not my intention to portray accused women solely as victims. Most were competent political actors who made conscious choices about how they framed their objections to war, their defense, and the historical memory of their cases. They expected that their cases would further the causes of internationalism, free speech, and workers' movements. In the process, their behavior and words challenged a wartime culture that in its worst moments stripped Americans of their right to disagree with those who governed them, demonized immigrants and people of color, and reduced women to their basest biological functions.

NOTES

Introduction

1. William English Walling to Anna Strunsky, 1917, 2–3. Papers of William English Walling, box 1, folder 3, State Historical Society of Wisconsin, Madison, Wisconsin. For studies of Walling's position on the war, see Michael Bassett, "The Socialist Party of America: Years of Decline" (Ph.D. diss., Duke University, 1963); Kenneth E. Hendrickson, "The Pro-war Socialists: The Social Democratic League and the Ill-Fated Drive for Industrial Democracy in America, 1917–1920," *Labor History* 11 (Summer 1970): 304–22; Robert D. Reynolds Jr., "The Millionaire Socialist: J.G. Phelps Stokes and His Circle of Friends" (Ph.D. diss., University of South Carolina, 1974); Robert D. Reynolds Jr., "Pro-War Socialists: Intolerant or Bloodthirsty," *Labor History* 17 (Summer 1976): 413–15; Jack Meyer Stuart, "William English Walling: A Study in Politics and Ideas" (Ph.D. diss., Columbia University, 1968); and James Weinstein, *The Decline of Socialism in America, 1912–1925* (New York: Monthly Review Press, 1967).

2. Anna Strunsky to William English Walling, 21 March 1917, 1–2. Anna Strunsky Walling Papers, Microfilm Edition, reel 1, Yale University, New Haven, CT.

3. Hendrickson, "The Pro-war Socialists," 304–22; Reynolds, "The Millionaire Socialist"; and Stuart, "William English Walling."

4. Leon Fink, *Progressive Intellectuals and the Dilemmas of Democratic Commitment* (Cambridge: Harvard University Press, 1998); Reynolds, "The Millionaire Socialist"; Stuart, "William English Walling"; and Arthur Zipser and Pearl Zipser, *Fire and Grace: The Life of Rose Pastor Stokes* (Athens: University of Georgia Press, 1989).

5. Hendrickson, "The Pro-war Socialists," 304–22; and Reynolds, "Pro-war Socialists: Intolerant or Bloodthirsty," 413–15.

6. Strunsky to Walling, 21 March 1917, 1–2.

7. Anna Strunsky, "Revolutionist and War," *Mother Earth* X (June 1915): 140.

8. Fink, *Progressive Intellectuals and the Dilemmas of Democratic Commitment,* 169–74.

9. The literature on American participation in World War I is extensive. See for example, Ellis W. Hawley, *The Great War and the Search For a Modern Order* (New York: St. Martin's Press, 1979); David Kennedy, *Over Here: The First World War and American Society* (New York: Oxford University Press, 1980); George K. Knoles, "American Intellectuals and World War I," *Pacific Northwest Quarterly* 68 (October 1968): 203–15; William T. Leuchtenburg, "The Progressive Movement and World War I," *Mississippi Historical Review* 39 (December 1952): 483–504; Ronald Schaffer, *America in the Great War: The Rise of the War Welfare State* (New York: Oxford, 1991); Stanley Shapiro, "The Great War and Reform: Liberals and Labor," *Labor History* 12 (Summer 1971): 223–44; and John A. Thompson, *Reformers and War: American Progressive Publicists and the First World War* (Cambridge: Harvard University Press, 1987).

10. Woodrow Wilson, "Address to Congress," 2 April 1917. Reprinted in *New York Times,* 3 April 1917, 1.

11. The most detailed discussions of wartime repression are Donald O. Johnson, *The Challenge to American Freedoms: World War I and the Rise of the American Civil Liberties Union* (Lexington: University of Kentucky Press, 1963); Thomas Lawrence, "Eclipse of Liberty: Civil Liberties in the United States During the First World War," *Wayne State Review* 21 (Spring 1974): 33–112; Paul Murphy, *World*

War I and the Origins of Civil Liberties (New York: W.W. Norton Co., 1979), 71–132; H. C. Peterson and Gilbert C. Fite, *Opponents of War, 1917–1918* (Seattle: University of Washington Press, 1957), 15–17; Richard Polenberg, *Fighting Faiths: The Abrams Case, The Supreme Court, and Free Speech* (New York: Penguin, 1987); and William Preston Jr., *Aliens and Dissenters: Federal Suppression of Radicals, 1903–1933* (Cambridge: Harvard University Press, 1963). For a recent study of how wartime repression and the Red Scare that followed affected African-Americans, see Theodore Kornweibel Jr., *"Seeing Red": Federal Campaigns against Black Militancy, 1919–1925* (Bloomington: Indiana University Press, 1998).

12. Quoted in Peterson and Fite, *Opponents of War*, 17.

13. Murphy, *World War I and the Origins of Civil Liberties*.

14. Quoted in Murphy, *World War I and the Origins of Civil Liberties*, 83.

15. Murphy, *World War I and the Origins of Civil Liberties*, 81–86.

16. David Rabban, "The Emergence of Modern First Amendment Doctrine," *The University of Chicago Law Review* 50 (Fall 1983): 1205–1355; David Rabban, "The First Amendment in Its Forgotten Years," *The Yale Law Journal* 90 (January 1981): 522–95. For a more complete account of pre-war free speech cases, see David M. Rabban, *Free Speech in Its Forgotten Years* (Cambridge: Cambridge University Press, 1997).

17. Rabban, "The First Amendment in Its Forgotten Years," 544.

18. For example, state authorities arrested strike leaders during the Paterson, New Jersey, and Lawrence, Massachusetts, strikes and charged them with murder, even though the strikers had defended themselves after police had shot at them. See Melvyn Dubofsky, *We Shall Be All: A History of the Industrial Workers of the World* (Chicago: Quadrangle Books, 1969).

19. Rabban, "The Emergence of Modern First Amendment Doctrine," 1205–1355.

20. James M. Mock, *Censorship 1917* (New York: Da Capo Press, 1972); and James R. Mock and Cedric Larson, *Words That Won the War* (Princeton: University of Princeton Press, 1939). See also Peterson and Fite, *Opponents of War*.

21. John Higham, *Strangers in the Land: Patterns of American Nativism, 1860–1925* (New York: Atheneum, [1953] 1969), 4.

22. Ibid., 194–263.

23. Kennedy, *Over Here*; and Michael Rogin, *Ronald Reagan: The Movie and Other Episodes of Political Demonology* (Berkeley: University of California Press, 1988).

24. See studies on the Americanization movement: Robert A. Carlson, *The Americanization Syndrome: A Quest for Conformity* (London: Croom Helm, 1987); George Edward Hartman, *The Movement to Americanize the Immigrant* (New York: AMS Press, [1948] 1967); and Gerd Korman, *Industrialization, Immigrants, and Americanizers: The View from Milwaukee, 1866–1921* (Madison: The State Historical Society of Wisconsin, 1967).

25. Donner, *The Age of Surveillance*; Lawrence, "Eclipse of Liberty," 33–112; Murphy, *World War I and the Origins of Civil Liberties*; and Preston, *Aliens and Dissenters*.

26. Polenberg, *Fighting Faiths*.

27. See, for example, Peterson and Fite, *Opponents of War*. Other studies ignore O'Hare's case.

28. There were approximately two thousand federal espionage cases. The number of women defendants was so small because many of these cases involved members of the IWW who were arrested en masse, most of whom were men. Women made up a significant proportion of the cases that involved the leadership of socialist or anarchist movements and of those cases that resulted in significant free speech decisions.

29. Mari Jo Buhle, *Women and American Socialism, 1880–1920* (Urbana: Univer-

sity of Illinois Press, 1981); and Sally Miller, ed., *Flawed Liberation: Socialism and Feminism* (Westport: Greenwood Press, 1981). See especially Miller's essay, "Women in the Party Bureaucracy: Subservient Functionaries," 13–36. Socialist women were the women who were most vulnerable to arrest under the wartime emergency laws. A few days after Congress declared war on Germany, the Socialist Party wrote the St. Louis Resolution, which firmly committed socialists to resisting the war. Feeling that the St. Louis Resolution was imprudent, most socialists ignored its call for direct action. Nonetheless, the Justice Department and local authorities used that document to indiscriminately prosecute Socialist Party members. Because it was not clear what utterances or actions caused arrest, socialist women faced an uncertain outcome each time they acted politically during the war. But the opposition of socialist women to the war in itself does not explain either the character of wartime anti-radicalism or why authorities arrested some women and left others untouched. For discussions of the St. Louis Resolution, see Bassett, "The Socialist Party of America"; and Weinstein, *The Decline of American Socialism in America*.

30. For a survey of the major espionage cases involving women as primary defendants, see Elizabeth Gurley Flynn, *The Rebel Girl: An Autobiography (1906–1929)* (New York: International Publishing, 1955), 180–83; and Kathleen Kennedy, "'We Mourn for Liberty in America': Socialist Women, Anti-militarism, and State Repression, 1914–1922" (Ph.D. diss., University of California, Irvine, 1992), 186–247.

31. Neil K. Basen, "Kate Richards O'Hare: The First Lady of American Socialism, 1901–1917," *Labor History* 21 (Spring 1980): 165–99; Edward J. Bommel, "Kate Richards O'Hare: A Midwestern Pacifist's Fight for Free Speech," *North Dakota Quarterly* 44 (Winter 1976): 5–19; Sally M. Miller, *From Prairie to Prison: The Life of Social Activist Kate Richards O'Hare* (Columbia: University of Missouri Press, 1993), 158–91; and Sally M. Miller, "Kate Richards O'Hare: Progression Toward Feminism," *Kansas History* 7 (Winter 1983): 263–79.

32. Nancy Krieger, "Queen of Bolsheviks: The Hidden History of Dr. Marie Equi," *Radical America* 17 (1983): 55–73.

33. Polenberg, *Fighting Faiths*, 126–32.

34. For historical studies of this metaphor, see Natalie Zemon Davis, *Society and Culture in Early Modern France* (Stanford: Stanford University Press, 1975); Jacqueline Dowd Hall, "Disorderly Women: Gender and Labor Militancy in the Appalachian South," *Journal of American History* 73 (September 1986): 335–83; and Carroll Smith-Rosenberg, *Disorderly Conduct: Visions of Gender in Victorian America* (New York: Alfred A. Knopf, 1985), 245–96.

35. For another discussion of the importance of the draft in defining women's sedition, see Susan Zeiger, "She Didn't Raise Her Boy to Be a Slacker: Motherhood, Conscription and the Culture of the First World War," *Feminist Studies* 22 (Spring 1996): 7–39.

36. Kennedy, *Over Here*, 148.

37. Ibid. These quotas caused minor problems in areas with heavy concentrations of exempted aliens.

38. For a definition of patriotic motherhood, see Barbara Steinson, *American Women's Activism During World War I* (New York: Garland Publishing Company, 1981).

39. Zeiger, "She Didn't Raise Her Boy to Be a Slacker," 7–39.

40. Billie Melman, "Introduction," in *borderlines: Genders and Identities in War and Peace 1870–1930,* ed. Billie Melman (New York: Routledge, 1998), 1–25.

41. The literature here is extensive. See in particular Sandra M. Gilbert, "Soldier's Heart: Literary Men, Literary Women, and the Great War," *Signs* 8 (Summer 1988): 422–50; Steven C. Hause, "More Minerva than Mars: The French

Women's Rights Campaign and the First World War"; and Margaret R. Higonnet and Patrice L.-R. Higonnet, "The Double Helix," both in *Behind the Lines: Gender and the Two World Wars,* ed. Margaret Randolph Higonnet, Jane Jenson, Sonya Michel, and Margaret Collins Weitz (New Haven: Yale University Press, 1987); and George Mosse, *Fallen Soldiers: Reshaping the Memory of the World Wars* (New York: Oxford University Press, 1990). For a further summary of this literature, see Melman, "Introduction," 1–25.

42. Margaret Randolph Higonnet et al., "Introduction," in *Behind the Lines,* 4.

43. Melman, "Introduction," 6. For examples of this scholarship, see Helen M. Cooper, Adrienne Auslander Munich, and Susan Merrill Squier, eds., *Arms and the Woman: War, Gender, and Literary Representation* (Chapel Hill: University of North Carolina Press, 1989); Miriam Cooke and Angela Woollacott, eds., *Gendering War Talk* (Princeton: Princeton University Press, 1993); and Frances Early, "New Historical Perspectives on Gendered Peace Studies," *Women's Studies Quarterly* 3 (Fall-Winter 1995): 22–31.

44. Higonnet et al., "Introduction," 1–17.

45. Melman, "Introduction," 8.

46. Joan W. Scott, "Rewriting History," in *Behind the Lines,* 25.

47. Evelyn Nakano, "From Servitude to Service Work: Historical Continuities in the Racial Division of Paid Reproductive Work," *Signs* (Autumn 1992): 405. Glenn defines social reproduction in the following way: "The term social reproduction is used by feminist scholars to refer to the array of activities and relationships involved in maintaining people both on a daily basis and inter-generationally. Reproductive labor includes activities such as purchasing household goods, preparing and serving food, laundering and repairing clothing, maintaining furnishings and appliances, socializing children, providing care and emotional support for adults, and maintaining kin and community ties."

48. Paula Baker, "The Domestication of Politics: Women and American Political Society, 1780–1920," in *Women, the State, and Welfare,* ed. Linda Gordon (Madison: University of Wisconsin Press, 1990), 73, 80–81. According to Baker, "the domestication of politics" represented an ironic victory. As government adopted white, middle-class women's view of its role, those functions traditionally performed by women were placed in the hands of trained professionals, who acquired their expertise through professional training often inaccessible to women.

49. For another interpretation of how the state appropriates moral authority, see Morton Keller, *Regulating a New Society: Public Policy and Social Change in America, 1900–1933* (Cambridge: Harvard University Press, 1994).

1. Loyal Mothers and Virtuous Citizens

1. Quoted in Barbara Steinson, *American Women's Activism in World War I* (New York: Garland Publishing, 1982), 177. The term "patriotic motherhood" is Steinson's.

2. For example, peace advocates argued that women's roles as mothers uniquely equipped them to negotiate international disputes that offered alternatives to the military solutions favored by men. Women's participation in politics was made necessary, peace advocates argued, by the failure of politics that warfare and the preparedness movement epitomized. Marie Louis Degen, *The History of the Woman's Peace Party* (New York: Garland Publishers, [1939] 1972); Kathleen Kennedy, "Declaring War on War: Gender and the American Socialist Attack on Militarism, 1914–1918," *Journal of Women's History* 7 (Summer 1995): 27–51; Linda Kay Schott, "Women Against War: Pacifism, Feminism, and Social

Justice in the United States, 1915–1941" (Ph.D. diss., Stanford University, 1985); and Steinson, *American Women's Activism in World War I.*

3. For a cautionary note about failing to distinguish between the many languages used by women in the early twentieth century, see Nancy Cott, "What's in a Name? The Limits of 'Social Feminism'; or Expanding the Vocabulary of Women's History," *Journal of American History* 76 (December 1986): 820–25.

4. Seth Koven and Sonya Michel, "Introduction: 'Mother Worlds,'" in *Mothers of a New World: Maternalist Politics and the Origins of Welfare States,* ed. Seth Koven and Sonya Michel (New York: Routledge, 1993), 4. See also, Katherine Arnup, Andree Lévesque, and Ruth Roach Pierson, eds., *Delivering Motherhood: Maternal Ideologies and Practices in the 19th and 20th Centuries* (New York: Routledge, 1990); Nancy Schrom Dye and Daniel Blake Smith, "'Mother Love' and Infant Death," *Journal of American History* 73 (September 1986): 329–53; Linda Gordon, ed., *Women, the State, and Welfare* (Madison: University of Wisconsin Press, 1990); Felicia A. Kornbluh, "The New Literature on Gender and the Welfare State: The U.S. Case," *Feminist Studies* 22 (Spring 1996): 171–97; and Molly Ladd-Taylor, *Mother-Work: Women, Child Welfare, and the State, 1890–1930* (Urbana: University of Illinois Press, 1994).

5. Koven and Michel, "Introduction: 'Mother Worlds,'" 4. See also, Cott, "What's in a Name?," 821.

6. Paula Baker, "The Domestication of Politics: Women and American Political Society, 1780–1920," *American Historical Review* 89:3 (June 1984): 620–47; Paula Baker, *The Moral Frameworks of Public Life: Gender, Politics, and the State in New York, 1870–1930* (New York: Oxford University Press, 1991), 24–57; Rebecca Edwards, *Angels in the Machinery: Gender in American Party Politics from the Civil War to the Progressive Era* (New York: Oxford University Press, 1997); Linda Kerber, *Women of the Republic: Intellect and Ideology in Revolutionary America* (New York: W.W. Norton & Co., 1980); Suzanne Lebsock, "Women and American Political Society," in *Women, Politics, and Change in Twentieth-Century America,* ed. Louise Tilly and Patricia Gurin (New York: Russell Sage Foundation, 1990); and Robyn Muncy, *Creating a Female Dominion in American Reform, 1890–1935* (Cambridge: Harvard University Press, 1992).

7. Baker, *The Moral Frameworks of Public Life;* and Lebsock, "Women and American Political Society," 42–45.

8. For example, unlike middle-class women, who defined the problem of women's wage work in relation to the home life and child care practices of working women, working-class women focused on job-related issues and sometimes joined radical and labor movements that focused on the class differences between women. But African-American women, who were more likely than their European-American counterparts to work outside the home while they were raising children, constructed definitions of working mothers that emphasized the compatibility between wage work and motherhood. How or if the concerns of middle-class white women and those of working-class women, women of color, and/or immigrant women merged into effective political coalitions is a source of some controversy among historians. The literature on this subject is extensive. See Eileen Boris, "The Power of Motherhood: Black and White Activist Women," *Yale Journal of Law and Feminism* 2 (Fall 1989): 25–49; Mari Jo Buhle, *Women and American Socialism: 1880–1920* (University of Illinois Press, 1983); Ellen Carol Dubois, "Working Women, Class Relations, and Suffrage Militance: Harriot Stanton Blatch and the New York Woman Suffrage Movement, 1894–1909," *Journal of American History* 74 (June 1987): 34–58; Nancy Schrom Dye, "Creating a Feminist Alliance: Sisterhood and Class Conflict in the New York Woman's Trade Union League, 1903–1914," *Feminist Studies* 3 (1975): 11–25; Noralee Frankel and Nancy S. Dye, ed., *Gender, Class, Race and Reform in the Progressive Era* (Lexing-

ton: University of Kentucky Press, 1992); Evelyn Brooks Higginbotham, *Righteous Discontent: The Women's Movement in the Black Baptist Church, 1880–1920* (Cambridge: Harvard University Press, 1993); Robin Miller Jacoby, " The Women's Trade Union League and American Feminism," *Feminist Studies* 3 (1976): 126–40; Alice Kessler-Harris, *Out to Work: A History of Wage Earning Women in the United States* (New York: Oxford University Press, 1982); Kathy Peiss, *Cheap Amusements: Working Women and Leisure in Turn-of-the-Century New York* (Philadelphia: Temple University Press, 1986); and Christine Stansell, *City of Women: Sex and Class in New York* (Urbana: University of Illinois Press, 1987).

9. Nancy Cott, *The Grounding of Modern Feminism* (New Haven: Yale University Press, 1987), 1–50; and Nancy Woloch, *Muller v. Oregon: A Brief History with Documents* (Boston: Bedford Books, 1996), 3–83.

10. See the articles in Margaret Randolph Higonnet, Jane Jensen, Sonya Michel, and Margaret Collins Weitz, ed., *Behind the Lines: Gender and the Two World Wars* (New Haven: Yale University Press, 1987); and Billie Melman, ed., *borderlines: Genders and Identities in War and Peace 1870–1930* (New York: Routledge, 1998).

11. For a theoretical discussion of this argument, see Margaret Randolph Higonnet and Patrice Higonnet, "The Double Helix," in *Behind the Lines*, 31–47.

12. Ronald C. Marchard, *The American Peace Movement and Social Reform* (Princeton: Princeton University Press, 1972).

13. Thomas Knock, *To End All Wars: Woodrow Wilson and the Quest for a New World Order* (Princeton: Princeton University Press, 1992), 48–104. For example, Knock argues that the WPP's "platform committee produced the earliest, and what must be acknowledged as the most comprehensive, manifesto on internationalism advanced by any American organization throughout the entire war" (p. 51). Wilson drew liberally from the ideas of the WPP as well as from those of other American peace organizations.

14. Ibid.

15. Schott, "Women Against War."

16. Ibid.

17. Susan Zeiger, "She Didn't Raise Her Boy to Be a Slacker: Motherhood, Conscription and the Culture of the First World War," *Feminist Studies* 22 (Spring 1996): 9.

18. Degen, *The History of the Woman's Peace Party*; Schott, "Women Against War"; and Steinson, *American Women's Activism in World War I.*

19. Zeiger, "She Didn't Raise Her Boy to Be a Slacker," 7–39.

20. "The Sum of All Villainies," *New Republic* (13 February 1915): 37.

21. David Kennedy, *Over Here: The First World War and American Society* (New York: Oxford University Press, 1980), 47.

22. See Herbert Croly, "The End of American Isolation," *New Republic* (7 November 1914): 9–10.

23. Eldon Eisenach, *The Lost Promise of Progressivism* (Lawrence: University of Kansas Press, 1994).

24. Theodore Roosevelt, "Is the Women's Peace Movement 'Silly and Base'?" *Literary Digest* 50 (1 May 1915): 1022.

25. Kennedy, *Over Here*, 66.

26. Allen F. Davis, "Welfare Reform and World War I," *American Quarterly* XIX (Fall 1967): 516–33; Charles Hirschfeld, "Nationalist Progressivism and World War I," *Mid-America* 45 (July 1963): 139–56; John M. Jordan, *Machine-Age Ideology: Social Engineering and American Liberalism, 1911–1939* (Chapel Hill: University of North Carolina Press, 1994), 68–92; Morton Keller, *Regulating a New Society: Public Policy and Social Change in America, 1900–1933* (Cambridge: Harvard University Press, 1994); George H. Knoles, "American Intellectuals and World War I," *Pacific Northwest Quarterly* (October 1968): 203–15; William T. Leuch-

tenburg, "The Progressive Movement and American Foreign Policy, 1898–1916," *Mississippi Valley Historical Review* 39 (December 1952): 483–504; Stanley Shapiro, "The Great War and Reform: Liberals and Labor," *Labor History* 11 (Summer 1971): 323–44; L. Moody Simms Jr., "World War I and the American Intellectual," *Social Science* 45 (June 1970): 57–62; Joseph M. Siracusa, "Progressivism, Imperialism, and the Leuchtenburg Thesis, 1952–1974," *Australian Journal of Politics and History* 20 (December 1974): 312–25; J.A. Thompson, "American Progressive Publicists and the First World War, 1914–1917," *Journal of American History* 58 (September 1971): 364–83; John A. Thompson, *Reformers and War: American Progressive Publicists and the First World War* (Cambridge: Cambridge University Press, 1987); and Walter I. Trattner, "Progressivism and World War I: A Reappraisal," *Mid-America* 44 (July 1962): 131–45.

27. Michael C.C. Addams, *The Great Adventure: Male Desire and the Coming of World War I* (Bloomington: Indiana University Press, 1990); Peter Filene, "In Time of War," in *The American Male*, ed. Elizabeth Pleck and Joseph Pleck (Englewood Cliffs, N.J.: Prentice Hall, 1980); and Arnaldo Testi, "The Gender of Reform Politics: Theodore Roosevelt and the Culture of Masculinity," *The Journal of American History* 81 (March 1995): 1509–33.

28. Baker, *The Moral Frameworks of Public Life*, xiv; Lebsock, "Women and American Political Society," 45–57. Baker concludes that this new expertise was not gender neutral because the new ethics of professionalism contained its own gender system. For a discussion of how this transformation affected woman's politics, see also Muncy, *Creating a Female Dominion*.

29. For changes in late nineteenth-century society, see David B. Danbom, *"The World of Hope": Progressives and the Struggle for an Ethical Public Life* (Philadelphia: Temple University Press, 1987); T.J. Jackson Lears, *No Place of Grace: Anti-Modernism and the Transition of American Culture, 1880–1920* (New York: Pantheon, 1981); and Robert H. Wiebe, *The Search for Order, 1917–1920* (New York: Hill and Wang, 1967). For a recent study that integrates the observations of women's historians about the influence of women on progressivism, see Eisenach, *The Lost Promise of Progressivism*.

30. Adams, *The Great Adventure*; Hirschfeld, "Nationalist Progressivism and the First World War," 139–56; Leuchtenburg, "The Progressive Movement and American Foreign Policy," 483–504; and Thompson, *Reformers and War*.

31. Burton J. Hendrick, *Life and Letters of Walter H. Page*, vol. II (Garden City, N.Y.: Doubleday, 1922), 218–19. For a discussion of Page's views on World War I and his influence in the Wilson administration, see Robert Osgood, *Ideals and Self-Interest in American Foreign Relations: The Great Transformation of the 20th Century* (Chicago: University of Chicago Press, 1953), 154–60.

32. John Higham, *Strangers in the Land: Patterns of American Nativism, 1886–1925* (New York: Atheneum, [1953] 1969); and Edward Saveth, "Race and Nationalism in American Historiography: The Late Nineteenth Century," *Political Science Quarterly* 54 (September 1939): 421–44.

33. Here my thesis revises that of Higham.

34. Gail Bederman, *Manliness and Civilization: A Cultural History of Gender and Race in the United States, 1880–1917* (Chicago: University of Chicago Press, 1995), 5. See also, Testi, "The Gender of Reform Politics."

35. Bederman, *Manliness and Civilization*, 200–201.

36. Thomas G. Dyer, *Theodore Roosevelt and the Idea of Race* (Baton Rouge: Louisiana State University Press, 1980).

37. Bederman, *Manliness and Civilization*, 179.

38. Edwards, *The Angel in the Machinery*, 12–75.

39. Linda Gordon, *Woman's Body, Woman's Right: Birth Control in America* (New York: Penguin Books, 1976). Calls for greater state intervention in mothering

were part of the political agendas of progressive women. For example,"scientific mothering" set the stage for increased state intervention in mothering and established a new framework for maternal politics as war approached. According to Ladd-Taylor, scientific mothering "maintained that [the] maternal instinct needed to be supplemented with scientific education."Ladd-Taylor, *Mother-Work*, 6–7. Such calls for greater intervention in mothering, Ladd-Taylor notes, were linked to concerns among white Protestants about the impact of new immigration and of poverty on the family and the nation.These concerns led to calls for white, middle-class women to bear more children and take greater responsibility for teaching immigrants and poor women how to mother.

40. These concerns about manliness and the potential threat that women posed to men's soldiering affected the policies of progressives during the war as they used the military to mold a new kind of man. For example, the Commission on Training Camp Activities (CTCA) was charged with protecting soldiers from illicit sexual activity and venereal disease.The progressives who ran the CTCA attacked these problems by reshaping manhood.They hoped, in Bristow's words, that"out of war would emerge a new American citizen, loyal first and foremost to the nation and united with other citizens through shared values." Nancy K. Bristow, *Making Men Moral: Social Engineering During the Great War* (New York: New York University Press, 1996), 17, 21.

41. Rear Admiral Goodrich, quoted in John Dewey,"Universal Service as Education II," *New Republic* (29 April 1916): 334.

42. Like Goodrich, Roosevelt also looked to the military to strengthen citizenship. He insisted that all men should undertake one half year of military service. Military training, he wrote,"would tend to social cohesion" and "a higher form of citizenship."By disciplining the body, military training created virtuous citizens capable of the "moral self-mastery" necessary for virtuous citizenry. Theodore Roosevelt, *The Works of Theodore Roosevelt*, vol. 18 (New York: Charles Scribner's Sons, 1926), 334.

43. John Gary Clifford, *The Citizen Soldier: The Plattsburgh Training Camp Movement, 1913–1920* (Lexington: University of Kentucky Press, 1972); and Michael Pearlman, *To Make Democracy Safe for America: Patricians and Preparedness in the Progressive Era* (Urbana: University of Illinois Press, 1984).

44. For a discussion of Roosevelt's changing views on women's participation in public life, see Doris Groshen Daniels, "Theodore Roosevelt and Gender Roles," *Presidential Studies Quarterly* 26 (Summer 1996): 648–65.

45. Roosevelt, *The Works of Theodore Roosevelt*, vol. 19 (New York: Charles Scribner's Sons, 1926), 140–51. Roosevelt told a suffrage leader, "Personally I believe in woman suffrage, but I am not an enthusiastic advocate of it because I do not regard it as a very important matter." John Milton Cooper, *Pivotal Decades: The United States, 1900–1920* (New York: W.W. Norton), 100.

46. For Roosevelt's discussion of the relationship between mothering and soldiering, see Roosevelt, *The Works of Theodore Roosevelt*, vol. 19, 165.

47. For a discussion of the category of nonmen, see Gerald Edwin Shenk, "'Work or Fight': Selective Service and Manhood in the Progressive Era" (Ph.D. diss., University of California, San Diego, 1992), 1–30.

48. See Roosevelt's discussion in Roosevelt, *The Works of Theodore Roosevelt*, vol. 18, 305.

49. Ibid., 207–208.

50. Pacifists provided one example of nonmen, according to Roosevelt. As nonmen, pacifists acted on impulse and were consequently easily controlled by others."In some of our big cities, since the war began, men have formed vegetarian societies, claiming to be exempt from service on the ground that they object to killing not merely men, but chickens," Roosevelt scornfully wrote in

one of his most famous passages condemning pacifists."Others among the leading apostles of applied pacifism are not timid men; on the contrary they are
brutal violent men, who are perfectly willing to fight, but only for themselves
and not for the nation. These rough-neck pacifists have always been the potent
allies of the parlor or milk-and-water pacifists; although they stand at the op-
posite end of the developmental scale. The parlor pacifist, the white-handed or
sissy type of pacifist, represents decadence, represents the rotting out of the
virile virtues among people who typify the unlovely senile side of civilization.
The rough-neck pacifist, on the contrary, is a mere belated savage, who has not
been educated to the virtues of national patriotism and of willingness to fight
for the national flag and national ideal." Roosevelt, *The Works of Theodore Roosevelt*, vol. 19, 173–74.

51. Edwards, *Angels in the Machinery*, 17.

52. On April 14, 1917, Wilson created the Committee on Public Information
and appointed George Creel as its head. Creel quickly established an effective
propaganda machine designed to"drive home the absolute justice of America's
cause, the absolute selflessness of America's aims." Rejecting the term propaganda, Creel insisted that his committee offered an "educational and informa-
tive" view of the Wilson administration's reasons for intervention. Using the
techniques of mass advertising, Creel promoted the war through movies, poster
art, and pamphlets. See William J. Breen, *Uncle Sam at Home: Civilian Mobilization, Wartime Federalism and the Council of National Defense, 1917–1919* (Westport:
Greenwood Press, 1984); George Creel, *How We Advertised America: The First Telling of the Amazing Story of the Committee on Public Information That Carried the
Gospel of Americanism to Every Corner of the Globe* (New York: Harper & Brothers,
1920); Leslie Midkiff DeBauche, *Reel Patriotism: The Movies and World War I* (Madison: University of Wisconsin Press, 1997); James R. Mock and Cedric Larson,
Words That Won the War (Princeton: University of Princeton Press, 1939); and
Stephen Vaughn, *Holding Fast the Inner Lines: Democracy, Nationalism, and the
Committee on Public Information* (Chapel Hill: University of North Carolina Press,
1980).

53. Michele J. Shover, "Roles and Images of Women in World War I Propaganda," *Politics and Society* 5 (1975): 470.

54. Claire A. Culleton,"Gender-Charged Munitions: The Language of World
War I Munitions Reports,"*Women's Studies International Forum* 11 (1988): 109–16;
and Shover,"Roles and Images of Women in World War I," 469–86. For a more
detailed analysis of the connections between pro-war rhetoric and poster art,
see Kathleen Kennedy,"'We Mourn for Liberty in America': Socialist Women,
Anti-militarism, and State Repression, 1914–1922" (Ph.D. diss., University of
California, Irvine, 1992), 14–68.

55. See, for example, Howard Chandler Christy, "I Want You for the Navy."
Reprinted in Shover, "Roles and Images of Women in World War I," 483; and
Christy, "If You Want To Fight! Join the Marines."Reprinted in unauthored pamphlet "Posters and Facsimiles." Edited by the National Archives, 3. Christy's
work replaced the paternal father of Uncle Sam with the seductive woman. For
an analysis of this transformation, see Kennedy, "'We Mourn for Liberty in
America,'" 14–68.

56. For a debate about the meaning of some of the most famous of these im-
ages—those of Red Cross nurses—see Sandra M. Gilbert,"Soldier's Heart: Lit-
erary Men, Literary Women, and the Great War," *Signs* 8 (Fall 1988): 422–50; and
Jane Marcus,"The Asylums of Antaeus: Women, War and Madness. Is There a
Feminist Fetishism?" in *The Difference Within: Feminism and Critical Theory*, ed.
Elizabeth Meese and Alice Parker (Amsterdam: John Benjamins, 1989), 49–81.

57. Nicoletta F. Gullace, "Sexual Violence and Family Honor: British Propa-

ganda and International Law during the First World War," *The American Histori-cal Review* 102 (June 1997): 716–25.

58. Steinson, *Women's Activism in World War I*, v.

59. Ibid., 163.

60. Alan Price, *The End of the Age of Innocence: Edith Wharton and the First World War* (New York: St. Martin's Press, 1996).

61. Steinson, *Women's Activism in World War I*, 163–219.

62. Ibid., 212.

63. Ibid., 179.

64. Ibid., 179.

65. Ibid., 210.

66. Ibid., 178.

67. Anne Morgan, quoted in Barbara Steinson, *American Women's Activism in World War I*, 215. For a discussion of the anti-suffrage movement, see Manuela Thurner, "'Better Citizens Without the Ballot': American Antisuffrage Women and Their Rationale During the Progressive Era," *Journal of Women's History* 5 (Spring 1993): 33–60.

68. For a suffrage response to this argument, see Rose Young, "Which Party Gave New York Women the Franchise?" National Woman's Suffrage Association Press Release, 7 February 1919, 1–4. Wisconsin Woman's Suffrage Association Papers, box 21, folder 1, Wisconsin Historical Society, Madison, WI.

69. For discussions of these positions, see Steinson, *American Women's Activism*.

70. See for example, "What Suffragists Think of Mr. Wood," Suffrage News Bulletin, 4 May 1917. Papers of the Wisconsin Woman's Suffrage Association, box 13, folder 3, Wisconsin Historical Society, Madison, WI. This bulletin responded to remarks made by Henry Wise Wood, who argued that the specific qualities that women brought to politics, such as gentleness, weakness, love, and mercy, hurt the war effort. For a discussion of women's political roles during the war, see Neil A. Wynn, *From Progressivism to Prosperity: World War I and American Society* (New York: Holmes & Meier, 1986).

71. Theodora Youmans to Mrs. Frances Schwartz, 22 May 1917. Wisconsin Woman's Suffrage Association Papers, box 13, Wisconsin Historical Society, Madison, WI.

72. Theodora Youmans, Wisconsin Woman's Suffrage Association Press Release, 7 April 1917. Wisconsin Woman's Suffrage Association Papers, box 13, folder 1, Wisconsin Historical Society, Madison, WI.

73. Harriot Stanton Blatch, *Mobilizing Woman-Power* (New York: The Woman's Press, 1918), 20. Roosevelt wrote the introduction to Blatch's book. Blatch later became disenchanted with the war's results. For an analysis of Blatch and her position on the war, see Ellen Carol Dubois, *Harriot Stanton Blatch and the Winning of Woman Suffrage* (New Haven: Yale University Press, 1997), 175–225.

74. Wynn, *From Progressivism to Prosperity*.

75. Vera Barman Whitehorse, "The Immigrant Woman and the Vote," *Immigrants in America Review* 1 (September 1915): 65. "They [immigrant children] learn more quickly than she [the immigrant mother] the language and customs of their new country," wrote Whitehorse, "and may then look upon her with scorn. Her authority over them is destroyed. The helpless mother can be deceived as well as scorned by her children, and she is powerless to protect them from the dangers she knows nothing of."

76. Mrs. James G. Dunning, quoted in Mrs. Rhodes, "Americanization Through Women's Organizations," *Immigrants in America Review* 1 (September 1915): 51. "Little has been done to reach the immigrant mother," wrote the chair of Patriotic Education of the Daughters of the American Revolution. "[S]he has been permitted to remain the embodiment of foreign ideas and ideals; her home is a

foreign home, and foreign homes are not reliable for the production of patriotic American citizens."

77. Grace H. Bagley, "Americanization as War Service," *Woman Citizen* (30 June 1917), 84.

78. Jessie Hooper to Hamilton, 1 March 1917, 3. Wisconsin Woman's Suffrage Association Papers, box 13, Wisconsin Historical Society, Madison, WI.

79. Some suffrage organizations did enforce loyalty within their ranks. See John D. Buerker, "The Politics of Mutual Frustration: Socialists and Suffragists in New York and Wisconsin," in *Flawed Liberation: Socialism and Feminism*, ed. Sally M. Miller (Westport: Greenwood Press, 1981); and Kathleen Kennedy, "Loyalty and Citizenship in the Wisconsin Woman's Suffrage Association, 1917–1919," *Mid-America* 76 (Spring/Summer 1994): 109–31.

80. The best study of this tradition is Higham, *Strangers in the Land*.

81. Whitehorse, "The Immigrant Woman and the Vote," 67.

82. For studies on the Americanization movement, see Robert A. Carlson, *The Americanization Syndrome: A Quest for Conformity* (London: Croom Helm, 1987); George Edward Hartman, *The Movement to Americanize the Immigrant* (New York: AMS Press, [1948] 1967); and Gerd Korman, *Industrialization, Immigrants, and Americanizers: The View from Milwaukee, 1866–1921* (Madison: The State Historical Society of Wisconsin, 1967).

83. Kennedy, "Loyalty and Citizenship in the Wisconsin Woman's Suffrage Association, 1917–1919," 109–32; and Kennedy, "'We Mourn for Liberty in America,'" 106–85.

84. Cott, *The Grounding of Modern Feminism*; Linda G. Ford, *Iron-Jawed Angels: The Suffrage Militancy of the National Woman's Party, 1912–1920* (Lanham, MD: University Press of America, 1991); and Christine Lunardini, *From Equal Suffrage to Equal Rights: Alice Paul and the National Woman's Party, 1910–1928* (New York: New York University Press, 1986), 106–33.

85. McClymer, *War and Welfare*, 76. See also, Michael Rogin, *Ronald Reagan the Movie and Other Episodes of Political Demonology* (Berkeley: University of California Press, 1987); and Ronald Schaffer, *America in the Great War: The Rise of the War Welfare State* (New York: Oxford University Press, 1991).

2. Motherhood and Subversion

1. Kathleen Diane Moum, "Harvest of Discontent: The Social Origins of the Nonpartisan League, 1880–1920" (Ph.D. diss., University of California, Irvine, 1986).

2. Neil K. Basen, "Kate Richards O'Hare: The 'First Lady' of American Socialism, 1901–1917," *Labor History* 21 (Spring 1980): 165–99; Bernard J. Brommel, "Kate Richards O'Hare: A Midwestern Pacifist's Fight for Free Speech," *North Dakota Quarterly* 44 (Winter 1976): 5–19; Sally M. Miller, *From Prairie to Prison: The Life of Social Activist Kate Richards O'Hare* (Columbia: University of Missouri Press, 1993), 127–91; Sally Miller, "Kate Richards O'Hare: Progression Towards Feminism," *Kansas History* 7 (Winter 1983): 263–79; and Erling N. Sannes, "'Queen of the Lecture Platform': Kate Richards O'Hare and North Dakota Politics, 1917–1921," *North Dakota History* 58 (Fall 1991): 2–19.

3. *United States vs. Kate Richards O'Hare, District of North Dakota* (December 1917). Cited in Walter Nells, ed., *Espionage Act Cases: With Certain Others on Related Points* (New York: National Civil Liberties Bureau, 1918).

4. Ibid., 46.

5. Thomas Lawrence, "Eclipse of Liberty: Civil Liberties in the United States During the First World War," *Wayne State Review* 21 (Spring 1974): 33–112.

6. David Rabban, "The Emergence of Modern First Amendment Doctrine,"

The University of Chicago Law Review 50 (Fall 1984): 1205–1355; and David Rabban, "The First Amendment in Its Forgotten Years," *The Yale Law Journal* 90 (January 1981): 519–95.

7. Ibid.

8. Paul L. Murphy, *World War I and the Origin of Civil Liberties in the United States* (New York: W.W. Norton & Co., 1979), 207.

9. Brommel, "Kate Richards O'Hare," 5–19; and H.C. Peterson and Gilbert C. Fite, *Opponents of War, 1917–1918* (Seattle: University of Washington Press, 1957), 35–36.

10. See also, Kate Richards O'Hare and Frank O'Hare, *World Peace: A Spectacle Drama in Three Acts* (St. Louis: National Rip-Saw Publishing Co., 1915).

11. Mari Jo Buhle, *Women and American Socialism 1870–1920* (Urbana: University of Illinois Press, 1983), 246–48; and Miller, *From Prairie to Prison*.

12. Miller, *From Prairie to Prison*, 20.

13. Kate Richards O'Hare, *The Sorrows of Cupid* (St. Louis: National Rip-Saw Publishing, 1913).

14. Miller, *From Prairie to Prison*, 146–47.

15. Brommel, "Kate Richards O'Hare," 5–19. Brommel fails to discuss the significance of the prosecution's strategy.

16. Murphy, *World War I and the Origin of Civil Liberties*, 207.

17. See, for example, "Mothers of Soldiers Brood Sows; Sammies Fit Only for Fertilizer, Said Mrs. O'Hare," *Bismarck Evening Tribune*, 6 December 1917, 1.

18. "Remarks of Judge Wade When Imposing Sentence Upon the Defendant," 1. Papers of the Department of Justice, RG 60, #9-19-603, sec. 1, folder 2, National Archives, Washington, DC.

19. Ibid., 17.

20. His remarks were not out of step with the specifics of O'Hare's critique of patriotic motherhood. O'Hare suggested that militarism alienated women from their labor, specifically the production and socialization of children. O'Hare argued that the combined forces of capitalism and militarism denied women the moral authority that was their "just earnings."

21. "Remarks of Judge Wade," 25.

22. Ibid., 24.

23. Ibid., 26.

24. Claude R. Rorbie to the Attorney General of the United States, 31 May 1919. Papers of the Department of Justice, RG 60, #9-16-603, folder 1, National Archives, Washington, DC. Rorbie agreed with Wade's understanding of his role in espionage prosecutions. Rorbie argued that shortening O'Hare's sentence would be an insult not only to American soldiers but also to Wade.

25. As President Wilson considered commuting the sentences of those arrested under the wartime laws, local officials scrambled to protect their convictions and sentences. In a letter to Attorney General Palmer, Wade reaffirmed his position, defining O'Hare as the most dangerous political activist in the United States. "Kate O'Hare is in my judgement, one of the most dangerous characters in the U.S.," he wrote. "She has no equal, in my judgement, in the matter of poisoning the minds of the struggling masses unless it be Debs. In fact I think she is more dangerous than Debs, because she is more subtle. She can convince any audience that she is a martyr to the cause of humanity, and she can do more to plant this seed of Bolshevism than Debs can. She can do more in this direction than a man who will get out openly and advocate bombs and destruction, because the man who advocates destruction directly does not get many followers, but Kate O'Hare in her speeches can convince her hearers, especially her ignorant hearers, that they are slaves." Martin Wade to Attorney General Palmer, 11 June 1919. Papers of the Department of Justice, RG 60, #9-19-603, folder 1, National Archives, Washington, DC.

26. "Kate Richards O'Hare Tells of Trial and Sentence," *New York Call*, 16 February 1918, 2.

27. "Kate R. O'Hare Tells Audience Story of Trial," *New York Call*, 27 February 1918, 1.

28. O'Hare, quoted in "Kate R. O'Hare Tells of Trial and Sentence," 2. See also Kate Richards O'Hare, "Guilty," in *Kate Richards O'Hare: Selected Writings and Speeches*, ed. Philip S. Foner and Sally M. Miller (Baton Rouge: Louisiana State University Press, 1982), 184–85.

29. Carol F. Karlsen, *The Devil in the Shape of a Woman: Witchcraft in Colonial New England* (New York: Random House Inc., 1987). In retrospect, O'Hare's comparison of her case to the Salem witchcraft trials was telling. As historian Carol Karlsen has shown, the Salem trials emerged from conflicts over the role of women in the community and fears of the influence women were thought to wield over young people. Accused witches were most often older women who did not conform to conventional maternal and/or gender roles; they symbolized the consequences to the community when it lost control of motherhood.

30. "Women to Fight Imprisonment of Kate O'Hare," *New York Call*, 27 June 1919, 1; and "'Free Kate O'Hare!' Is Women's Appeal at Protest Meeting," *New York Call*, 29 June 1919, 1. The Kate Richards O'Hare Defense Committee included Mary Harris Bloor, Elizabeth Gurley Flynn, and Meta Stern Lilienthal. Also active were Agnes Smedley and Theresa Malkiel.

31. Anita Block, "Kate Richards O'Hare," *New York Call*, 23 December 1917. See also Meta Lilienthal to "Friend of Justice," 17 April 1919. Papers of the New York Bureau of Legal Advice, box 3, folder 27, Tamiment Institute of Labor Library, New York, NY. Lilienthal wrote: "Kate Richards O'Hare, far from being a criminal, is a woman of superior qualities, good virtuous [sic] and noble, a woman who has given the best part of her life for the common cause of humanity. She is moreover, a wife and mother. Her imprisonment means that a happy home has been broken up, that a devoted husband has been robbed of his wife, that four young children have been deprived of their mother. I appeal to you, not so much in behalf of Kate Richards O'Hare, the writer, the orator, the organizer, the leader of men and women, as in behalf of Kate Richards O'Hare, the loving wife, the worthy mother."

32. For a discussion of the responses of socialist women to World War I, see Kathleen Kennedy, "Declaring War on War: Gender and the American Socialist Attack on Militarism, 1914–1918," *Journal of Women's History* 7 (Summer 1995): 27–51.

33. Theresa Malkiel, "Kate Richards O'Hare: A Prisoner," *The New Call Magazine*, 14 December 1919, 4.

34. O'Hare was not the "only mother," as she claimed, imprisoned under the Espionage Act. Minnie Geibel was sentenced to five years in prison and fined two thousand dollars for allegedly making seditious remarks. Geibel spent ten months in prison. See "Application for Executive Clemency," 12 March 1919. Records of the Office of the Pardon Attorney, RG 304, #33-422, folder 1, National Archives, Washington, DC.

35. Kate Richards O'Hare, "Dear Sweethearts," 17 August 1919. Kate Richards O'Hare Papers, Microfilm Edition, reel 1, Arthur and Elizabeth Schlesinger Library, Cambridge, MA.

36. For a further discussion of this strategy, see Kathleen Kennedy, "'We Mourn for Liberty in America': Socialist Women, Anti-militarism, and State Repression, 1914–1922" (Ph.D. diss. University of California, Irvine, 1992).

37. Kate Richards O'Hare, "Dear Sweethearts," 20 April 1919. Kate Richards O'Hare Papers, Microfilm Edition, reel 1, Arthur and Elizabeth Schlesinger Library, Radcliffe College, Cambridge, MA.

38. Ibid., 3.

39. Kate Richards O'Hare, "Dear Sweethearts," 26 April 1919. Kate Richards O'Hare Papers, Microfilm Edition, reel 1, Arthur and Elizabeth Schlesinger Library, Radcliffe College, Cambridge, MA.

40. Ibid., 2.

41. Kate Richards O'Hare, "Dear Sweethearts," 31 January 1920. Kate Richards O'Hare Papers, Microfilm Edition, reel 1, Arthur and Elizabeth Schlesinger Library, Radcliffe College, Cambridge, MA. See also letters dated 15 June 1919 and 17 August 1919 for further references to her growing friendship with Goldman. For a discussion of Goldman and O'Hare's friendship, see Bonnie Stepenoff, "Mother and Teacher as Missouri State Penitentiary Inmates: Goldman and O'Hare, 1917–1920," *Missouri Historical Review* 91 (July 1991): 402–21.

42. "Address of Miss Emma Goldman at Kate Richards O'Hare Testimonial Dinner," 17 November 1919. Alexander Berkman Papers, Tamiment Institute of Labor History, New York, NY. See also Emma Goldman, *Living My Life,* vol. II (New York: Dover Publications Inc., 1970), 677.

43. Candice Falk, *Love, Anarchy, and Emma Goldman* (New York: Holt, Rinehart, and Winston, 1984); and Goldman, *Living My Life*.

44. See Committee for Florence Kimble, Post #7, American Legion, Libson, ND, to the Attorney General, Records of the Office of the Pardon Attorney, RG 304, #33–422, 1; and "Petition Directed by Lloyd Spetz," Post #1, American Legion, ND, Papers of the Department of Justice, #33–422, National Archives, Washington, DC.

45. Melvin Hildeth, Attorney General North Dakota to the Attorney General of the United States, 15 February 1919. Papers of the Department of Justice, RG 60, #9-19-603, folder 1, National Archives, Washington, DC.

46. North Dakota State Representative H. Herbush was less subtle in his evaluation of O'Hare's moral claims. "This prison has within its walls bootleggers, rapists, murders and other criminals," he wrote to the Department of Justice, "but we hope that its walls will not be disgraced by the presence of this woman." H. Herbush to Department of Justice, 22 March 1918. Papers of the Department of Justice, RG 60, 9-19-603, folder 1, National Archives, Washington, DC.

47. Memorandum to the Department of Justice, 12. Papers of the Department of Justice, RG 60, #9-19-603; folder 1, National Archives, Washington, DC.

48. For a further discussion of this point, see Michael Rogin, *Ronald Reagan The Movie And Other Episodes in Political Demonology* (Berkeley: University of California Press, 1987), 44–80.

49. Ibid.

50. Miller, *From Prairie to Prison*, 154–57.

51. Frank O'Hare to Eugene Debs, 27 December 1917. Reprinted in Eugene V. Debs, *Correspondences: The Letters of Eugene Debs,* vol. II, ed. Robert J. Constantine (Urbana: University of Illinois Press, 1990), 349. For biographical information on Frank O'Hare, see Peter Buckingham, *Rebel Against Injustice: The Life of Frank P. O'Hare* (Columbia: University of Missouri Press, 1996).

52. Debs, *Correspondences,* vol. II, 350.

53. Eugene Debs to Frank O'Hare, 2 January 1918. Reprinted in Debs, *Correspondences,* vol. 2, 356.

54. Ibid., 355.

55. Ibid., 359.

56. Eugene Debs to Frank O'Hare, 12 January 1918. Reprinted in Debs, *Correspondences,* vol. II, 363.

57. Kate Richards O'Hare, "Dear Sweethearts," 7 December 1919. Kate Richards O'Hare Papers, Microfilm Edition, reel 1, Arthur and Elizabeth Schlesinger Library, Radcliffe College, Cambridge, MA. Foreman was a schoolteacher and

socialist who was driven out of Oregon by neighbors. After she was arrested in Texas for disparaging remarks about the Red Cross, Foreman served two years in an Oklahoma prison. Apparently she was in ill health even before her conviction; her time in prison completely destroyed her health. For further information about her case, see Elizabeth Gurley Flynn, *The Rebel Girl: An Autobiography* (New York: International Publishing, 1955), 251. Foreman's prison letters are in the Papers of the Socialist Party of America, Microfilm Edition, reel 9, University of California, Irvine, CA.

58. Kate Richards O'Hare to Otto Branstetter, 8 February 1920. Papers of the Socialist Party of America, reel 9, University of California, Irvine CA.

59. Ibid., 2.

60. Kennedy, "'We Mourn for Liberty in America,'" 248–330; Nick Salvatore, *Eugene V. Debs: Citizen and Socialist* (Urbana: University of Illinois Press, 1982); and John Sherman, "'This Is a Crusade!' Socialist Party Amnesty Campaigns to Free Eugene V. Debs, 1919–1921," in *Culture, Gender, Race, and U.S. Labor History*, ed. Ronald C. Kent, Sara Markham, David R. Roediger, and Herbert Shapiro. (Westport: Greenwood Press, 1993), 24–41.

61. Otto Branstetter to Kate Richards O'Hare, 14 February 1920, 1. Socialist Party of America Papers, Microfilm Edition, reel 9, University of California, Irvine, CA. Despite this controversy, Branstetter and O'Hare were friends. Both developed their careers in the Midwest. Their friendship perhaps led Branstetter to relent and commit additional resources to O'Hare's defense.

62. Otto Branstetter to Kate Richards O'Hare, 14 February 1920. Papers of the Socialist Party of America, Microfilm Edition, reel 9, University of California, Irvine, CA.

63. Kate Richards O'Hare to Otto Branstetter, 24 February 1920, 1. Socialist Party of America Papers, Microfilm Edition, reel 9, University of California, Irvine, CA.

64. Ibid., 2.

65. Ibid., 1.

66. Otto Branstetter to Frank P. O'Hare, 26 February 1920. Papers of the Socialist Party of America, Microfilm Edition, reel 9, University of California, Irvine, CA.

67. Frank P. O'Hare to Otto Branstetter, March 1920. Papers of the Socialist Party of America, Microfilm Edition, reel 9, University of California, Irvine, CA. Frank asked Branstetter to burn this letter, which Branstetter obviously decided against. At this time Branstetter was under attack for his amnesty campaign and may have kept and filed the letter for that reason.

68. Brommel, "Kate Richards O'Hare," 5–9; and Miller, "Kate Richards O'Hare," 263–73. See also Kate Richards O'Hare, *In Prison* (Seattle: University of Washington Press, [1923] 1976).

69. Otto Branstetter to Frank O'Hare, 26 February 1920; Otto Branstetter to Kate Richards O'Hare, 26 February 1920; and Otto Branstetter to Kate Richards O'Hare, 10 April 1920. Socialist Party of America Papers, Microfilm Edition, reel 9, University of California, Irvine, CA.

70. Brommel, "Kate Richards O'Hare," 17–19.

71. Morris Hillquit to Adolph F. Germer, 12 February 1918, 1. Morris Hillquit Papers, State Historical Society of Wisconsin, Madison, WI.

72. Kennedy, "'We Mourn for Liberty in America,'" 248–330; and Sherman, "'This Is a Crusade!'," 24–41. Hillquit's argument that the party treated all cases equally was not true. After 1919, the party focused the majority of its efforts on the case of Eugene Debs.

73. David A. Shannon, *The Socialist Party of America: A History* (New York: Macmillan, 1955), 25–26.

74. Morris Hillquit to Nina and Lawrence Hill, 10 April 1917. Morris Hillquit Papers, Wisconsin Historical Society, Madison, WI.

75. A. Germer to Morris Hillquit, 9 April 1919. Morris Hillquit Papers, State Historical Society, Madison, WI.

76. James Weinstein, *The Decline of Socialism in America, 1912–1925* (New York: Monthly Review Press, 1967), 177–234.

77. Basen, "Kate Richards O'Hare: The 'First Lady' of American Socialism," 165–69; Buhle, *Women and American Socialism, 1870–1920*; and Miller, "Kate Richards O'Hare: Progression Toward Feminism," 263–79.

78. Shannon, *The Socialist Party of America*, 25.

79. For a discussion of southwestern socialism, see James R. Green, *Grass Roots Socialism: Radical Movements in the Southwest, 1895–1943* (Baton Rouge: Louisiana State University Press, 1978).

80. Marla Martin Hanley, "The Children's Crusade of 1922: Kate O'Hare and the Campaign to Free Radical War Dissenters in the Era of America's First Red Scare," *Gateway Heritage* 10 (Summer 1989): 34–43.

81. Flynn, *The Rebel Girl*, 292–96.; and Mary Heaton Vorse, *A Footnote to Folly: Reminiscences of Mary Heaton Vorse* (New York: Farrar and Rinehart Inc., 1935), 393–407. For information on Mary Heaton Vorse, see Dee Garrison, *Mary Heaton Vorse: The Life of an American Insurgent* (Philadelphia: Temple University Press, 1989). Vorse, a journalist, became involved in the labor movement when she covered the Lawrence, Massachusetts, strike in 1912. Vorse was friends with Flynn and provided publicity for her endeavors and other labor activities.

82. The signs the children carried included, "My Daddy Didn't Want to Kill," "My Mother Died of Grief," and "Is the Constitution Dead?" Flynn, *The Rebel Girl*, 293.

83. Flynn, *The Rebel Girl*, 293; and Vorse, *A Footnote to Folly*, 393–407.

84. Shannon, *The Socialist Party of America*, 25.

85. Buhle, *Women and American Socialism*, 1–145; Mary P. Ryan, *Cradle of the Middle Class: The Family in Oneida County New York, 1790–1865* (Cambridge: Cambridge University Press, 1981); and Carroll Smith-Rosenberg, *Disorderly Conduct: Visions of Gender in Victorian America* (New York: Alfred A. Knopf, 1985).

86. Kate Richards O'Hare, *Kate Richards O'Hare: Selected Writings and Speeches*, ed. Philip S. Foner and Sally M. Miller (Baton Rouge: Louisiana State University Press, 1982); and O'Hare, *The Sorrows of Cupid*.

87. The parade was led by children carrying a banner that read, "A Little Child Shall Lead Them," underscoring this point.

88. Flynn, *The Rebel Girl*, 293; and Vorse, *A Footnote to Folly*, 293–307.

89. Otto Branstetter, "The Children's Crusade: Supplemental Report on Amnesty Work by the National Executive Committee to National Convention," 20 January 1922, 1–9. Socialist Party of America Papers, Microfilm Edition, reel 9, University of California, Irvine, CA.

90. Ibid., 8.

91. Ibid.

92. Ibid., 9–10.

93. Sherman, "'This Is a Crusade!'," 24–41.

94. Hanley, "The Children's Crusade of 1922," 34–43.

95. Buhle, *Women and American Socialism*, 246–87.

96. Kate Richards O'Hare, "Idealist and Concubine," *Erie Truth*, 13 August 1921. Kate Richards O'Hare Papers, Microfilm Edition, reel 1, State Historical Society of Wisconsin, Madison, WI.

97. Richard Polenberg, *Fighting Faiths: The Abrams Case, The Supreme Court, and Free Speech* (New York: Penguin, 1987), 154–96.

98. Ibid.

99. Ibid., 126–32.

100. Lucy Robins, *War Shadows: A Documental Story of the Struggle for Amnesty* (New York: Central Labor Bodies Conference for the Release of Political Prisoners, 1922), 230–31.

101. Polenberg, *Fighting Faiths*, 127–31.

102. Smedley was a journalist who was increasingly interested in left-wing causes. She was indicted under the Espionage Act for her participation in the Indian independence movement. The American government outlawed that movement because it potentially embarrassed England, and because it suspected members of the movement received aid from Germany. Steimer met Smedley after they were both arrested for distributing birth control information. She later joined the Communist Party and moved to China. For more information on Smedley, see Joan Jensen, *Passage from India: Asian Immigration in North America* (New Haven: Yale University Press, 1988); and Janice Mackinnon and Stephen Mackinnon, *Agnes Smedley: The Life and Times of an American Radical* (Berkeley: University of California Press, 1988). Smedley's case is discussed in chapter 5.

103. Mollie Steimer to Agnes Smedley, no date. Elizabeth Gurley Flynn Papers, Microfilm Edition, reel 1, Wisconsin Historical Society, Madison, WI. Steimer wrote this letter after meeting a representative for the Workers Defense Union, most likely Elizabeth Gurley Flynn. Steimer's case is discussed further in chapter 5.

104. As Polenberg shows in his study, Steimer was the most stubborn of the four anarchists who were convicted in the Abrams case. She refused to agree to deportation despite the fact that deportation was her only hope for an early release from prison. Steimer eventually agreed not to oppose her deportation and after serving thirty months of a fifteen-year sentence was deported to the Soviet Union. Polenberg, *Fighting Faiths*, 326–28.

105. Buhle, *Women and American Socialism*, 257–84; and Walter Rideout, *The Radical Novel in the United States, 1900–1954* (Cambridge: Harvard University Press, 1956).

106. Kathy Peiss, "'Charity Girls' and City Pleasures: Historical Notes on Working-Class Sexuality, 1880–1920," in *Unequal Sisters: A Multicultural Reader in U.S. Women's History*, ed. Ellen Carol Dubois and Vicki L. Ruiz (New York: Routledge, 1990); and Christine Stansell, *City of Women: Sex and Class in New York 1789–1860* (Urbana: University of Illinois Press, 1987).

107. For discussions on anarchist approaches to marriage, see Falk, *Love, Anarchy, and Emma Goldman*; Margaret S. Marsh, *Anarchist Women, 1870–1920* (Philadelphia: Temple University Press, 1981); and Polenberg, *Fighting Faiths*, 126–32.

108. Paula Baker, "The Domestication of Politics: Women and American Political Society, 1780–1920," *American Historical Review* 89 (June 1984): 620–47; and Suzanne Lebsock, "Women and American Political Society," in *Women, Politics, and Change in Twentieth-Century America*, ed. Louise Tilly and Patricia Gurin (New York: Russell Sage Foundation, 1990).

3. Liberty with Strings

1. Emma Goldman to Agnes Inglis, 31 March 1917, 1–2, Emma Goldman Papers, Microfilm Edition, reel 57, University of California, Berkeley, CA.

2. Ibid.

3. In 1909, for example, after arresting Goldman for "conspiracy, making unlawful threats, using force and violence, and disturbing the public peace,"

federal authorities investigated the possibility of deportation. For information about her arrest, see Emma Goldman, *Living My Life,* vol. 1 (New York: Dover Publications Inc., 1970), 446.

4. Richard Drinnon, *Rebel in Paradise: A Biography of Emma Goldman* (Chicago: University of Chicago Press, 1961), 165–88; and Alice Wexler, *Emma Goldman: An Intimate Life* (New York: Pantheon Books, 1984), 87–172.

5. Ibid. See also Bonnie Baaland, *Emma Goldman: Sexuality and the Impurity of the State* (Montreal: Black Rose Books, 1993); Marian J. Motton, *Emma Goldman and the American Left: "Nowhere at Home"* (New York: Twayne, 1992); Alix Kates Shulman, "Dancing in the Revolution: Emma Goldman's Feminism," *Socialist Review* 12 (March-April 1982): 1–32; and David Waldstreicher, *Emma Goldman: Political Activist* (New York: Chelsea House Publishers, 1990). For an interesting discussion of how the memory of Emma Goldman has been reinvented over time, see Oz Frankel, "Whatever Happened to 'Red Emma'? Emma Goldman, from Alien Rebel to American Icon," *The Journal of American History* 83 (December 1996): 903–42.

6. Richard Gid Powers, *Secrecy and Power: The Life of J. Edgar Hoover* (New York: The Free Press, 1987), 81–91. Here Powers draws from the works of Stanley Coben and Emile Durkheim. See Stanley Coben, "A Study in Nativism: The American Red Scare of 1919–1920," *Political Science Quarterly* (March 1964): 52–75; and Emile Durkheim, *The Division of Labor in Society* (New York: The Free Press, 1964). Hoover was just beginning his career with the Justice Department when he wrote the department's brief in support of Goldman's deportation. According to Powers, Hoover used the deportation of Goldman as a springboard for his career in the Justice Department.

7. Powers, *Secrecy and Power,* 81–91.

8. Thomas McCarthy to Mr. Fitts, 29 May 1917, 3–4. Emma Goldman Papers, Microfilm Edition, reel 57, University of California, Berkeley, CA. See also W.M. Offley to A.B. Bielaski, 31 May 1917, 1–2. Emma Goldman Papers, Microfilm Edition, reel 57, University of California, Berkeley, CA. Offley wrote that "it begins to appear that the failure of the Government to act in the premises is being accepted either as an admission of weakness or as evidence of our inability to prevent a continuance of efforts." Offley, while speaking generally of anti-war activity, referred to Goldman as "the ring leader of this particular faction" and called for her immediate arrest.

9. "The No Conscription League," *Mother Earth* (June 1917): 113.

10. My reconstruction of these events comes from Drinnon, *Rebel in Paradise,* 184–200; Goldman, *Living My Life,* 609–14; and Wexler, *An Intimate Life,* 226–44.

11. Alexander Berkman immigrated to the United States from Russia in 1888 and met Goldman in 1889. Immediately upon his arrival in the United States he joined the anarchist movement. He was convicted of attempting to murder Henry Clay Frick, who managed a strike-ridden steel plant in Homestead, Pennsylvania. Berkman spent a year in jail. For more information on Berkman, see Wexler, *An Intimate Life,* 54–70.

12. Goldman, *Living My Life,* 611.

13. "Tattler," "Notes from the Capital: Emma Goldman," *Nation* CIV (28 June 1917); "Uncle Sam's Obstreperous Niece," *Literary Digest* LV (18 August 1917); "Emma Goldman and A. Berkman Behind the Bars," *New York Times,* 16 June 1917, 1, 10; and "Convict Berkman and Miss Goldman; Both Off to Prison," *New York Times,* 10 July 1917.

14. "Emma Goldman and A. Berkman Behind the Bars," 1.

15. Ibid., 2.

16. Ibid., 1. It is possible that Goldman intentionally chose to wear a purple dress, but Goldman claimed that she had no time to choose what she would

wear. For Goldman's description of this incident, see Goldman, *Living My Life*, 609–14.

17. Ibid.

18. See, "Emma Goldman and Alexander Berkman Behind the Bars," 1; and "Soldiers Face Riots in Seizing Slackers," *New York Times*, 16 June 1917, 10.

19. Ibid.

20. See "Emma Goldman and A. Berkman Behind the Bars," 1, 10.

21. Emma Goldman, "Speech Against Conscription, Forward Hall," 14 June 1917, #830214178, 11. For Goldman's version of this speech, see #840305204. Other copies of Goldman's speeches are: "Meeting of No-Conscription League," 4 June 1917; and "Speech [Against Conscription]," Harlem River Casino, New York, 18 May 1917. All of these documents are reprinted in the Emma Goldman Papers, Microfilm Edition, reel 57, University of California, Berkeley, CA.

22. *United States vs. Emma Goldman and Alexander Berkman* (July 9, 1917), 52–54. Emma Goldman Papers, Micofilm Edition, reel 58, University of California, Berkeley, CA.

23. Michael Rogin, *Ronald Reagan the Movie and Other Episodes in Political Demonology* (Berkeley: University of California Press, 1987), 67.

24. Ibid., xiii.

25. Carol F. Karlsen, *The Devil in the Shape of a Woman: Witchcraft in Colonial New England* (New York: Vintage Books, 1987), xii. As Rogin notes, "American countersubversion has taken its shape from the pervasiveness of . . . the definition of American identity against racial, ethnic, class, and gender aliens." Rogin, *Ronald Reagan the Movie*, xiv. Rogin argues that explanations of countersubversion must take gender into account.

26. Karlsen, *The Devil in the Shape of a Woman*, 118.

27. John Higham, *Strangers in the Land: Patterns of American Nativism, 1860–1925* (New York: Atheneum, [1953] 1969); and Rogin, *Ronald Reagan the Movie*.

28. "Emma Goldman and A. Berkman Behind the Bars," 1.

29. Ibid., 54.

30. I am using the definition of nonman suggested by Edwin Shenk in "'Work or Fight': Selective Service and Manhood in the Progressive Era" (Ph.D. diss., University of California, San Diego, 1992), 27. Shenk uses the following table to illustrate the differences between "manly" and "unmanly" characteristics:

MANLY	UNMANLY
agency	latency
powerful	powerless
volition	instinct, impulse
structure	chaos
organization	disorganization
self discipline	controlled by others
physical perfection	illness, crippled
balance	distortion
fairness	inequity

31. Goldman, *Living My Life*, 614. See also Goldman to Agnes Inglis, 10 July 1917. Emma Goldman Papers, Yale University, New Haven, CT; and "The Trial and Conviction of Emma Goldman and Alexander Berkman," *Mother Earth* XVII (July 1917): 150–67.

32. "The Trial and Conviction of Emma Goldman and Alexander Berkman," 150–67; and *United States vs. Emma Goldman and Alexander Berkman*.

33. Goldman, *Living My Life*, 598.

34. "The Trial and Conviction of Emma Goldman and Alexander Berkman," 150.

35. Ibid., 159.

36. Ibid., 153–54.

37. Ibid., 157–58.

38. "Convict Berkman and Miss Goldman; Both Off to Prison," 1.

39. "Uncle Sam's Obstreperous Niece," 55.

40. Goldman served from February 1918 to September 1919.

41. Implicated in the Mooney case—a pre-war case in which Tom Mooney was convicted of throwing a bomb into a San Francisco preparedness parade—Berkman fought extradition to California. Although he was never tried in the case, the threat of a murder charge lingered. This possibility further exhausted Goldman, who coordinated Berkman's defense while awaiting the outcome of their appeal. For information on Mooney's case, see Richard H. Frost, *The Mooney Case* (Palo Alto: Stanford University Press, 1968).

42. Constantine M. Panunzio, *The Deportation Cases of 1919–1920* (New York: Da Capo Press, 1970); and Louis F. Post, *The Deportation Delirium of Nineteen-Twenty: A Personal Narrative of an Historic Official Experience,* introduction by Moorfield Story (New York: Da Capo Press, 1970).

43. Frances Early, *War's Heretics: The Feminist Pacifists and Civil Libertarians of the Bureau of Legal Advice, 1917–1920* (Syracuse: Syracuse University Press, 1997); Post, *The Deportation Delirium of Nineteen Twenty.* As Powers points out, the immigration laws under which deportation fell protected the interests of the American government, thereby allowing the Justice Department to deport aliens for simply holding unpopular political beliefs. The government did not have to prove that such individuals acted against the government. Powers, *Secrecy and Power,* 69–76.

44. Powers, *Secrecy and Power,* 81. Powers argues that most of those who were deported were "faceless" members of organizations that the Justice Department defined as subversive. Many of those who were deported had never been convicted of a crime.

45. Ibid., 81.

46. This distinction was not necessary because under immigration law all alien anarchists were subject to deportation.

47. After her release from prison, Goldman toured the Midwest, denouncing the government's systematic violation of civil liberties and commenting on poor prison conditions. It was during this tour that her former friend Louis B. Post signed her deportation order.

48. "Deposition to the Court," U.S. Military Intelligence Reports, Microfilm Edition, reel 3, #10-110-154, National Archives, Washington, DC. Kershner had apparently misrepresented the number of years he had resided in the country when he applied for citizenship.

49. The principles of *feme covert* were outlined in Sir William Blackstone's *Commentaries,* published in 1765. According to Blackstone, "the very beginning or guide to the status of the woman is suspended during the course of marriage, or at least is incorporated and consolidated into that of the husband; under whose wing, protection, and cover she performs everything." The underlying premise of *feme covert* is noted in a state court ruling that justified coverture as "a civil disqualification at common law, arising from a want of free agency in the wife as much as from the want of judgement in an idiot." Both are quoted in Nancy Woloch, *Women and the American Experience: A Concise Edition* (New York: McGraw-Hill, 1996), 46. Although there are few studies on how coverture affected immigration law as late as 1915, the Supreme Court upheld its basic prin-

ciples when it ruled as constitutional an act of Congress that "any woman marrying a foreigner should take the nationality of her husband." The Court ruled that in upholding the constitutionality of the law it was maintaining an "ancient principle of [merging] the identity of husband and wife." See Edward S. Cowin, *The Constitution and What It Means*, 14th ed., revised by Harold W. Chase and Craig Ducet (Princeton: Princeton University Press, 1978), 89. For discussions of the status of women under immigration laws, see Candice Lewis Bredbenner, *A Nationality of Her Own: Women, Marriage, and the Law of Citizenship* (Berkeley: University of California Press, 1998); and Virginia Sapiro, "Women, Citizenship and Naturalization Policies in the United States,"*Politics and Society* 13 (1984): 1–26.

50. Post, *The Deportation Delirium of Nineteen-Twenty*, 12–16.

51. Drinnon, *Rebel in Paradise*; and Wexler, *Emma Goldman: An Intimate Life*.

52. Post, *The Deportation Delirium of Nineteen-Twenty*.

53. Harvey O'Connor, *Revolution in Seattle: A Memoir* (New York: Monthly Review Press, 1964).

54. Agent Wright to the Justice Department, 30 August 1917. U.S. Military Intelligence Reports, Microfilm Edition, reel 4, #10110-219, National Archives, Washington, DC.

55. See for example, "Women I.W.W. in Jail, 'Happy to Pay the Price,'" *Seattle Star*, 8 September 1917, 1. For information on Olivereau's case, see chapter 5.

56. It was not unusual for federal agents to invoke Goldman's name when they attempted to define the threat posed by individual women. See Report by Agent Martin, "Re Alexander Berkman, Rosa Spanier and Helen Boardman—Anarchist Matters," 14 August 1917, 2–4. Military Intelligence Reports, Microfilm Edition, reel 3, #10110-154, National Archives, Washington, DC. Martin notes that Spanier "worship[ped] Emma Goldman," although she denied that she was an anarchist.

57. For references to the Guillotine Club see, "Report from Allen Pinkerton," 10 December 1917, #85020525; H. Van Deman, Chief of Military Intelligence, to Major Nicholas Biddle, 13 December 1917, #8708125; A. Bruce Bielaski to Hintor C. Glabaugh, 29 December 1917, #880606023; Inspectors Brady and Cahill to Lieutenant W.C. Campbell, 11 January 1918, #810402046; Inspector Brady to Lieutenant Campbell, 13 January 1918, #60-810402048. All of these documents are in Department of Justice Papers, RG 165, National Archives, Washington, DC, and are reprinted in Emma Goldman Papers, Microfilm Edition, reel 60, University of California, Berkeley, CA. The members of the Guillotine Club were also referred to as the "Goldman Women."

58. Agents 101 and 102, "Report from L.A.," 2 January 1918, 1–2, #810402039. In Department of Justice Papers, RG 165, National Archives, Washington, DC. Reprinted in the Emma Goldman Papers, Microfilm Edition, reel 60, University of California, Berkeley, CA.

4. The Venom of a Bolshevik Woman

1. Jonathan Dembo, *Unions and Politics in Washington State, 1885–1935* (New York: Garland Publishers, 1983), 160–65; and Richard Gid Powers, *Not Without Honor: The History of American Anticommunism* (New York: The Free Press, 1996), 1–15.

2. Dembo, *Unions and Politics in Washington State*, 163.

3. James Weinstein, *The Decline of Socialism in America 1912–1925* (New York: Monthly Review Press, 1967), 119–289.

4. Kathleen Ann Sharp, "Rose Pastor Stokes: Radical Champion of the Ameri-

can Working Class, 1879–1933" (Ph.D. diss., Duke University, 1979); and Arthur Zipser and Pearl Zipser, *Fire and Grace: The Life of Rose Pastor Stokes* (Athens: The University of Georgia Press, 1989). Despite her national reputation as a socialist, Stokes, unlike O'Hare, did not assert herself as a leader in the American left until her wartime trial and conviction under the newly amended Espionage Act.

5. Mari Jo Buhle, *Women and American Socialism, 1870–1920* (Urbana: University of Illinois Press, 1981), 320.

6. Rose Pastor Stokes to Jessie Ashley, 16 June 1916. Papers of Rose Pastor Stokes, Tamiment Institute of Labor History, New York, NY. Newspapers quoted Stokes as saying that she had distributed information on birth control because she "wanted to do what Emma Goldman did." See *New York Herald,* 6 May 1916.

7. Jessie Ashley to Rose Pastor Stokes, 17 June 1916. Papers of Rose Pastor Stokes, Tamiment Institute of Labor History, New York, NY. Jessie Ashley joined the socialist movement in 1906. Ashley was especially active in the suffrage and birth control movements. She was a founder of the National Birth Control League of America and contributed to the *Birth Control Review.* Ashley died suddenly of pneumonia in 1919. See "Jessie Ashley: A Victim of Pneumonia," *New York Call,* 2 January 1919. For Goldman's reaction to Stokes's activity, see Zipser and Zipser, *Fire and Grace,* 137.

8. Anna Strunsky Walling noticed this change in Stokes as early as 1915. She wrote to her husband, William English Walling, "Rose—I wonder if she has changed or I had never known her—she appeared to me so self-conscious and without sufficient breadth in life, now I find her an experienced, understanding, subtle woman, quick to absorb and quick to give. She is very versatile with a great deal of abandon—quite a different person of the Rose I thought she was three years ago." Anna Strunsky Walling to William English Walling, 1915. Papers of William English Walling, State Historical Society, Wisconsin, Madison, WI.

9. Robert Dwight Reynolds Jr., "The Millionaire Socialists: J.G. Phelps Stokes and His Circle of Friends" (Ph.D. diss., University of South Carolina, 1974); Sharp, "Rose Pastor Stokes"; and Zipser, *Fire and Grace.* For a discussion of Stokes's marriage, see Patrick Renshaw, "Rose of the World: The Pastor-Stokes Marriage and the American Left, 1905–1925," *New York History* 62 (October 1981): 428–37.

10. Rose Pastor Stokes to Chairman of Executive Committee of Woman's Peace Party of New York, 17 March 1917, 1. Papers of Rose Pastor Stokes, Tamiment Institute of Labor History, New York, NY.

11. Rose Pastor Stokes, "A Confession," *Century Magazine* 95 (November 1917): 457.

12. The St. Louis Resolution is reprinted in Alexander Trachtenberg, ed., *The American Socialists and the War* (New York: Garland Publishing, [1917] 1973), 38–41. See also "Proceeding of the Emergency Convention of the Socialist Party of America," 1917. Papers of the Socialist Party of America, Microfilm Edition, reel 9, University of California, Irvine, CA. For discussions of how the St. Louis Resolution was received, see Michael E.R. Bassett, "The Socialist Party of America: Years of Decline" (Ph.D. diss., Duke University, 1963); Kathleen Kennedy, "'We Mourn for Liberty in America': Socialist Women, Anti-militarism, and State Repression, 1914–1922" (Ph.D. diss., University of California, Irvine, 1992), 72–82; and James Weinstein, *The Decline of Socialism in America, 1912–1925* (New York: Monthly Review Press, 1967).

13. Stokes, "A Confession," 457.

14. Ray Ginger, *The Bending Cross: A Biography of Eugene Victor Debs* (New Brunswick: Rutgers University Press, 1949), 346. Ginger discusses the friendship between Debs and Stokes and argues that their friendship survived the

divisions caused in part by the war because Debs understood her "sincerity and her unflagging devotion to the workers' welfare, he realized that her support of the war sprang from her belief that it was, in truth, a war for democracy."

15. Stokes explained her reasons for working for Hillquit's campaign in "Rose Stokes for Hillquit," *New York Call*, 1 November 1917. Stokes argued that among other reasons for supporting Hillquit and other socialist candidates was her dismay at the government's efforts to curb dissent. "The issue of freedom of speech, press and assemblage is also vitally involved in this campaign," Stokes explained, "I believe a certain amount of restraint in time of war to be imperative, but here, to my mind, the government has erred not on the liberal but on the reactionary side and I believe that Hillquit's election would serve as a corrective of that policy."

16. Rose Pastor Stokes Comes Back," *Living Men*, 2 (February 1918): 6–7.

17. "Speech Delivered by Rose Pastor Stokes at New Star Casino," 10 November 1918. Papers of Rose Pastor Stokes, Tamiment Institute of Labor History, New York, NY.

18. Reynolds, "Millionaire Socialists"; and Zipser and Zipser, *Fire and Grace*, 161–218.

19. WED Stokes to Charles Warren, 4 March 1918. Papers of the Department of Justice, RG 60, #9-19-1755, folder 2, National Archives, Washington, DC.

20. WED Stokes was still bitter over Stokes's support of a waiters' strike that affected one of his hotels. Rose Pastor Stokes's biographers suggest that the anti-Semitism of WED Stokes also played a role in his attacks. See Zipser and Zipser, *Fire and Grace*, 90–91.

21. United States Circuit Court of Appeals, Eighth Circuit, #5255, *Rose Pastor Stokes, Plaintiff in Error vs. United States of America, Defendant in Error to the District Court of the United States for the Western District of Missouri*, 70. Papers of Rose Pastor Stokes, box 9, folder 12, Yale University, New Haven, CT. Stokes's trial took place on May 22, 1918. A complete transcript of her trial is available at Yale University.

22. Ibid.

23. Ibid. The entire text of the letter Stokes wrote to the *Star* reads as follows:

> I see that it is, after all necessary to send a statement for publication over my own signature, and I trust that you will give it space in your columns.
> A headline in this evening's issue of the story reads: 'Mrs. Stokes for the Government and Against the War at the Same Time.' I am for the government. In the interview that follows I am quoted as having said that "I believe the government of the United States should have the unqualified support of every citizen in its war aims."
> I made no such statement, and I believe no such thing. No government which is for the profiteers can also be for the people. I am for the people, while the government is for the profiteers.
> I expect my working class point of view to receive no sympathy from your paper, but I do expect that the traditional courtesy of publication by newspapers of a signed statement of correction, which even our most bourbon papers grant, will be extended to this statement by yours.

Attorney General to President of the United States, 9 July 1918, 2. Papers of the Department of Justice, RG 60, 9-19-1755, folder 1, National Archives, Washington, DC.

24. For a sympathetic survey of Stokes's defense strategy, see "Defense Contends R.P. Stokes Is Loyal," *New York Call*, 22 May 1917; "Mrs. Stokes Tells of Early Life's Hardship," *New York Call*, 23 May 1918; and "Mrs. Stokes Case to Jury Today Is Belief," *New York Call*, 24 May 1918. Stokes continued to argue that although she said nothing disloyal and did not believe in opposing the war, she did oppose the Espionage Act. See Rose Pastor Stokes to Mrs. Colt, 6 July 1918. Rose Pastor Stokes Papers, Tamiment Institute of Labor History, New York, NY.

25. *Rose Pastor Stokes, Plaintiff in Error*, 35. Because the *Star* was distributed in military camps, prosecutors argued that draft-aged men had probably read Stokes's letter and were likely to have been influenced by it.

26. Ibid., 291.

27. For examples of these press reports, see "Divided on Rose Pastor Stokes," *Kansas City Times*, 28 March 1918; "Rose Pastor Stokes Turns Again," *Kansas City Star*, 17 March 1918; "Says Masses Will Revolt After War," *Kansas City Post*, 17 March 1918; and "Thinks War's End Is More Distant," *Kansas City Journal*, 17 March 1918. Rienke is quoted in the *Kansas City Times*. Of these reports, the *Kansas City Journal's* was the most positive and the *Kansas City Star's* was the most negative. These clippings are also available in the Papers of the Department of Justice, RG 60, #9-19-1755, folder 4, National Archives, Washington, DC. See also coverage by the *New York Times*, which claims that Stokes was "hissed by some and some in the audience walked out." The *Times* claimed that Stokes called the war a "capitalist war" and emphasized her return to socialism. *New York Times*, 18 March 1918.

28. Stokes's biographers note that Stokes received a letter from Annette Moore, chair of the Kansas City Woman's Club's Program Committee, that claimed that those members who had testified against Stokes were motivated by their dislike of Reinke and hoped to embarrass her by misconstruing Stokes's remarks. See Zipser and Zipser, *Fire and Grace*, 187.

29. Ibid., 160–65; and "Exhibits Submitted with Memorandum to the President as to Persons Imprisoned for Violating of War Laws by the NCLB," undated. Papers of the Department of Justice, RG 60, #197009-1, folder 1, National Archives, Washington, DC.

30. *Rose Pastor Stokes, Plaintiff in Error*, 352.

31. Ibid., 192.

32. Ibid., 232.

33. Ibid., 33; 291

34. Ibid., 35; 299.

35. See Committee for Florence Kimble, Post #7, American Legion, Libson, ND to Attorney General, Records of the Office of the Pardon Attorney, RG 104, #33-422, 1; and "Petition Directed by Lloyd Spetz, Post #1, American Legion, ND, Records of the Office of the Pardon Attorney, RG 104, #33-422, National Archives, Washington, DC.

36. *Rose Pastor Stokes, Plaintiff in Error*, 305.

37. This is not to say that prosecutors did not describe male defendants as individuals with the potential to infect the population with ideas bred from their personalities. But the process by which males did so was understood as a feminine process and their participation in this process was perceived as a perversion of their masculinity.

38. *Rose Pastor Stokes, Plaintiff in Error*, 35.

39. John R. Hutchinson, *Champions of Charity: War and the Rise of the Red Cross* (Boulder: Westview Press, 1996), 256.

40. Ibid., 256–57. As Hutchinson argues, "support for the Red Cross was seen as an instrument for ridding the nation of 'undesirable' influences."

41. Ibid., 352–54.

42. *Rose Pastor Stokes, Plaintiff in Error*, 34.

43. Ibid. In his appeal of her conviction, Stokes's lawyer, Seymour Stedman, argued that these remarks as well as those that directly accused Stokes of violating patriotic motherhood were particularly prejudicial.

44. Ibid, 308–22.

45. "Ten Years for Criticism," *Literary Digest* L (15 June 1918): 13.

46. Ibid. See also *New York Times*, 25 March 1918.

47. After Stokes's arrest, Graham Stokes released the following statement that clarified his disagreement with his wife: "Mrs. Stokes had emphasized the danger to the democratic movements of the times that lies in government interference with the free expression of their views by honest and high minded radicals. I share Mrs. Stokes's recognition of that danger, and yet I do recognize no less the danger to the democratic movement that lies in the utterances of honest, earnest, and high minded radicals." Letter to the Editor, *Kansas City Star*, 25 March 1918.

48. "Rose Pastor Stokes, Plaintiff in Error," 352.

49. Charlotte Perkins Gilman to Thomas Gregory, 9 June 1918, 1. Papers of the Department of Justice, RG 60, #9-19-1755, box 802, folder 1, National Archives, Washington, DC.

50. "Pippa," "Poverty and Brains Made a Socialist of Rose Pastor Stokes," *New York Call*, 26 May 1918. Anna Pastor was a teacher and labor organizer. The *New York Call*'s coverage of Stokes's trial was generally sympathetic and touted her return to socialism as evidence of the party's position that the war served the interests of the capitalist class.

51. For descriptions of Debs's defense of O'Hare and Stokes in his Canton, Ohio, speech and at his trial, see David Karsner, *Debs: His Authorized Life and Letters* (New York: Boni and Liveright, 1919), 37, 230–31. Stokes was dismayed by Debs's conviction and she attended his trial and offered support throughout. For her reaction to his indictment, see Rose Pastor Stokes to Comrade Jump, 4 June 1918. Papers of Rose Pastor Stokes, Tamiment Institute of Labor History, New York, NY.

52. Rose Pastor Stokes to Anna Strunsky Walling, no date. Papers of Anna Strunsky Walling, Microfilm Edition, reel 1, Yale University, New Haven, CT. See also Rose Pastor Stokes to Mrs. Alpha Loveall, 15 June 1918. Papers of Rose Pastor Stokes, Tamiment Labor Library, New York University, New York, NY. Stokes responded to Loveall's admonishment that she should be humiliated by her conviction with the following: "In these days, our fundamental liberties are taken from us, it seems that the only place for decent person is in prison. I am therefore not humiliated by my conviction and sentence. Indeed I feel I can do more for our lost liberties in prison, in these days, than out."

53. Rose Pastor Stokes, quoted in "Rose Pastor Stokes Dies at 54," *New York Sun*, 20 June 1933.

54. Rose Pastor Stokes to Helen Phelps, 7 June 1923. Papers of Rose Pastor Stokes, Tamiment Institute of Labor History, New York, NY.

55. For Stokes's feelings about Graham's family, see Rose Pastor Stokes to Comrade Drake, 14 October 1918. Papers of Rose Pastor Stokes, Tamiment Institute of Labor History, New York, NY.

56. Part of the letter is reprinted in "Rose Pastor Stokes Tells History of Conviction," *New York Call*, 11 July 1918, 1.

57. "R.P. Stokes Denounces Enemies of Freedom," *New York Call*, 2 August 1918, 2.

58. Ibid.

59. "Memo for Attorney General," 22 September 1920, 1–2. Papers of the Department of Justice, RG 60, box 802, #9-19-1755-58, folder 1, National Archives, Washington, DC.

60. English, Assistant District Attorney to R.P. Stewart, 21 April 1921, 1–2. Papers of the Department of Justice, RG 60, #9-19-1755-66, box 805, folder 1, National Archives, Washington, DC.

61. Mr. O'Brian to Solicitor General, 19 May 1919, 1. Papers of the Department of Justice, RG 60, #9-16-603, box 802, folder 1, National Archives, Washington, DC.

62. F. Guyon to J. Spellancy, Assistant Attorney General, 27 December 1919; 24 January 1920; and 12 November 1919, 1. Papers of the Department of Justice, RG 60, #9-16-603, box 802, folder 1, National Archives, Washington, DC.

63. Stokes, "A Confession," 457.

64. Buhle, *Women and American Socialism*, 320.

65. Michael Rogin, *Ronald Reagan the Movie and Other Episodes in Political Demonology* (Berkeley: University of California, 1987), 81–114. Rogin discusses, albeit implicitly, the link between Wilson's perception of himself as "the spiritual body of the nation" and his policies, especially his crusade for international liberalism. The Sedition Act formalized this link because it conflated criticism of Wilson's policies with disloyalty.

66. Robert K. Murray, *Red Scare: A Study in National Hysteria* (New York: McGraw Hill Book Co., 1955).

5. Disorderly Conduct

1. Harvey O'Connor, *Revolution in Seattle: A Memoir* (New York: Monthly Review Press, 1964), 97. For information on O'Connor, see Jessie Lloyd O'Connor, Harvey O'Connor, and Susan M. Bowler, *Harvey and Jessie: A Couple of Radicals* (Philadelphia: Temple University Press, 1988).

2. O'Connor, *Revolution in Seattle*, 98–123.

3. Sadler avoided Socialist Party politics because of her disdain for fundraising. She did, however, represent the state of Washington at the St. Louis Convention and served on the committee that wrote the St. Louis Resolution. She voted against the majority resolution because it did not oppose defensive wars. Instead, Sadler supported a resolution written by Louis Boudin that uniformly condemned war. During the war, Sadler helped organize Seattle's branch of the People's Council and served on Thomas Mooney's defense committee. She later joined the Communist Party. "Proceedings of the Emergency Convention of the Socialist Party of America," St. Louis, 1917. Papers of the Socialist Party of American, Microfilm Edition, reel 9. For Sadler's connection to the Communist Party, see Lena Morrow Lewis to Bertha Hale White, 10 November 1921. Socialist Party of America Papers, Microfilm Edition, reel 9, University of California, Irvine.

4. Paul Avrich, *The Haymarket Tragedy* (Princeton: Princeton University Press, 1984); and Bruce Nelson, *Beyond the Martyrs: A Social History of Chicago's Anarchist Movement, 1890–1900* (New Brunswick: Rutgers University Press, 1989). The Haymarket riot occurred when police attempted to disrupt an anarchist rally in 1884. A bomb was thrown into the crowd that killed several police officers. Although the identity of the bomb thrower remains unknown, several anarchist leaders were executed for the crime. Along with the assassination of President McKinley, this event triggered a wave of state repression against anarchist and radical speech.

5. Agent Wright to the Justice Department, 30 August 1917. U.S. Military Intelligence Reports, Microfilm Edition, #10110-19, reel 1, National Archives, Washington, DC.

6. Ibid, 7.

7. Skid Road was an old logging road that developed into an important meeting place for Seattle's working class. For a discussion of the importance of Skid Road in the history of Seattle, see Murray Morgan, *Skid Road: An Informal Portrait of Seattle* (New York: Viking Press, 1951).

8. The modern school movement was based on the ideas of Spanish anar-

chist Francisco Ferrer. Proponents argued that children learned best in an un-structured environment that contrasted with the highly disciplined structure of early-twentieth-century schools. Olivereau assisted William Thurston Brown, who set up a modern school in Portland, Oregon. Paul Avrich, *The Modern School Movement: Anarchism and Education in the United States* (Princeton: Princeton University Press, 1980), 362.

9. Sarah E. Sharbach, "Louise Olivereau and the Seattle Radical Commu-nity" (Master's thesis, University of Washington, 1986).

10. Albert Gunns, *Civil Liberties in Crisis: The Pacific Northwest, 1917–1940* (New York: Garland Publishing, 1983), 27.

11. For information about Root, see Samuel Flagg Bemis, *The American Secre-tary of State and Their Diplomacy* (New York: Cooper Square, 1963); Philip C. Jes-sup, *Elihu Root* (New York: Dodd, Mead & Co., 1938); and Richard William Leo-pold, *Elihu Root and the Conservative Tradition* (Boston: Little Brown, 1954).

12. Sharbuck, "Louise Olivereau."

13. Wilson, quoted in Sharbach, "Louise Olivereau," 24. For more informa-tion on the activity of loyalty leagues in Seattle, see Jonathan Dembo, *Unions and Politics in Washington State, 1885–1935* (New York: Garland, 1983), 145–65. The Northwest was the focus of American shipbuilding during the war. In 1917, strikes in the Seattle shipyards and in the logging industry jeopardized wartime shipbuilding. The war department sent Colonial Brice P. Disque to help solve these labor disputes. He brokered a settlement that included the American Federation of Labor, company management, and the army. His solu-tion, Dembo argues, effectively destroyed IWW influence in the lumber industry. However, rumors persisted that these strikes were connected to the Bolshevik Revolution.

14. Gunns, *Civil Liberties in Crisis*, 4.

15. Robert Z. Tyler, *Rebels of the Woods: The I.W.W. in the Pacific Northwest* (Eu-gene: University of Oregon Press, 1967), 116–54. See also Melvyn Dubofsky, *We Shall Be All: A History of the Industrial Workers of the World*, 2nd ed. (Urbana: Univer-sity of Illinois Press, 1988); and Patrick Renshaw, "The I.W.W. and the Red Scare, 1917–1924," *Journal of Contemporary History* 3 (1968): 63–72. Many of these raids were conducted to find evidence for the trial of IWW members in Chicago.

16. Louise Olivereau quoted in Jessie Lloyd, "One Woman's Resistance," in *Revolution in Seattle: A Memoir*, by Harvey O'Connor (New York: Monthly Re-view Press, 1964), 249–50.

17. "Allen Arrests Anti-Drafter," *Seattle Star*, 7 September 1917, 1.

18. Alfred Bettman, "Supplemental Memorandum to Mr. O'Brien: U.S. vs. Louise Olivereau," 28 April 1919, 1. Records of the Office of the Pardon Attorney, RG 104, #33-422, folder 5, National Archives, Washington, DC.

19. Theodore Roosevelt, *The Works of Theodore Roosevelt*, vol. 19 (New York: Charles Scribner's Sons, 1926), 200–201.

20. See for example, "Woman Tells U.S. Jury She Is Anarchist," *Seattle Post Intelligencer*, 29 November 1917, 1.

21. "Women I.W.W. In Jail: 'Happy to Pay the Price,'" *Seattle Star*, 8 September 1917, 3; and *Seattle Times*, 30 November 1917.

22. Presiding Judge Jeremiah Neterer refused to allow Olivereau to question potential jurors about their prejudices against anarchism. Neterer dismissed Olivereau's questions as either "immaterial" or "not an issue." Sharbach, "Louise Olivereau," 54.

23. Louise Olivereau, quoted in Minnie Parkhurst, *The Louise Olivereau Case Trial and Speech to Jury in Federal Court of Seattle Washington, November, 1917* (Se-attle: Parkhurst Press, 1917), 21.

24. Ibid.

25. Robert L. Friedheim, *The Seattle General Strike* (Seattle: University of Washington Press, 1964), 10.

26. Parkhurst, *The Louise Olivereau Case*, 48.

27. Frances Early, *War's Heretics: The Feminist Pacifists and Civil Libertarians of the Bureau of Legal Advice, 1917–1920* (Syracuse: Syracuse University Press, 1997). See also Gerald Edwin Shenk, "'Work or Fight': Selective Service and Manhood in the Progressive Era" (Ph.D. diss., University of California, San Diego, 1992).

28. Wood's comments are reprinted in Sharbuck, "Louise Olivereau," 62. For more information about Wood, see Albert Gunns, *Civil Liberties in the Northwest*, 36–40. Wood represented Dr. Marie Equi during her appeal.

29. "Louise Olivereau Speech Before Jury," *The Seattle Daily Call*, 4 December 1917, 4.

30. Ibid., 4.

31. Ibid., 4.

32. A copy of Olivereau's trial transcript is in the Minnie Parkhurst Papers, boxes 2 and 3. University of Washington, Seattle, WA. The quote is from pages 135–37.

33. Ibid., 141.

34. Lloyd, "One Woman's Resistance," 250.

35. "Woman Anarchist Quickly Convicted for Attack on Military Draft Statute," *Seattle Post Intelligencer*, 1 December 1917, 1.

36. Ibid.

37. "Woman Anarchist Quickly Convicted," 1.

38. Ibid., 1.

39. Strong was the subject of a recall campaign initiated by the Minute Men, who objected to her associations with the labor movement. Her case will be further discussed in the next chapter. For information on Strong, see Bryce E. Nelson, *Good Schools: The Seattle Public School System, 1901–1930* (Seattle: University of Washington Press, 1988); Anna Louise Strong, *I Change Worlds: The Remaking of An American* (New York: Henry Holt and Company, 1935); and Tracy B. Strong, *Right in Her Soul: The Life of Anna Louise Strong* (New York: Random House, 1983).

40. Strong, *I Change Worlds*, 64.

41. "Miss Olivereau Confesses Guilt," *Seattle Daily Call*, 8 September 1917, 1.

42. Louise Olivereau, "Letter to the Editor," *Seattle Daily Call*, 15 September 1917, 3.

43. Emma Goldman to Ellen Kennan, 21 December 1917, Emma Goldman Papers, Microfilm Edition, reel 57, University of California, Berkeley, CA.

44. Louise Olivereau, quoted in "One Woman's Resistance," 252.

45. Sharbuck, "Louise Olivereau," 60.

46. Parkhurst's papers contain several letters from Olivereau. See also Gunns, *Civil Liberties in Crisis*, 27.

47. Parkhurst, *The Louise Olivereau Case*, 30.

48. The birth control movement was not the only civil rights movement that directly implicated issues of gender. Most significantly, the anti-lynching campaign of Ida B. Wells linked gender and sexuality to civil rights and civil liberties issues. For further information on Wells's activities, see Gail Bederman, *Manliness and Civilization: Cultural History of Gender and Race in the United States, 1880–1917* (Chicago: University of Chicago Press, 1995); Early, *War's Heretics*; and Jacqueline Jones Royster, *Southern Horrors and Other Writings: The Anti-lynching Campaigns of Ida B. Wells, 1892–1900* (New York: Bedford, 1997), 1–46.

49. Lloyd, "One Woman's Resistance," 248.

50. O'Connor, *Revolution in Seattle*, 99.

51. Strong, *I Change Worlds*, 63–64.

52. *Industrial Worker*, 8 December 1917. See also, Friedheim, *The Seattle General Strike*, 10. In Friedheim's words, the leadership of the IWW "were indignant that anyone would think that they would trust an emotional, irresponsible girl in such an important undertaking" as distributing anti-conscription flyers.

53. Sharbuck, "Louise Olivereau," 65–67.

54. Ibid., 260.

55. Ibid., 129.

56. Ibid., 147–49.

57. Ibid., 58.

58. Margaret Marsh, *Anarchist Women, 1870–1920* (Philadelphia: Temple University Press, 1981). Steimer immigrated from the Ukraine in 1912 and became involved in anarchism through her interactions with radical youth groups.

59. Michael Les Benedict, *The Blessing of Liberty: A Concise History of the Constitution of the United States* (Lexington: D.C. Heath, 1996), 265; and Richard Polenberg, *Fighting Faiths: The Abrams Case, the Supreme Court, and Free Speech* (New York: Penguin Books, 1987), 197–242.

60. Polenberg, *Fighting Faiths*, 125.

61. Ibid., 43–53. Press reports buttressed the Justice Department's case by linking the distribution of the pamphlets with a disturbance in New York's predominantly immigrant east side that had occurred on the night after the distribution of the pamphlets. There was no direct link between the pamphlets and the disturbance; the disturbance was caused by the cancellation of a scheduled meeting of the Socialist Party. As in Goldman's case, these reports had the effect of associating the pamphlet's distribution with social disorder whether or not federal authorities ever claimed that the pamphlets had caused that disorder. This link between the pamphlets and social disorder was only strengthened by the fact that the defendants were self-identified anarchists and Jewish immigrants.

62. Ibid., 82–117.

63. The Supreme Court focused on the call of the defendants for a general strike, noting that if the strike occurred it would hurt the war effort. Benedict, *The Blessing of Liberty*, 265.

64. Polenberg, *Fighting Faiths*, 118–19.

65. Ibid., 118–25.

66. Steimer, quoted in "Sentenced to Twenty Years in Prison," undated pamphlet, Political Prisoner Defense and Relief Committee, 21. Papers of the Department of Justice, RG 65, #362977, National Archives, Washington, DC. This pamphlet reprinted Clayton's questioning of Steimer.

67. Polenberg, *Fighting Faiths*, 118–25.

68. For studies on masculinity, see Ava Baron, ed., *Work Engendered: Toward a New History of American Labor* (Ithaca: Cornell University Press, 1991); Bederman, *Masculinity and Civilization*; Shenk, "'Work or Fight': Selective Service and Manhood in the Progressive Era."

69. Polenberg, *Fighting Faiths*, 131.

70. Ibid., 126–32.

71. B. Faulhaer, "American Anarchist Federated Commune and Mollie Steimer: Memo to Justice Department," 30 September 1919, 1. Papers of the Department of Justice, RG 65, #362977, National Archives, Washington, DC.

72. D.J. Scully, "Mollie Stiner [*sic*]: Bolshevik Activities: Memo to Justice Department," 25 September 1919, 1–2. Papers of the Department of Justice, RG 65, #362977, National Archives, Washington, DC.

73. Ibid., 130.

74. Michael Hunt, *Ideology and U.S. Foreign Policy* (New Haven: Yale University Press, 1987), 116. For information on the American response to the Russian Civil War, see David Fogleson, *America's Secret War Against Bolshevism: U.S. Intervention in the Russian Civil War, 1917–1920* (Chapel Hill: University of North Carolina Press, 1998).

75. John Preston quoted in Joan M. Jensen, *Passage from India: Asian Indian Immigrants in North America* (New Haven: Yale University Press, 1988), 224.

76. Jensen, *Passage from India*, 196–225.

77. Ibid., 226–45.

78. Jensen, *Passage from India*, 196–245; and Janice R. MacKinnon and Stephen R. MacKinnon, *Agnes Smedley: The Life and Times of an American Radical* (Berkeley: University of California Press, 1988), 31–68.

79. Jensen, *Passage from India*, 232–36. The People's Council was an organization of pacifists and socialists that attempted to organize labor in opposition to the war and the Wilson administration's attack on civil liberties. The Justice Department believed that the People's Council violated the Espionage Act and treated membership in the People's Council as evidence of disloyalty. Harriet Hyman Alonso, "Gender and Peace Politics in the First World War: The People's Council of America," *International History Review* XIX (February 1997): 83–104; and Ronald Marchard, *The American Peace Movement and Social Reform* (Princeton: Princeton University Press, 1972).

80. Ronald Gottesman, "Agnes Smedley," in *Notable American Women, 1607–1950: A Biographical Dictionary*, vol. III, ed. Edward T. James, Janet Wilson James, and Paul S. Boyer (Cambridge: Harvard University Press), 300–302; and Mark Seldon, "Agnes Smedley," in *Encyclopedia of the American Left*, ed. Mari Jo Buhle and Paul Buhle (New York: Garland, 1990), 705–706.

81. MacKinnon and MacKinnon, *Agnes Smedley*, 31–50.

82. Jensen, *Passage from India*, 196–225; and MacKinnon and MacKinnon, *Agnes Smedley*, 31–52.

83. MacKinnon and MacKinnon, *Agnes Smedley*, 31–52; and John Preston, "Indian Nationalist Party Case: Violation of Espionage Act," 11. Papers of the Department of Justice, RG 60, #193421, sec. 1, folder 2, National Archives, Washington, DC.

84. Supreme Court of the United States, *Agnes Smedley and Sallenanath Ghose vs. Thomas D. MacCarthy, U.S. Marshal in the Southern District of New York, Appeal for the U.S. District Court For the Southern District of New York* (October 1918), 1–3. Papers of the Department of Justice, RG 60, #193424, folder 1, National Archives, Washington, DC.

85. MacKinnon and Mackinnon, *Agnes Smedley*, 31–52.

86. Jensen, *Passage from India*, 196–245; and MacKinnon and MacKinnon, *Agnes Smedley*, 31–52.

87. "Memorandum to the Office of Solicitor General," 5 December 1918. Papers of the Department of Justice, RG 60, #193421, sec. 1, folder 1, National Archives, Washington, DC.

88. MacKinnon and MacKinnon, 31–52, 60–61; Agnes Smedley, *Daughter of Earth* (New York: The Feminist Press, [1929] 1986), 302–400.

89. Preston, "Indian Nationalist Party Case," 17–18.

90. John Preston to Attorney General Thomas Gregory, 3 September 1918, 9. Papers of the Department of Justice, RG 60, #193421, folder 2. See also telegram from Preston, John Preston to Thomas Gregory, 5 November 1918. Papers of the Department of Justice, RG 60, #193424, sec. 1, folder 1, National Archives, Washington, DC.

91. Alonso, "Gender and Peace Politics in the First World War," 83–104.

92. John Preston to Attorney General, Thomas Gregory, 27 March 1919, 1. Pa-

pers of the Department of Justice, RG 60, #193424-49, sec. 2, folder 1, National Archives, Washington, DC.

93. Alex C. King to the Attorney General, 16 October 1919, 5. Papers of the Department of Justice, RG 60, #193424, sec. 2, folder 1, National Archives, Washington, DC.; and O'Brien to Mr. Brown, 10 October 1918. Papers of the Department of Justice, RG 60, #193424, sec. 1, folder 1, National Archives, Washington, DC.

94. Larve Boucu to Attorney General, 25 October 1918, 1–2. Papers of the Department of Justice, RG 60, #193424-321/2, sec. 1, folder 1, National Archives, Washington, DC.

6. "Conduct Unbecoming"

1. Bryce T. Nelson, *Good Schools: The Seattle Public School System, 1901–1930* (Seattle: University of Washington Press), 1988.

2. Glenda Choat, "Anna Louise Strong: From Progressive to Radical" (Master's thesis, Western Washington State College, 1977); Stephanie Ogle, "Anna Louise Strong: The Seattle Years" (Master's thesis, Seattle University, 1973); Anna Louise Strong, *I Change Worlds: The Remaking of An American* (New York: Henry Holt and Company, 1935); and Tracy B. Strong, *Right in Her Soul: The Life of Anna Louise Strong* (New York: Random House, 1983).

3. Nelson, *Good Schools*, 13–14.

4. Choat, "Anna Louise Strong," 29–32.

5. Strong, *I Change Worlds*, 64.

6. *Seattle Times*, 28 November 1917.

7. Strong, *I Change Worlds*, 64.

8. Ibid.

9. Keith Murray, "The Charles Neiderhauser Case: Patriotism in the Seattle Schools, 1919," *Pacific Northwest Quarterly* 74 (January 1983): 11–17; and Nelson, *Good Schools*.

10. Robyn Muncy, *Creating A Female Dominion in American Reform, 1890–1935* (New York: Oxford University Press, 1991). See Joyce Antler, *The Educated Woman and Professionalization: The Struggle for a New Feminine Identity, 1890–1920* (New Haven: Yale University Press, 1987); Ellen Fitzpatrick, *Endless Crusade: Women Social Scientists and Progressive Reform* (New York: Oxford University Press, 1990); Regina Morantz-Sanchez, *Sympathy and Science: Women Physicians in American Medicine* (New York: Oxford University Press, 1985); Rosalind Rosenberg, *Beyond Separate Spheres: Intellectual Roots of Modern Feminism* (New Haven: Yale University Press, 1982); and Judith A. Trolander, *Professionalism and Social Change: From Settlement House Movement to Neighborhood Centers, 1886 to the Present* (New York: Columbia University Press, 1987).

11. Nelson, *Good Schools*, 13. Nelson notes that fourteen women ran for the school board between 1900 and 1917 and only Strong was elected.

12. See, for example, Theodore Roosevelt, "Is the Women's Peace Movement 'Silly and Base'?" *Literary Digest* 50 (1 May 1915): 1022; and "The Sum of All Villainies," *New Republic* (13 February 1915): 37.

13. Muncy also suggests that the super-patriotism of the 1920s adversely affected the female dominion because conservative critics linked women's welfare work to socialism. See Muncy, *Creating the Female Dominion*, 124–57.

14. Ibid., 93–123.

15. Fitzpatrick, *Endless Crusade*.

16. Molly Ladd-Taylor, *Mother-Work: Women, Child Welfare, and the State, 1890–1930* (Urbana: University of Illinois Press, 1994). As Ladd-Taylor argues, ideas

about what motherhood should be were increasingly informed by professional and scientific standards during this time.

17. In "The District Court of the United States, For the Northern District of Illinois, Eastern Division" (June 1918). Socialist Party of America Papers, Microfilm Edition, reel 7, University of California, Irvine, CA; and "First Chicago Woman Is Held For Sedition," *Chicago News*, 6 June 1918.

18. "The District Court of the United States," 1, 5.

19. Ibid., 5.

20. "First Chicago Woman is Held For Sedition," 1.

21. See, for example, Sandra M. Gilbert, "Soldier's Heart: Literary Men, Literary Women, and the Great War," *Signs* 8 (Summer 1988): 422–50; and John F. Hutchinson, *Champions of Charity: War and the Rise of the Red Cross* (Denver, CO: Westview Press, 1996).

22. "The District of the United States," 1–8.

23. For information on Landis's role in wartime cases, see H.C. Peterson and Gilbert C. Fite, *Opponents of War, 1917–1918* (Seattle: University of Washington Press, 1957), 28–29, 118–19, and 237–40.

24. In *District Court of the United States For the Northern District of Illinois, Eastern Division, United States of America vs. Ruth Lighthall* (November 1918). Socialist Party of America Papers, Microfilm Edition, reel 7, University of California, Irvine, CA; and "Ruth Insists She Is Going to Talk All She Wants," *Tulsa Democrat*, 23 June 1918.

25. Ibid.

26. Michael Rogin, *Ronald Reagan the Movie and Other Episodes in Political Demonology* (Berkeley: University of California Press, 1987), 59. Lighthall's indictment is a good example of Rogin's argument that countersubversion transformed "potentially political discontent into problems of personal life."

27. Unsigned to Theodore Lunde, 11 January 1919, 1. Socialist Party of America Papers, Microfilm Edition, reel 8, University of California, Irvine, CA.

28. Lighthall to Seymour Stedman, 22 January 1919, 1. Socialist Party of America Papers, Microfilm Editon, reel 8, University of California, Irvine, CA.

29. Ibid., 2.

30. Unsigned to Lighthall, 31 January 1919, 1. Socialist Party of America Papers, Microfilm Edition, reel 9, University of California, Irvine, CA.

31. Nancy Krieger, "Queen of the Bolsheviks: The Hidden History of Dr. Marie Equi," *Radical America* 17 (1983): 55–73; and Robert L. Tyler, *Rebels of the Woods: The I.W.W. in the Pacific Northwest* (Eugene: University of Oregon, 1967), 139–41. For other discussions of Equi, see Helen Camp, *Iron in Her Soul: Elizabeth Gurley Flynn and the American Left* (Pullman: Washington State University Press, 1995); and Elizabeth Gurley Flynn, *The Rebel Girl: An Autobiography* (New York: International Publishers, 1955), 252.

32. Krieger, "Queen of the Bolsheviks," 55–73; and Tyler, *Rebels of the Woods*, 139–41.

33. Ibid.

34. Carroll Smith-Rosenberg, *Disorderly Conduct: Visions of Gender in Nineteenth Century America* (New Haven: Yale University Press, 1985), 217–96.

35. Krieger, "Queen of the Bolsheviks"; and Tyler, *Rebels of the Woods*.

36. "Dr. Equi in Tears on the Stand," *Oregon Journal*, 19 November 1918, 14.

37. Dr. Equi Is Guilty of Disloyalty," *Oregon Journal*, 21 November 1918, 1.

38. Ibid., 2.

39. Ibid.

40. Ibid.

41. Nelson, *Good Schools*; and Peterson and Fite, *Opponents of War, 1917–1918*, 102–12.

42. Alexander Trachtenberg, ed., *The American Labor Year Book 1919–1920* (New York: The Rand School, 1920), 89.

43. For a survey of these laws, see Howard K. Beale, *Are American Teachers Free? An Analysis of Restraints upon the Freedom of Teaching in American Schools* (New York: Octagon Books, 1972), 22–40; and Bessie Louise Pierce, *Public Opinion and the Teaching of History in the United States* (New York: Alfred A. Knopf, 1926). The *New York Call* referred to these laws as the "bloody five." Meta Stern Lilienthal, "The Militarist Laws from the Mother's Point of View," *New York Call*, 27 May 1916. For a survey of the political battles within New York City's schools that does not, however, discuss the issue of loyalty, see Diane Ravitch, *The Great School Wars: New York City, 1805–1973, A History of the Public Schools as Battlefield of Social Change* (New York: Basic Books, Inc., 1974). For cases of those New York teachers accused of disloyalty, see New York Bureau of Legal First Aid, *Scrapbook*, 1917, Newspaper Clippings, box 3. Tamiment Institute of Labor History, New York, NY; and Charles Howlett, "Quaker Conscience in the Classroom: The Mary S. McDowell Case," *Quaker History* 83 (Fall 1994): 99–115.

44. Michael C. C. Addams, *The Great Adventure: Male Desire and the Coming of World War I* (Bloomington: Indiana University Press, 1992); Gail Bederman, *Manliness & Civilization: A Cultural History of Gender and Race in the United States, 1880–1917* (Chicago: University of Chicago Press, 1995); Joe L. Dubbert, *A Man's Place: Masculinity in Transition* (Englewood Cliffs, NJ: Prentice Hall, 1979); Peter Filene, "In Time of War" in *The American Male*, ed. Elizabeth Pleck and Joseph Pleck (Englewood Cliffs, NJ: Prentice Hall, 1980); Kathleen Kennedy, "'We Mourn for Liberty in America': Socialist Women, Anti-militarism, and State Repression, 1914–1922" (Ph.D. diss., University of California, Irvine, 1992); Gerald Edwin Shenk, "'Work or Fight': Selective Service and Manhood in the Progressive Era" (Ph.D. diss., University of California, San Diego, 1992); and Arnaldo Testi, "The Gender of Reform Politics: Theodore Roosevelt and the Culture of Masculinity," *The Journal of American History* 81 (March 1995): 1509–33.

45. Lewis Todd, *Wartime Relations of the Federal Government and the Public Schools, 1917–1918* (New York: Arno Press, 1971), 197–220.

46. Ibid.

47. For further discussion of Foreman's case, see Beale, *Are American Teachers Free?*, 25; James Green, "The 'Salesman-Soldiers' of the 'Appeal Army': A Profile of Rank and File Socialist Agitators," in *Socialism and the Cities*, ed. Bruce M. Stave (Port Washington, NY: Kennikat Press, 1975), 17; Flynn, *The Rebel Girl: An Autobiography*, 251; and Flora Foreman to *The Liberator*, 20 November 1918. New York Bureau of Legal First Aid, *Scrapbook*, Clippings. Tamiment Institute of Labor History, New York, NY. Foreman's prison letters are in the Papers of the Socialist Party of America.

48. "German Teacher on Trial For Disloyalty," *New York Times*, 18 May 1918, 13.

49. A.E. Palmer, "Summary of Charges," 24 April 1918. Papers of the New York Bureau of Legal First Aid, box 5, Tamiment Institute of Labor History, New York, NY. See also Preston and Fite, *Opponents of War*, 110.

50. Charles Recht, "To Chairmen and Members of the Bureau of Legal Advice." Papers of the New York Bureau of Legal First Aid, box 1, Tamiment Institute of Labor History, New York, NY.

51. Palmer, "Summary of Charges"; "Pippa," "Cited Teacher Says She Never Discussed the War," *New York Call*, 2 April 1918; and "Draft of a Pamphlet for Pignol Case." Papers of the New York Bureau of Legal First Aid, box 5, Tamiment Institute of Labor History, New York, NY.

52. Palmer, "Summary of Charges," 3.

53. Charles Recht, "Department of Education City of New York. In the Matter of Charges Preferred by John L. Tildsley Against Gertrude A.M. Pignol, "A Teacher

Respondent."Papers of the New York Bureau of Legal First Aid, box 5, Tamiment Institute of Labor History, New York, NY.

54. Charles Recht, "To Chairman and Members of the Bureau of Legal Advice." New York Bureau of Legal First Aid Papers, box 5, Tamiment Institute of Labor History, New York, NY.

55. Recht may have been paraphrasing John H. Finley, State Commissioner of Education, who in an address to the State Teachers Association, stated that "the same degree of loyalty is asked of the teacher as of the soldier. If he cannot give that, his place is not in the public school." John H. Finley, quoted in Charles Howlett, "Quaker Conscience in the Classroom," 109.

56. "Pippa," "Cited Teacher Says She Never Discussed War," 1.

57. Charles Recht, quoted in "New York Bureau of Legal Advice Year Book, 1918," 6. Papers of Frances Witherspoon and Tracy Mygatt, box 10, Swarthmore Peace Collection, Swarthmore, PA.

58. Ibid.

59. For information on McDowell's case, see Beale, *Are American Teachers Free?* 28–29; Howlett, "Quaker Conscience in the Classroom," 99–115; and "Quaker Teacher Is Put on Trial Before Board for Her Pacifist Views," *New York Call*, 16 May 1918, 1, 3.

60. Beale, *Are American Teachers Free?*, 29; and Howlett, "Quaker Conscience in the Classroom," 106.

61. Howlett, "Quaker Conscience in the Classroom," 107.

62. *McDowell v. Board of Education*, quoted in Howlett, "Quaker Conscience in the Classroom," 109.

63. *New York Times*, 14 June 1923.

64. Howlett, "Quaker Conscience in the Classroom," 110.

65. Hughan's books include, Jessie Wallace Hughan, *American Socialism of the Present Day* (New York: John Lane, 1911); Jessie Wallace Hughan, *A Study of International Government* (New York: Thomas & Crowell Co., 1923); and Jessie Wallace Hughan, *What Is Socialism?* (New York: Vanguard Press, 1928).

66. Frances Early, "Revolutionary Pacifism and War Resistance: Jessie Wallace Hughan's 'War Against War,'" *Peace and Change* 30 (July 1995): 307–28; "Jessie Wallace Hughan, 1875–1955," unpublished biography. Jessie Wallace Hughan Papers, Swarthmore College Peace Collection, Swarthmore, PA; and Kennedy, "'We Mourn for Liberty in America,'" 155–58.

67. Jessie Wallace Hughan, "The Logic of Pacifism," *Intercollegiant Socialist Society* (October-November, 1916): 11.

68. Jessie Wallace Hughan, "War Against War," *New Review* (15 August 1915): 188.

69. Ibid.

70. "Another Dove for Peace," *New York World*, June 1915, 1.

71. Clipping, *Tribune*, 26 March 1917. Helen Summer Woodbury Papers, box 9, folder 7, State Historical Society of Wisconsin, University of Wisconsin, Madison.

72. Ibid.

73. For discussions of the Woman's Peace Party, see Marie Louise Degen, *The History of the Woman's Party* (New York: Garland Publishers, [1939] 1972); Linda Kay Schott, "Women Against War: Pacifism, Feminism, and Social Justice in the United States, 1915–1941" (Ph.D. diss., Stanford University, 1985); and Barbara Steinson, *American Women's Activism in World War I* (New York: Garland Publishers, 1982).

74. Unsigned and undated letter. Jessie Wallace Hughan Papers, Swarthmore College Peace Collection, Swarthmore, PA.

75. Unsigned and undated letter. Jessie Wallace Hughan Papers, Swarthmore College Peace Collection, Swarthmore, PA.

76. Associate Superintendent John L. Tildsley to Jessie Wallace Hughan, 2 July 1918. Jessie Wallace Hughan Papers, Swarthmore College Peace Collection, Swarthmore, PA. See also "Reminiscences of Tracy Mygatt and Francis Witherspoon." Interviewed by John T. Mason. Oral History Research Office, Columbia University, 1966. Specifically, school officials denied Hughan promotions and raises. During the War her superintendent continuously forced her to defend her anti-war activities, always under the threat of dismissal.

Conclusion

1. Richard Polenberg, *Fighting Faiths: The Abrams Case, the Supreme Court, and Free Speech* (New York: Penguin Books, 1987), 130.

2. Natalie Zemon Davis, *Society and Culture in Early Modern France* (Stanford: Stanford University Press, 1975); Jacqueline Dowd Hall, "Disorderly Women: Gender and Labor Militancy in the Appalachian South," *Journal of American History* 73 (September 1986): 335–83; and Carroll Smith-Rosenberg, *Disorderly Conduct: Visions of Gender in Victorian America* (New York: Alfred A. Knopf, 1985), 245–96.

3. The most recent examples are Michael C.C. Adams, *The Great Adventure: Male Desire and the Coming of World War I* (Bloomington: Indiana University Press, 1990); and Susan Zeiger, "She Didn't Raise Her Boy to Be a Slacker: Motherhood, Conscription and the Culture of the First World War," *Feminist Studies* 22 (Spring 1996): 7–39.

4. Michael Rogin, *Ronald Reagan the Movie and Other Episodes in Political Demonology* (Berkeley: University of California, 1988), 63.

5. For an explanation of why members of the National Woman's Party were not charged under the wartime laws, see Christine Lunardini, *From Equal Suffrage to Equal Rights: Alice Paul and the National Woman's Party, 1910–1928* (New York: New York University Press, 1986), 123–33.

6. For a survey of these cases, see H.C. Peterson and Gilbert C. Fite, *Opponents of War, 1917–1918* (Seattle: University of Washington Press, 1957).

7. Mrs. G.A. Harris to Winnie Branstetter, undated, 1. Socialist Party of America Papers, Microfilm Edition, reel 9, University of California, Irvine. I have corrected the spelling and punctuation, but have preserved Harris's style.

BIBLIOGRAPHY

Primary Sources

ARCHIVAL COLLECTIONS

American Union Against Militarism. Papers. Swarthmore College Peace Collection. Swarthmore, PA.

Berger, Meta. Papers. State Historical Society of Wisconsin. Madison, WI.

Berkman, Alexander. Papers. Tamiment Institute of Labor History. New York, NY.

Department of Justice. Papers. Record Group 60. National Archives. Washington DC.

Department of Justice. Papers. Record Group 65. National Archives. Washington DC.

Department of Justice. Papers. Record Group 165. National Archives. Washington DC.

Emergency Peace Federation Papers. Swarthmore College Peace Collection. Swarthmore, PA.

Flynn, Elizabeth Gurley. Papers. Microfilm Edition. State Historical Society of Wisconsin. Madison, WI.

————. Papers. Microfilm Edition. Tamiment Institute of Labor History. New York, NY.

Freeman, Elisabeth. Papers. Swarthmore College Peace Collection. Swarthmore, PA.

Goldman, Emma. Papers. Microfilm Edition. University of California, Berkeley. Berkeley, CA.

————. Papers. Microfilm Edition. Arthur and Elizabeth Schlesinger Library. Cambridge, MA.

————. Papers. Tamiment Institute of Labor History. New York, NY.

Hillquit, Morris. Papers. Microfilm Edition. State Historical Society of Wisconsin. Madison, WI.

Hughan, Jessie Wallace. Papers. Swarthmore College Peace Collection. Swarthmore, PA.

Lewis, Lena Morrow. Papers. Microfilm Edition. Tamiment Institute of Labor History. New York, NY.

Mygatt, Tracy, and Frances Witherspoon. Papers. Swarthmore College Peace Collection. Swarthmore, PA.

Nearing, Scott. Papers. Swarthmore College Peace Collection. Swarthmore, PA.

New York Bureau of Legal First Aid. Papers. Tamiment Institute of Labor History. New York, NY.

Office of the Pardon Attorney. Papers. Record Group 104. National Archives, Washington, D.C.

O'Hare, Kate Richards. Papers. Microfilm Edition. Arthur and Elizabeth Schlesinger Library. Cambridge, MA.

————. Papers. Microfilm Edition. State Historical Society of Wisconsin. Madison, WI.

People's Council of Democracy and Peace. Papers. Microfilm Edition. Swarthmore College Peace Collection. Swarthmore, PA.

Roe, Gwyneth K. Papers. State Historical Society of Wisconsin. Madison, WI.

Secor, Lella Faye. Papers. Swarthmore College Peace Collection. Swarthmore, PA.

Simons, Algie, and May Wood Simons. Papers. State Historical Society of Wisconsin. Madison, WI.

Socialist Party of America. Papers. Microfilm Edition. University of California, Irvine. Irvine, CA.

Stokes, Rose Pastor. Papers. Microfilm Edition. Tamiment Institute of Labor History. New York, NY.

———. Papers. Microfilm Edition. Yale University Library. New Haven, CT.

U.S. Military Intelligence Reports: Surveillance of Radicals in the United States, 1917–1945. Papers. Microfilm Edition. National Archives. Washington DC.

Walling, Anna Strunsky. Papers. Microfilm Edition. Yale University Library. New Haven, CT.

Walling, William English. Papers. State Historical Society of Wisconsin. Madison, WI.

Wisconsin Woman's Suffrage Association. Papers. State Historical Society of Wisconsin. Madison, WI.

Woman's Peace Party. Papers. Microfilm Edition. Swarthmore College Peace Collection. Swarthmore, PA.

Woodbury, Helen Sumner. Papers. State Historical Society of Wisconsin. Madison, WI.

PERIODICALS AND NEWSPAPERS

American Socialist, 1914–1917.
Blast, 1917.
Four Lights, 1916–1918.
Mother Earth, 1915–1917.
New Republic, 1914–1920.
New York Call, 1914–1923.
New York Times, 1914–1920.
Oregon Journal, 1917.
Seattle Post Intelligencer, 1917.
Seattle Star, 1917.
Seattle Times, 1917.

PRINTED MATERIAL

Bagley, Grace H. "Americanization as War Service." *The Woman Citizen* (30 June 1917): 84.

Blatch, Harriot Stanton. *Mobilizing Woman-Power*. New York: The Womans Press, 1918.

Creel, George. *How We Advertised America: The First Telling of the Amazing Story of the Committee on Public Information That Carried the Gospel of Americanism to Every Corner of the Globe*. New York: Harper & Brothers, 1920.

Debs, Eugene V. *Correspondences: Letters of Eugene Debs*. Vol. II. Edited by Robert Constantine. Urbana: University of Illinois, 1990.

Dewey, John. "Universal Service as Education II." *New Republic* (29 April 1916): 334.

Flynn, Elizabeth Gurley. *The Rebel Girl: An Autobiography*. New York: International Publishing, 1955.

Goldman, Emma. *Living My Life*. New York: Dover Publications, Inc., 1970.

Hendrick, Burton J. *Life and Letters of Walter H. Page*. Vol. 2. Garden City, NY: Doubleday, Page, and Company, 1922.

Hughan, Jessie Wallace. *American Socialism of the Present Day*. New York: John Lane, 1911.

———. *A Study of International Government*. New York: Thomas & Crowell Co., 1923.

———. "The Logic of Pacifism." *Intercollegiant Socialist Society* (October-November 1916): 11–14.

———. "War Against War." *New Review* (15 August 1915): 187–88.

———. *What Is Socialism?* New York: Vanguard Press, 1928.

Mason, John T. Interviewer. "Reminiscences of Tracy Mygatt and Frances Witherspoon." Oral History Research Office. Columbia University. 1966.

Nells, Walter, ed. *Espionage Act Cases: With Certain Others on Related Points*. New York: National Civil Liberties Bureau, 1918.

O'Connor, Harvey. *Revolution in Seattle: A Memoir*. New York: Monthly Review Press, 1964.

O'Hare, Kate Richards. *In Prison*. Seattle: University of Washington Press [1923] 1976.

———. *Kate Richards O'Hare: Selected Writings and Speeches*. Edited by Philip S. Foner and Sally M. Miller. Baton Rouge: Louisiana State University Press, 1982.

———. *The Sorrows of Cupid*. St. Louis: National Rip-Saw Publishing Company, 1913.

O'Hare, Kate Richards and Frank P. O'Hare. *World Peace: A Spectacle Drama in Three Acts*. St. Louis: National Rip-Saw Publishing Co., 1915.

Parkhurst, Minnie. *The Louise Olivereau Case Trial and Speech to Jury in Federal Court of Seattle Washington, November 1917*. Seattle: Parkhurst Press, 1917.

Post, Louis P. *The Deportation Delirium of Nineteen-Twenty: A Personal Narrative of an Historic Official Experience*. Introduction by Moorfield Story. New York: Da Capo Press, 1970.

Rhodes, Mrs. "Americanization Through Women's Organizations." *Immigrants in America Review* 1 (September 1915): 51.

Robins, Lucy. *War Shadows: A Documental Story of the Struggle for Amnesty*. New York: Central Labor Bodies Conference for the Release of Political Prisoners, 1922.

Roosevelt, Theodore. "Is the Women's Peace Movement 'Silly and Base'?" *Literary Digest* (1 May 1915): 1022.

———. *The Works of Theodore Roosevelt*. Vol. 18. New York: Charles Scribner's Sons, 1926.

———. *The Works of Theodore Roosevelt*. Vol. 19. New York: Charles Scribner's Sons, 1926.

"Rose Pastor Stokes Comes Back." *Living Men* 2 (February 1918): 6–7.

Smedley, Agnes. *Daugher of Earth*. New York: The Feminist Press, [1929], 1986.

Stokes, Rose Pastor. "A Confession." *Century Magazine* 95 (November 1917): 457.

Strong, Anna Louise. *I Change Worlds: The Remaking of An American*. New York: Henry Holt and Company, 1935.

"Tattler," "Notes from the Capital: Emma Goldman."*Nation* CIV (28 June 1917): 54.

"Ten Years for Criticism." *Literary Digest* 57 (15 June 1918): 13.

Trachtenberg, Alexander. *The American Labor Year Book 1919–1920*. New York: The Rand School, 1920.

——, ed. *The American Socialists and the War*. New York: Garland Publishing, [1917], 1973.

"Uncle Sam's Obstreperous Niece." *Literary Digest* 55 (18 August 1917).

Vorse, Mary Heaton. *A Footnote to Folly: Reminiscences of Mary Heaton Vorse*. New York: Farrar and Rinehart Inc., 1935.

Whitehorse, Vera Barman. "The Immigrant Woman and the Vote." *Immigrants in America Review* 1 (September 1915): 65.

Secondary Works, Articles, and Theses

Adams, Michael C.C. *The Great Adventure: Male Desire and the Coming of World War I*. Bloomington: Indiana University Press, 1990.

Alonso, Harriet Hyman. "Gender and Peace Politics in the First World War: The People's Council of America." *International History Review* XIX (February 1997): 83–104.

Antler, Joyce. *The Educated Woman and Professionalization: The Struggle for a New Feminine Identity, 1890–1920*. New Haven: Yale University Press, 1987.

Arnup, Katherine, Andree Lévesque, and Ruth Roach Pierson, eds. *Delivering Motherhood: Maternal Ideologies and Practices in the 19th and 20th Centuries*. London: Routledge, 1990.

Avrich, Paul. *The Haymarket Tragedy*. Princeton: Princeton University Press, 1984.

——. *The Modern School Movement: Anarchism and Education in the United States*. Princeton: Princeton University Press, 1980.

Baaland, Bonnie. *Emma Goldman: Sexuality and the Impurity of the State*. Montreal: Black Rose Books, 1993.

Baker, Paula. "The Domestication of Politics: Women and American Political Society, 1780–1920." *American Historical Review* 89 (June 1984): 620–47.

——. *The Moral Framework of Public Life: Gender, Politics, and the State in New York, 1870–1930*. New York: Oxford University Press, 1991.

Basen, Neil K. "Kate Richards O'Hare: The First Lady of American Socialism, 1901–1917." *Labor History* 21 (Spring 1980): 165–99.

Bassett, Michael E.R. "The Socialist Party of America: Years of Decline." Ph.D. diss., Duke University, 1963.

Beale, Howard K. *Are American Teachers Free? An Analysis of Restraints Upon the Freedom of Teaching in American Schools*. New York: Octagon Books, 1972.

Benedict, Michael Les. *The Blessing of Liberty: A Concise History of the Constitution of the United States*. Lexington: D.C. Heath, 1996.

Bommel, Edward J. "Kate Richards O'Hare: A Midwestern Pacifist's Fight for Free Speech." *North Dakota Quarterly* 44 (Winter 1976): 5–19.

Boris, Eileen. "The Power of Motherhood: Black and White Activist Women." *Yale Journal of Law and Feminism* 2 (Fall 1989): 25–49.

Bredbenner, Candice Lewis. *A Nationality of Her Own: Women, Marriage, and the Law of Citizenship*. Berkeley: University of California Press, 1998.

Breen, William J. *Uncle Sam at Home: Civilian Mobilization, Wartime Federalism, and the Council of National Defense, 1917–1919.* Westport: Greenwood Press, 1984.

Bristow, Nancy K. *Making Men Moral: Social Engineering During the Great War.* New York: New York University Press, 1996.

Buckingham, Peter H. *Rebel Against Injustice: The Life of Frank P. O'Hare.* Columbia: University of Missouri Press, 1996.

Buerker, John D. "The Politics of Mutual Frustration: Socialists and Suffragists in New York and Wisconsin." In *Flawed Liberation: Socialism and Feminism,* edited by Sally M. Miller. Westport: Greenwood Press, 1981.

Buhle, Mari Jo. *Women and American Socialism 1880–1920.* Urbana: University of Illinois Press, 1983.

Camp, Helen. *Iron in Her Soul: Elizabeth Gurley Flynn and the American Left.* Pullman: Washington State University Press, 1995.

Carlson, Robert A. *The Americanization Syndrome: A Quest for Conformity.* London: Croom Helm, 1987.

Choat, Glenda. "Anna Louise Strong: From Progressive to Radical." Master's thesis, Western Washington State College, 1977.

Clifford, John Garry. *The Citizen Soldier: The Plattsburgh Training Camp Movement, 1913–1920.* Lexington: University of Kentucky Press, 1972.

Coben, Stanley. "A Study in Nativism: The American Red Scare of 1919–1920." *Political Science Quarterly* 79 (March 1964): 52–75.

Cooke, Miriam and Angela Woollacott, ed. *Gendering War Talk.* Princeton: Princeton University Press, 1993.

Cooper, Helen M., Adrienne Auslander Munich, and Susan Merrill Squier, eds. *Arms and the Woman: War, Gender, and Literary Representation.* Chapel Hill: University of North Carolina Press, 1989.

Cooper, John Milton. *Pivotal Decades: The United States, 1900–1920.* New York: W.W. Norton, 1990.

Cott, Nancy. *The Grounding of Modern Feminism.* New Haven: Yale University Press, 1987.

———. "What's in a Name? The Limits of 'Social Feminism'; or Expanding the Vocabulary of Women's History." *Journal of American History* 76 (December 1986): 809–29.

Culleton, Claire A. "Gender-Charged Munitions: The Language of World War I Munitions Reports." *Women's Studies International Forum* 11 (1988): 109–16.

Danbom, David B. *"The World of Hope": Progressives and the Struggle for an Ethical Public Life.* Philadelphia: Temple University Press, 1987.

Daniels, Doris Groshen. "Theodore Roosevelt and Gender Roles." *Presidential Studies Quarterly* 26 (Summer 1996): 648–65.

Davis, Allen F. "Welfare Reform and World War I." *American Quarterly* XIX (Fall 1967): 516–33.

Davis, Natalie Zemon. *Society and Culture in Early Modern France.* Stanford: Stanford University Press, 1975.

DeBauche, Leslie Midkiff, *Reel Patriotism: The Movies and World War I.* Madison: University of Wisconsin Press, 1997.

Degen, Marie Louis. *The History of the Woman's Peace Party.* New York: Garland Publishers, [1939], 1972.

Dembo, Jonathan. *Unions and Politics in Washington State, 1885–1935.* New York: Garland Publishers, 1983.

Donner, Frank. *The Age of Surveillance: The Aims and Methods of the American Political Intelligence System*. New York: Alfred A. Knopf, 1980.

Drinnon, Richard. *Rebel in Paradise: A Biography of Emma Goldman*. Chicago: University of Chicago Press, 1961.

Dubbert, Joe L. *A Man's Place: Masculinity in Transition*. Englewood Cliffs, NJ: Prentice Hall, 1979.

Dubofsky, Melvyn. *We Shall Be All: A History of the Industrial Workers of the World*. Chicago: Quadrangle Books, 1969.

Dubois, Ellen Carol. *Harriot Stanton Blatch and the Winning of Woman's Suffrage*. New Haven: Yale University Press, 1997.

————. "Working Women, Class Relations, and Suffrage Militancy: Harriot Stanton Blatch and the New York Woman Suffrage Movement, 1894–1909." *Journal of American History* 74 (June 1987): 34–58.

Dye, Nancy Schrom and Daniel Blake Smith. "'Mother Love' and Infant Death." *Journal of American History* 73 (September 1986): 329–53.

Dye, Nancy Schrom, "Creating a Feminist Alliance: Sisterhood and Class Conflict in the New York Woman's Trade Union League, 1903–1914." *Feminist Studies* 3 (1975): 11–25.

Dyer, Thomas G. *Theodore Roosevelt and the Idea of Race*. Baton Rouge: Louisiana State University Press, 1980.

Early, Frances H. "Feminism, Peace, and Civil Liberties: Women's Role in the Origins of the World War I Civil Liberties Movement." *Women's Studies: An Interdisciplinary Journal* 18 (1990) 34–58.

————. "New Historical Perspectives on Gendered Peace Studies." *Women's Studies Quarterly* 3 (Fall-Winter 1995): 22–31.

————. *War's Heretics: The Feminist Pacifists and Civil Libertarians of the Bureau of Legal First Aid*. Syracuse: University of Syracuse Press, 1997.

————. "Revolutionary Pacifism and War Resistance: Jessie Wallace Hughan's 'War Against War.'" *Peace and Change* 30 (July 1995): 307–28.

Edwards, Rebecca. *Angels in the Machinery: Gender and Party Politics from the Civil War to the Progressive Era*. New York: Oxford University Press, 1997.

Eisenach, Eldon J. *The Lost Promise of Progressivism*. Lawrence: University of Kansas Press, 1994.

Falk, Candice. *Love, Anarchy, and Emma Goldman*. New York: Holt, Rinehart, and Winston, 1984.

Filene, Peter. "In Time of War." In *The American Male*, edited by Elizabeth Pleck and Joseph Pleck. Englewood Cliffs, NJ: Prentice Hall, 1980.

Fink, Leon. *Progressive Intellectuals and the Dilemmas of Democratic Commitment*. Cambridge: Harvard University Press, 1998.

Fitzpatrick, Ellen. *Endless Crusade: Women Social Scientists and Progressive Reform*. New York: Oxford University Press, 1990.

Fogleson, David. *America's Secret War Against Bolshevism: U.S. Intervention in the Russian Civil War, 1917–1920*. Chapel Hill: University of North Carolina Press, 1998.

Ford, Linda G. *Iron-Jawed Angels: The Suffrage Militancy of the National Woman's Party, 1912–1920*. Lanham, MD: University Press of America, 1991.

Frankel, Noralee, and Nancy Schrom Dye, eds. *Gender, Class, Race, and Reform in the Progressive Era*. Lexington: University of Kentucky Press, 1992.

Frankle, Oz. "Whatever Happened to 'Red Emma'? Emma Goldman from Alien

Rebel to American Icon." *The Journal of American History* 83 (December 1996): 903–42.

Friedheim, Robert L. *The Seattle General Strike.* Seattle: University of Washington Press, 1964.

Frost, Richard H. *The Mooney Case.* Palo Alto: Stanford University Press, 1968.

Garrison, Dee. *Mary Heaton Vorse: The Life of An American Insurgent.* Philadelphia: Temple University Press, 1989.

Gavin, Lettie. *American Women in World War I: They Also Served.* Boulder: University Press of Colorado, 1997.

Gilbert, Sandra M. "Soldier's Heart: Literary Men, Literary Women, and the Great War." *Signs* 8 (Fall 1988): 422–50.

Ginger, Ray. *The Bending Cross: A Biography of Eugene Victor Debs.* New Brunswick: Rutgers University Press, 1949.

Glenn, Evelyn Nakano. "From Servitude to Service Work: Historical Continuities in the Racial Division of Paid Reproductive Labor." *Signs* (Autumn 1992).

Gordon, Linda. *Heroes of Their Own Lives: The Politics and History of Family Violence.* New York: Viking, 1988.

———. *Woman's Body, Woman's Right: Birth Control in America.* New York: Penguin Books, 1976.

———, ed. *Women, the State, and Welfare.* Madison: University of Wisconsin Press, 1990.

Green, James R. *Grass Roots Socialism: Radical Movements in the Southwest, 1895–1943.* Baton Rouge: Louisiana State University Press, 1978.

———. "The 'Salesman-Soldiers' of the 'Appeal Army': A Profile of Rank and File Socialist Agitators." In *Socialist and the Cities,* edited by Bruce M. Stave. Port Washington, NY: Kennikat Press, 1975.

Greenwald, Maurine W. *Women, War, and Work: The Impact of World War I on Women Workers.* Westport: Greenwood, 1981.

Gullace, Nicoletta F. "Sexual Violence and Family Honor: British Propaganda and International Law During the First World War." *The American Historical Review* 102 (June 1997): 714–47.

Hall, Jacqueline Dowd. "Disorderly Women: Gender and Labor Militancy in the Appalachian South." *Journal of American History* 73 (September 1986): 335–83.

Hanley, Marla Martin. "The Children's Crusade of 1922: Kate O'Hare and the Campaign to Free Radical War Dissenters in the Era of America's First Red Scare." *Gateway Heritage* 10 (Summer 1989): 34–43.

Hartman, George Edward. *The Movement to Americanize the Immigrant.* New York: AMS Press, [1948], 1967.

Hawley, Ellis Wayne. *The Great War and the Search for Modern Order: A History of the American People and Their Institutions, 1917–1933.* New York: St. Martin's Press, 1979.

Hendrickson, Kenneth E. "The Pro-War Socialists: The Social Democratic League and the Ill-Fated Drive for Industrial Democracy in America, 1917–1920." *Labor History* 11 (Summer 1970): 304–22.

Higginbotham, Evelyn Brooks. *Righteous Discontent: The Women's Movement in the Black Baptist Church, 1880–1920.* Cambridge: Harvard University Press, 1993.

Higham, John. *Strangers in the Land: Patterns of American Nativism, 1886–1925.* New York: Atheneum, [1953], 1969.

Higonnet, Margaret Randolph, Jane Jenson, Sonya Michel, and Margaret Collins Weitz, eds. *Behind the Lines: Gender and the Two World Wars.* New Haven: Yale University Press, 1987.

Hirschfeld, Charles. "Nationalist Progressivism and World War I." *Mid-America* 45 (July 1963): 139–56.

Howlett, Charles. "Quaker Conscience in the Classroom: The Mary S. McDowell Case." *Quaker History* 83 (Fall 1994): 99–115.

Hunt, Michael. *Ideology and U.S. Foreign Policy.* New Haven: Yale University Press, 1987.

Hutchinson, John R. *Champions of Charity: War and the Rise of the Red Cross.* Boulder: Westview Press, 1996.

Jacoby, Robin Miller. "The Women's Trade Union League and American Feminism." *Feminist Studies* 3 (1976): 126–40.

Jensen, Joan. *Passage from India: Asian Immigration in North America.* New Haven: Yale University Press, 1988.

Jessup, Philip C. *Elihu Root.* New York: Dodd, Mead & Co., 1938.

Jordan, John M. *Machine-Age Ideology: Social Engineering and American Liberalism, 1911–1939.* Chapel Hill: University of North Carolina Press, 1994.

Karlsen, Carol F. *The Devil in the Shape of a Woman: Witchcraft in Colonial New England.* New York: Random House Inc., 1987.

Karsner, David. *Debs: His Authorized Life and Letters.* New York: Boni and Liveright, 1919.

Keller, Morton. *Regulating a New Society: Public Policy and Social Change in America, 1900–1933.* Cambridge: Harvard University Press, 1994.

Kennedy, David. *Over Here: The First World War and American Society.* New York: Oxford University Press, 1980.

Kennedy, Kathleen. "'Declaring War on War': Gender and the American Socialist Attack on Militarism, 1914–1918." *Journal of Women's History* 7 (Summer 1995): 27–51.

———. "Loyalty and Citizenship in the Wisconsin Woman's Suffrage Association, 1917–1919." *Mid-America* 76 (Spring/Summer 1994): 109–31.

———. "'We Mourn for Liberty in America': Socialist Women, Anti-militarism, and State Repression, 1914–1922." Ph.D. diss., University of California, Irvine, 1992.

Kerber, Linda. *Women of the Republic: Intellect and Ideology in Revolutionary America.* New York: W.W. Norton & Co., 1980.

Kessler-Harris, Alice. *Out to Work: A History of Wage Earning Women in the United States.* New York: Oxford University Press, 1990.

Knock, Thomas. *To End All Wars: Woodrow Wilson and the Quest for a New World Order.* Princeton: Princeton University Press, 1992.

Knoles, George H. "American Intellectuals and World War I." *Pacific Northwest Quarterly* 59 (October 1968): 203–15.

Korman, Gerd. *Industrialization, Immigrants, and Americanizers: The View from Milwaukee, 1866–1921.* Madison: The State Historical Society of Wisconsin, 1967.

Kornbluh, Felicia A. "The New Literature on Gender and the Welfare State: The U.S. Case." *Feminist Studies* 22 (Spring 1996): 171–97.

Kornweibel, Theodore Jr. *"Seeing Red": Federal Campaigns Against Black Militancy, 1919–1925.* Bloomington: Indiana University Press, 1998.

Koven, Seth, and Sonya Michel. "Introduction: 'Mother Worlds.'" In *Mothers of a*

New World: Maternalist Politics and the Origins of Welfare States, edited by Seth Koven and Sonya Michel. New York: Routledge, 1993.

Krieger, Nancy. "Queen of Bolsheviks: The Hidden History of Dr. Marie Equi." *Radical America* 17 (1983): 55–73.

Kunzel, Regina G. *Fallen Women, Problem Girls: Unmarried Mothers and the Professionalization of Social Work, 1890–1945.* New Haven: Yale University Press, 1993.

Ladd-Taylor, Molly. *Mother-Work: Women, Child Welfare, and the State, 1890–1930.* Urbana: University of Illinois Press, 1994.

Lawrence, Thomas. "Eclipse of Liberty: Civil Liberties in the United States During the First World War." *Wayne State Review* 21 (Spring 1974): 33–112.

Lears, T.J. Jackson. *No Place of Grace: Anti-Modernism and the Transition of American Culture, 1880–1920.* New York: Pantheon, 1981.

Lebsock, Suzanne. "Women and American Political Society." In *Women, Politics, and Change in Twentieth-Century America,* edited by Louise Tilly and Patricia Gurin. New York: Russell Sage Foundation, 1990.

Leopold, Richard William. *Elihu Root and the Conservative Tradition.* Boston: Little Brown, 1954.

Leuchtenburg, William T. "The Progressive Movement and American Foreign Policy." *Mississippi Valley Historical Review* 39 (December 1952): 483–504.

London, Joan. *Jack London and His Times: An Unconventional Biography.* New York: The Book League of America, 1939.

Lunardini, Christine. *From Equal Suffrage to Equal Rights: Alice Paul and the National Woman's Party, 1910–1928.* New York: New York University Press, 1986.

Mackinnon, Janice, and Stephen Mackinnon. *Agnes Smedley: The Life and Times of an American Radical.* Berkeley: University of California Press, 1988.

Marchard, Ronald. *The American Peace Movement and Social Reform.* Princeton: Princeton University Press, 1972.

Marcus, Jane. "The Asylums of Antaeus: Women, War and Madness. Is There a Feminist Fetishism?" In *The Differences Within: Feminism and Critical Theory,* edited by Elizabeth Meese and Alice Parker. Amsterdam: John Benjamins, 1989.

Marsh, Margaret S. *Anarchist Women, 1870–1920.* Philadelphia: Temple University Press, 1981.

May, Elaine Tyler. *Homeward Bound: American Families in the Cold War Era.* New York: Basic Books, 1988.

McClymer, John F. *War and Welfare: Social Engineering in America, 1890–1925.* Westport: Greenwood Press, 1980.

Melman, Billie, ed. *borderlands: Genders and Identities in War and Peace 1870–1930.* New York: Routledge, 1998.

Miller, Sally M. *From Prairie to Prison: The Life of Social Activist Kate Richards O'Hare.* Columbia: University of Missouri Press, 1993.

———. "Kate Richards O'Hare: Progression Toward Feminism." *Kansas History* 7 (Winter 1983): 263–79.

———, ed. *Flawed Liberation: Socialism and Feminism.* Westport: Greenwood Press, 1981.

Mock, James R., and Cedric Larson. *Words That Won the War.* Princeton: University of Princeton Press, 1939.

Mock, James M. *Censorship 1917.* New York: Da Capo Press, 1972.

Morantz-Sanchez, Regina. *Sympathy and Science: Women Physicians in American Medicine*. New York: Oxford University Press, 1990.

Morgan, Murray. *Skid Road: An Informal Portrait of Seattle*. New York: Viking Press, 1951.

Mosse, George L. *Fallen Soldiers: Reshaping the Memory of the World Wars*. New York: Oxford University Press, 1990.

Motton, Marian J. *Emma Goldman and the American Left: "Nowhere at Home."* New York: Twayne, 1992.

Mould, David H. *American Newsfilm 1914–1919: The Underexposed War*. New York: Garland Publishing Inc., 1983.

Moum, Kathleen Diane. "Harvest of Discontent: The Social Origins of the Nonpartisan League, 1880–1920." Ph.D. diss., University of California, Irvine, 1986.

Muncy, Robyn. *Creating a Female Dominion in American Reform*. Cambridge: Harvard University Press, 1992.

Murphy, Paul. *World War I and the Origins of Civil Liberties in the United States*. New York: W.W. Norton Co., 1979.

Murray, Keith. "The Charles Neiderhauser Case: Patriotism in the Seattle Schools, 1919." *Pacific Northwest Quarterly* 74 (January 1983): 11–17.

Murray, Robert K. *Red Scare: A Study in National Hysteria*. New York: McGraw Hill Book Co., 1955.

Nelson, Bruce. *Beyond the Martyrs: A Social History of Chicago's Anarchist Movement, 1890–1900*. New Brunswick: Rutgers University Press, 1989.

Nelson, Bryce. *Good Schools: The Seattle Public School System, 1901–1930*. Seattle: University of Washington Press, 1988.

O'Connor, Jessie Lloyd, Harvey O'Conner, and Susan M. Bowler. *Harvey and Jessie: A Couple of Radicals*. Philadelphia: Temple University Press, 1988.

Ogle, Stephanie. "Anna Louise Strong: The Seattle Years." Master's thesis, Seattle University, 1973.

Osgood, Robert. *Ideals and Self-Interest in American Foreign Relations: The Great Transformation of the 20th Century*. Chicago: University of Chicago Press, 1953.

Panunzio, Constantine M. *The Deportation Cases of 1919–1920*. New York: Da Capo Press, 1970.

Pearlman, Michael. *To Make Democracy Safe for America: Patricians and Preparedness in the Progressive Era*. Urbana: University of Illinois Press, 1984.

Peiss, Kathy. "'Charity Girls' and City Pleasures: Historical Notes on Working-Class Sexuality, 1880–1920." In *Unequal Sisters: A Multicultural Reader in U.S. Women's History*, edited by Ellen Carol Dubois and Vicki L. Ruiz. New York: Routledge, 1990.

———. *Cheap Amusements: Working Women and Leisure in Turn-of-the-Century New York*. Philadelphia: Temple University Press, 1986.

Peterson, H.C., and Gilbert C. Fite. *Opponents of War, 1917–1918*. Seattle: University of Washington Press, 1957.

Pierce, Bessie Louise. *Public Opinion and the Teaching of History in the United States*. New York: Alfred A. Knopf, 1926.

Polenberg, Richard. *Fighting Faiths: The Abrams Case, the Supreme Court, and Free Speech*. New York: Penguin Books, 1987.

Powers, Richard Gid. *Not Without Honor: The History of American Anticommunism*. New York: The Free Press, 1996.

———. *Secrecy and Power: The Life of J. Edgar Hoover*. New York: The Free Press, 1987.

Preston, William. Jr. *Aliens and Dissenters: Federal Suppression of Radicals, 1903–1933*. Cambridge: Harvard University Press, 1963.

Price, Alan. *The End of the Age of Innocence: Edith Wharton and the First World War*. New York: St. Martin's Press, 1996.

Rabban, David M. "The Emergence of Modern First Amendment Doctrine." *The University of Chicago Law Review* 50 (Fall 1983): 1205–1355.

———. "The First Amendment in Its Forgotten Years." *The Yale Law Journal* 90 (January 1981): 522–95.

———. *Free Speech in Its Forgotten Years*. Cambridge: Cambridge University Press, 1997.

Ravitch, Diane. *The Great School Wars: New York City, 1805–1973, A History of the Public Schools as Battlefield of Social Change*. New York: Basic Books, Inc., 1974.

Renshaw, Patrick. "Rose of the World: The Pastor-Stokes Marriage and the American Left, 1905–1925." *New York History* 62 (October 1981): 428–37.

———. "The I.W.W. and the Red Scare, 1917–1924." *Journal of Contemporary History* 3 (1968): 63–72.

Reynolds, Robert D. Jr. "The Millionaire Socialist: J.G. Stokes and His Circle of Friends." Ph.D. diss., University of South Carolina, 1974.

———. "Pro-War Socialists: Intolerant or Bloodthirsty?" *Labor History* 17 (Summer 1976): 413–15.

Rideout, Walter. *The Radical Novel in the United States, 1900–1954*. Cambridge: Harvard University Press, 1956.

Rogin, Michael Paul. *Ronald Reagan the Movie and Other Episodes of Political Demonology*. Berkeley: University of California Press, 1987.

Rosenberg, Rosalind. *Beyond Separate Spheres: Intellectual Roots of Modern Feminism*. New Haven: Yale University Press, 1982.

Royster, Jacqueline Jones. *Southern Horrors and Other Writings: The Anti-lynching Campaigns of Ida B. Wells, 1892–1900*. New York: Bedford, 1997.

Ryan, Mary P. *Cradle of the Middle Class: The Family in Oneida County New York, 1790–1865*. Cambridge: Cambridge University Press, 1981.

Salvatore, Nick. *Eugene V. Debs: Citizen and Socialist*. Urbana: University of Illinois Press, 1982.

Sannes, Erling N. "'Queen of the Lecture Platform': Kate Richards O'Hare and North Dakota Politics." *North Dakota Quarterly* 58 (Fall 1991): 2–19.

Sapiro, Virginia. "Women, Citizenship and Naturalization Policies in the United States." *Politics and Society* 13 (1984): 1–26.

Saveth, Edward. "Race and Nationalism in American Historiography: The Late Nineteenth Century." *Political Science Quarterly* 54 (September 1939): 421–44.

Schott, Linda Kay. "Women Against War: Pacifism, Feminism, and Social Justice in the United States, 1915–1941." Ph.D. diss., Stanford University, 1985.

Shannon, David A. *The Socialist Party of America: A History*. New York: Macmillan, 1955.

Shapiro, Stanley. "The Great War and Reform: Liberals and Labor." *Labor History* 11 (Summer 1971): 323–44.

Sharbach, Sarah. "Louise Olivereau and the Seattle Radical Community." Master's thesis, University of Washington, 1986.

Sharp, Kathleen Ann. "Rose Pastor Stokes: Radical Champion of the American Working Class, 1879–1933." Ph.D. diss., Duke University, 1979.

Shenk, Edward, "'Work or Fight': Selective Service and Manhood in the Progressive Era." Ph.D. diss., University of California, San Diego, 1992.

Sherman, John. "'This Is a Crusade!': Socialist Party Amnesty Campaigns to Free Eugene V. Debs, 1919–1921." In *Culture, Gender, Race, and U.S. Labor History*, edited by Ronald C. Kent, Sara Markham, David R. Roediger, and Herbert Shapiro. Westport: Greenwood Press, 1993.

Shover, Michele J. "Roles and Images of Women in World War I Propaganda." *Politics and Society* 5 (1975): 469–86.

Shulman, Alix Kates. "Dancing in the Revolution: Emma Goldman's Feminism." *Socialist Review* 12 (March-April 1982): 1–32.

Simms, L. Moody Jr. "World War I and the American Intellectual." *Social Science* 45 (June 1970): 57–62.

Siracusa, Joseph M. "Progressivism, Imperialism, and the Leuchtenburg Thesis, 1952–1974." *Australian Journal of Politics and History* 20 (December 1974): 312–24.

Skocpol, Theda. *Protecting Soldiers and Mothers: The Political Origins of Social Policy in the United States.* Cambridge: Harvard University Press, 1992.

Smith-Rosenberg, Carroll. *Disorderly Conduct: Visions of Gender in Victorian America.* New York: Alfred A. Knopf, 1985.

Stansell, Christine. *City of Women: Sex and Class in New York.* Urbana: University of Illinois Press, 1987.

Steinson, Barbara. *American Women's Activism in World War I.* New York: Garland Publishing, 1982.

Stepenoff, Bonnie. "Mother and Teacher as Missouri State Penitentiary Inmates: Goldman and O'Hare, 1917–1920." *Missouri Historical Review* 91 (July 1991): 402–21.

Strong, Tracy B. *Right in Her Soul: The Life of Anna Louise Strong.* New York: Random House, 1983.

Stuart, Jack Meyer. "William English Walling: A Study in Politics and Ideas." Ph.D. diss., Columbia University, 1968.

Testi, Arnaldo. "The Gender of Reform Politics: Theodore Roosevelt and the Culture of Masculinity." *The Journal of American History* 81 (March 1995): 1509–33.

Thom, Deborah. *Rude Girls and Good Girls: Women Workers in World War I.* New York: Harvill Press, 1998.

Thompson, John A. "American Progressive Publicists and the First World War, 1914–1917." *Journal of American History* 58 (September 1971): 364–83.

———. *Reformers and War: American Progressive Publicists and the First World War.* Cambridge: Cambridge University Press, 1987.

Thurner, Manuela. "'Better Citizens Without the Ballot': American Antisuffrage Women and Their Rationale During the Progressive Era." *Journal of Women's History* 5 (Spring 1993): 33–60.

Todd, Lewis. *Wartime Relations of the Federal Government and the Public Schools, 1917–1918.* New York: Arno Press, 1971.

Trattner, Walter L. "Progressivism and World War I: A Reappraisal." *Mid-America* 44 (July 1962): 131–45.

Trolander, Judith A. *Professionalism and Social Change: From Settlement House*

Movement to Neighborhood Centers, 1886 to the Present. New York: Columbia University Press, 1987.

Tyler, Robert Z. *Rebels of the Woods: The I.W.W. in the Pacific Northwest.* Eugene: University of Oregon Press, 1967.

Vaughn, Stephen. *Holding Fast the Inner Lines: Democracy, Nationalism, and the Committee on Public Information.* Chapel Hill: University of North Carolina Press, 1980.

Waldstreicher, David. *Emma Goldman: Political Activist.* New York: Chelsea House Publishers, 1990.

Weinstein, James. *The Decline of Socialism in America, 1912–1925.* New York: Monthly Review Press, 1967.

Wexler, Alice. *Emma Goldman: An Intimate Life.* New York: Pantheon Books, 1984.

Wiebe, Robert H. *The Search for Order, 1917–1920.* New York: Hill and Wang, 1967.

Wynn, Neil A. *From Progressivism to Prosperity: World War I and American Society.* New York: Holmes & Meier, 1986.

Zeiger, Susan. "She Didn't Raise Her Boy to Be a Slacker: Motherhood, Conscription, and the Culture of the First World War." *Feminist Studies* 22 (Spring 1996): 7–39.

Zipser, Arthur, and Pearl Zipser. *Fire and Grace: The Life of Rose Pastor Stokes.* Athens: University of Georgia Press, 1989.

INDEX

KATHLEEN KENNEDY is Assistant Professor of History and Director of Women's Studies at Western Washington University. She has published in *Journal of Women's History*, *Mid America*, and *Journal of Lesbian and Gay Studies*.

☙❧